GALVESTON BAY

HOUSTON
CITY OF DESTINY

HOUSTON
CITY OF DESTINY

BY THE EDITORIAL STAFF OF
UNIBOOK, INC.

ORY MAZAR NERGAL
EDITOR-IN-CHIEF

EDITED BY
FRED NAHAS

FOREWORD BY
LOUIE WELCH

CONSULTING EDITORS
ROY H. CULLEN
GENERAL MAURICE HIRSCH

MACMILLAN PUBLISHING CO., INC.
NEW YORK
COLLIER MACMILLAN PUBLISHERS
LONDON

EDITORIAL STAFF

ORY MAZAR NERGAL
Editor-in-Chief

FRED NAHAS
Editor

The Hon. LOUIE WELCH
Foreword

ROY H. CULLEN
General MAURICE HIRSCH
Consulting Editors

C. JACK MAHONEY
General Editor

CHARLES V. KRIEGER
General Editor, Production

DR. MARJORY MACCORQUODALE
Managing Editor

CHRISTINE B. STANLEY
PATRICIA S. SOLLOCK
Senior Editors

PETER ELEK
Associate Editor

RICHARD H. HILL
Executive Editor

DORIS ANDERSON, KWADWO A. APORI, STEPHANIE B. BALL, MARGI A. DAY, RICHARD EVANGELOU, VICKI FALDE, WILLIAM GOLOBI, CHARLES HEINEKE, ROBERT RITCHIE
Assistant Editors

KATHY A. ABRAHAM, FLORI C. FONG, BETTE E. LLOYD, ANNA M. MORRISON
Production Assistants

Copyright © 1980 by Unibook, Inc.
2323 South Voss Road, Houston, Texas 77057
(713) 977-2950

Macmillan Publishing Co., Inc.
866 Third Avenue, New York, N.Y. 10022
Collier Macmillan Canada, Ltd.

Library of Congress Cataloging in Publication Data
Unibook, inc.
    Houston, city of destiny.
    Includes index.
    1. Houston, Tex. I.Nahas, Fred. II.Title.
F394.H84U54 1980 976.4'1411 80-19958
ISBN 0-02-620900-4

10 9 8 7 6 5 4 3 2 1

Printed in the United States of America

CONTENTS

FOREWORD

Writing a book on Houston is like trying to take the ultimate portrait of the city skyline. Just when the photographer thinks he has captured the perfect view of the downtown profile, new buildings seem to spring up overnight and a brand-new picture is required.

Houston won't stay still for you very long. That's the quality which makes our city so exciting. Houston is an on-going urban adventure that has a habit of surpassing even the most expert projection or expectation. In fact, events move so quickly that even the most involved Houstonian sometimes feels like an awed spectator wondering what surprise the city has in store just around the corner.

There's something about Houston that inspires heroic and unique action, and makes it a city of destiny. For example, at the turn of the century, Houstonians set out to make their city a seaport. That was a rather formidable task since Houston is fifty miles from the Gulf of Mexico. A sluggish stream called Buffalo Bayou was widened and deepened and became the Houston Ship Channel. Houston is now the third largest seaport in the nation and second in value of foreign trade.

Within a quarter of a century after its founding, the Texas Medical Center had become renowned for medical excellence the world over.

The first domed stadium in history was built in Houston and soon acquired a reputation as the eighth wonder of the world.

Houston was the command post for man's great adventure to the moon. In fact, the very first word from the moon was "Houston." The Apollo 11 astronauts were calling home to report man's first landing on another world.

Perhaps Houston's secret is the fact that it thrives on new ideas, and provides an atmosphere where dreams can come true. Houston is an open community where talent, initiative, and effort will take you as far as you dare to go.

In any frame of reference, Houston is a growth community and has a great deal more growing to do. Houston is prosperous and, because of this, is growing at a rate that has put it in the company of world cities. In fact, the Houston area has virtually doubled in population every twenty years since the turn of the century, and so it is not unreasonable to expect that the population will double again by the year 2000.

Houston grows up and out. The two tallest buildings outside New York or Chicago are now being built in Houston's booming downtown area, which forms a strong nucleus for the city. Major activity centers with a variety of office buildings, famous stores, hotels, and other facilities create their own skylines, which dot the Houston landscape into the suburban areas. These activity centers are tied together by one of the world's finest freeway systems, and will ultimately be served by a rapid transit system. The activity centers give Houstonians an opportunity to work, shop, and be entertained within a few miles of their homes. A wide range of neighborhoods and living accommodations provide for an unexcelled quality of life in Houston.

LEFT: *This spacious building is the student center at the University of Houston.*

Dynamic economic growth has become the norm for Houston. The city's economic diversification, one of its great strengths, will continue to broaden the financial base into the foreseeable future. Houston is an energy capital, a leader in finance, retailing, engineering, construction, and manufacturing. It is a headquarters city for national and multinational corporations, a center of science and technology and medical facilities. Houston is a national and international hub for air traffic, as well as a vitally important port city. Houston's fame and its facilities have made it a leading convention and tourist center.

Perhaps most noteworthy is Houston's sudden and dramatic emergence as a world city. Houston know-how in fields like energy technology, engineering, science and medicine is sought around the world, while the people of many countries come to Houston to take in the city's unexcelled economic opportunity. In fact, this international activity has been so intense that Houston's consular corps has grown rapidly to become one of the largest in the nation.

Houston has thrived because it is a free market city. There is a partnership between the local government and the private sector that is perhaps unique in the world. There is planning and regulation, but primarily there is the freedom to let new ideas take root and develop.

Houston is a city with young concepts where fresh new talent is appreciated and sought. The resulting influx has made Houston a virtual melting pot of national, as well as international cultures. This has brought a great diversity to our culture.

Houston is quite a story, as you will see in the pages ahead. Of course, there is little doubt that there will have to be a sequel to this book. Houston will see to it.

Louie Welch

PART I THE INTRODUCTION

covers Houston's location and area, climate and nature, flora and fauna. It describes the city's site on the upper Texas Gulf Coast prairie, in the Sunbelt of the southwestern United States, and goes on to relate the extent and environs which are the setting of the story of the City of Houston, which follows.

SETTING

Houston, Texas is a way of life and a state of mind. Many of its citizens, including the 1,000 or more persons arriving each week, hope to capture a piece of the American Dream, which is becoming increasingly elusive elsewhere in the nation.

Houston, like Texas, has mammoth proportions— in size, in spirit and in reputation. The largest city in the South and the fourth largest in area in the United States, Houston now ranks fifth and is quickly overtaking Philadelphia as the fourth most populous city in the nation. The acknowledged World Capital of Energy, the city sprawls over 556 square miles, mostly in Harris County (546), with dabs in Fort Bend (8) and Montgomery (2) counties.

Houston, by far the fastest growing major city in the United States, thrives on hope, opportunity, enthusiasm, tolerance and growth—the foundations of our nation. Many of our great cities, including Houston, arose because of these factors. Life in Houston continues to be characterized by the freedom, exuberance, audacity and anticipation that have always been a part of the city's heritage. An outwardly slow-paced city in constant motion, Houston changes swiftly. The prospect of endless growth intoxicates, and few stop to question the city's rate of progress. In the economic context, growth and Houston have become interchangeable words.

Geographically, Houston is situated on a wide expanse of level land twenty-five miles west of Galveston Bay. Downtown, and a few other business districts, are clutters of mushrooming tall, contemporary office buildings, which provide the area with an impressive skyline.

Yet Houston spreads in all directions from its center area, fanning out well beyond the Interstate 610 Loop and the north, west and south Belt, both designed to provide access from the city's outskirts to its hub.

Seen from the air, Houston presents a remarkable vista of greenery with seemingly endless neighborhoods of single and two story houses, dramatically punctuated by a sprinkle of unique, modern, high-rise office park clusters all over the city. Arterial highways spread from the center to the suburbs and connect it with the rest of the state and nation. Also linking the city to the nation and to the rest of the world is the Houston Ship Channel, which begins four miles east of downtown and connects the city with the Gulf of Mexico, 50 miles away. Much of Houston's major industry is located adjacent to this vital waterway.

Moving clockwise from the ship channel to the southeast, we find the independent city of Pasadena; NASA's Lyndon B. Johnson Manned Space Center lies some 30 miles farther to the southeast.

New buildings seem to virtually pop up overnight as construction activity keeps on changing Houston's appearance.

William P. Hobby Airport is just west of the Gulf Freeway, which connects Houston with Galveston. Sandwiched between heavily populated southwest Houston and the central business district is the Texas Medical Center, a small city within itself. Houston's architectural wonder, the Astrodome, is very much in evidence, with its adjacent Astroworld and the rest of the Astrodomain, further to the south and west of the Medical Center.

Office building clusters rise near the western section of the Loop 610, surrounded by residential neighborhoods such as Bellaire, West University Place and River Oaks, including some of Houston's many shopping complexes, such as Galleria I and II. Past Memorial Park and directly west of downtown

A building reflecting Houston's fortunes as well as its clouds.

An angle of the Port of Houston's Turning Basin.

Houston, the residential area of west, northwest and north Houston emerges, stretching out as far as the eye can see. Twenty miles directly north of downtown is the Houston Intercontinental Airport and further, to the northeast, is Lake Houston. Finally, due east from downtown, stands the San Jacinto Monument, reaching high, with the Texas Lone Star at its top.

In 1970, Houston had a population of almost 1.2 million. In 1980, statisticians estimated it at 1.7 million, up 41 percent, an increase of newcomers endlessly flowing there from throughout the world. During a decade when the national trend indicated a decline of urban center populations, Houston was the only city among the nation's eight largest to increase its numbers.

Houston means different things to different people. It has been called Baghdad on the Bayou, Energy Capital of the World, Space City U.S.A., and City of the Future. Undoubtedly, it is the hub of the booming Sunbelt. But no single epithet, word or phrase, can capture the essence of this city that holds many meanings for the region, the nation, and the world.

A city of destiny, Houston is continually re-defining its course. It embodies a new frontier of growth in a nation whose destiny has followed that of its frontiers. Black gold—oil—catapulted Houston into the forefront of the twentieth century. The city's industrial capacities, its status as the center of a rich agricultural region and its teeming port had already sent it well on its way. Houston became an international city. The Port of Houston, which is the gateway to the American Southwest, is an important factor in the city's international connections. The Texas Medical Center, ranking among the largest and most advanced health care complexes in the United States, is another factor. The NASA LBJ Space Center, home of the astronauts and nerve center of the United States' manned space flight program and Space Shuttle project, adds further to Houston's international stature.

The Houston Center reaches upwards toward the sky at Fannin and McKinney streets, and is the first building of a 33-block project that is being developed.

The city's continually diversifying economic base, a key factor in Houston's growth, mirrors the international flavor of the city. At once sophisticated and innocent, Houston is a city of contrasts, where cowboy chic vies with more cosmopolitan modes of behavior. To describe Houston is to talk about its pickup trucks and industry, theaters and symphony orchestra, urban cowboys and executive jetsetters, education and finance, medicine and agriculture, NASA and the port.

Houston is a city full of vitality. Indeed, the estimated median age of its populace is under 28. It is significant and somehow symbolic that, more than ten years ago, Apollo 11 astronaut Neil Armstrong's first, and now-famous, words from the moon were "Houston, Tranquility base here. The *Eagle* has landed." Houston stood on the threshold of a world emerging into the space age.

Houston, city of the future, continues to grow in part because of its location. Situated in a unique geographical area, Houston occupies a fortuitous expanse in the south central part of the North American continent. Three distinctive geographical sections of the continent converge within the Houston area. The flat, low-lying coastal plain sweeps westward from the Gulf of Mexico toward Houston, which lies near its fertile center. To the north, the coastal prairie merges with the farmlands of the nation's grain belt, the broad plains of mid-America. The woodlands, which begin at the Atlantic Ocean, spread westward to the Houston city limits and give way, further west of the city, to vast rolling plains. These in turn break upward into escarpment, the foothills of the Rocky

A young couple explores Memorial Park.

Mountains and, beyond, the great desert lands of the West.

Houston is located fifty miles west of the Gulf of Mexico, twenty-five miles from Galveston Bay on Buffalo Bayou. Its official coordinates are 95°22′ west longitude and 29°46′ north latitude. Some 365 miles west of New Orleans and 240 miles southeast of Dallas, Houston is practically equidistant from Chicago (1,110 miles) and Denver, (1,050 miles), Boston (1,890 miles) and San Francisco (1,960 miles), New York City (1,675 miles) and Los Angeles (1,575 miles). Austin, the state capital, sits amid rolling hills 160 miles to Houston's northwest; San Antonio, eighth largest American city and oldest in Texas, is 190 miles to its southwest.

One of many Texas contrasts: cattle grazing amidst the oil wells.

With an official elevation of 49′ (15 meters), Houston's terrain ranges from sea level to 90′ (27 meters). Thus, it is pancake flat, posing no barrier to the city's relentless course of outward expansion.

The most prominent bodies of water in the city are Lake Houston, the city's primary water source, Buffalo Bayou, a segment of the San Jacinto River and the ship channel. The channel connects the Port of Houston Turning Basin, four miles down Buffalo Bayou from the central business district, to Galveston Bay. In addition, numerous smaller creeks and bayous (pronounced "by-ohs" in Texas) flow sluggishly through the city.

Blessed with an abundance of water and proximity to a major water body, Houston receives an average of 48 inches (122 cm) of rainfall annually. Fine mists emanating from the Gulf of Mexico produce occasional nighttime ground fog. Heavy fog of limited duration occurs an average of 16 times per year and light fog—62 times. Prevailing southeasterly winds from the Gulf also moderate Houston temperatures throughout the year, giving the city enjoyably mild winters and seasonably cool summer nights.

Black-eyed Susans herald the advent of spring in Houston.

As a result, Houston's mild Sunbelt climate permits outdoor activities throughout the year and contributes to the characteristic Houstonian ease and friendliness. The sun shines in the city three-fifths of the time, some 230 days per year. Springtime and autumn are especially mild, dry and clear. With a normal average annual temperature of 69° Fahrenheit (F), 20° Centigrade (C), Houston is the most air-conditioned city in the world. Summer temperatures, however, seldom reach 100° F (38° C). The normal daily maximum temperature during the five warm months (May through September) is 92° F (33° C) and the summer's normal daily minimum temperature is 73° F (23° C).

Houston's winters, as mild as summers in the extreme northwestern and northeastern sections of the United States, occasionally receive cold Arctic air blasts, locally called "blue northers." Of short duration, usually overnight, the blue northers may be accompanied by light frost with the thermometer approaching the freezing point. Temperatures reach 32° F or lower on an average of only ten days per year. The longest cold spell on record occurred in early 1951, when temperatures of 32° F or lower lasting 123 hours straight were recorded. Overall, the normal daily minimum temperature during January and February, Houston's winter months, is 45° F (7° C); the normal daily maximum, 65° F (18° C).

Like temperature extremes, such weather extremes as snowfall, extended dry periods, tornadoes and windstorms are rarities in Houston. Most of the city's precipitation is in the form of rain showers. The amount of rainfall varies substantially from one section of Houston to another on any rainy day. Thunder squalls and tropical storms, however, occasionally pass through the area during their summer spawning season.

With its subtropical climate, a diversity of native plants and animals abound in Houston. As with other aspects of the city, Houston's flora and fauna reflect elements of the tropical and continental, native and foreign.

Although mostly an ultramodern concrete, glass and steel city, Houston surprises newcomers and oldtimers alike with its vistas of lush greenery. Many of its native trees and shrubs are evergreen. Chief among these are shade trees such as live and laurel oaks, Eastern red cedar, loblolly pine, red bay and sweet bay magnolia. The ornamental American and dahoon holly, Jerusalem thorn, Southern magnolia and Texas mountain laurel trees also retain their foliage throughout the year.

The dogwood and redbud are among the most strikingly beautiful of the deciduous ornamental trees native to the woodlands and are popular in gardens throughout the city. Pecan and shagbark hickory trees also rank high on lists of Houstonians' favorite

The armadillo, known throughout Texas, can roll into a ball within its armor.

leaf-shedding ornamentals. Simultaneously, Houstonians prefer a variety of native deciduous trees for shade: American elm, black and water hickory, Carolina linden, chalk and red maple, Eastern cottonwood, sweet gum, sycamore and post, willow, red and overcup oaks. Stands of oak, many of them draped with Spanish moss, are common sights in the city.

Throughout Houston, oaks and pines coexist with such native evergreen shrubs as the yaupon holly and the Southern and bayberry wax myrtle. Deciduous shrubs like sumacs and various types of hawthorn grow profusely alongside such native plants as the palmetto, a short palm with fan-like leaves that gives a jungle-like appearance to an otherwise typical pine and oak forest.

Random honeysuckle and dewberry plants dot grassy areas with mesquite and huisache trees. Prickly pear cactus appears where the soil is more sandy, sometimes in clusters. Chinese tallow, a rapid growing import, appears in many yards and in the surrounding countryside. Although trees ranging from palm to eucalyptus are found in many Houston yards, the most common of the native species are the magnolia, elm, mimosa, hickory, willow and sweet gum trees. The unique yucca, with needle-pointed leaves that can cause pain when touched, is often found in local yards. Although landscaping heavily favored tropical species as recently as twenty years ago, the popularity of such plants as banana trees and oleanders is giving way to more continental species.

Situated in an area of flourishing wildflowers, Houston's fields, roadsides and gardens are vibrant from spring to fall with numerous native and imported species. Throughout the years, travelers on foot, horseback, covered wagon and automobile have introduced a number of species from areas as distant as Europe and the West Indies. As many as 3,000 species of flowering plants alone, excluding common weeds and shrubs and trees, abound in the Houston area. Such colorful wildflowers as the bluebonnet (the Texas state flower) and Indian paintbrush herald spring in Houston. The blossoms of evening primrose yield to the blooming of daisies, blue curls, dandelions, blue-eyed grass, wine cups, Turk's caps, fire wheels, horsemint and black-eyed Susans.

The interesting resurrection fern grows on the top side of large oak limbs and remains in a curled-up position while it is dry, looking quite dead. After a thundershower, however, it uncurls, spreads its leaves and reveals itself as a healthy fern.

Numerous organizations promote the cultivation of native and more recently introduced flora in the city. The Houston Garden Club specializes in developing private and public gardens. Each spring the River Oaks Garden Club sponsors the Azalea Trail, a tour of homeowners' gardens displaying several striking varieties of blooming azaleas.

The animal life of Houston is as varied as its plant life. Among the numerous varieties of insects that inhabit the city are the cicada, distinguished by a constant monotonous singing during the summer. During late spring, mayflies and June bugs appear. In the summer, various butterflies, dragonflies, moths and bees buzz and flit among the plants. During autumn, monarch butterflies fly south through the city on their annual trek to Mexico for the winter, creating a colorful sight.

Bullfrogs, whose large tadpoles swim in the creeks and ponds of the area, croak loudly throughout springtime and summertime nights. Other amphibians include the gray and green tree frogs, cricket frogs,

Raccoons are well-known nighttime adventurers in Houston.

The Houston toad is an amphibian facing extinction.

A Houston winter resident, the yellow-bellied sapsucker.

Gulf Coast toads, spade foot toads, leopard frogs and narrow-mouthed toads. The Houston toad, a rarity in the city whose name it bears, is threatened with extinction. It still inhabits a few protected areas in South Texas, however.

Houston's bayous harbor such reptiles as red-eared turtles, snapping turtles, water snakes and garter snakes. Green snakes, box turtles, and ground skinks exist in the woods. Hognose snakes are fairly common in some areas. The green anole, a four to five-inch long lizard which changes color to match its background, visits many local yards; during spring, the males sit on fences or brick walls, displaying their pink throat fans and bobbing their heads up and down. One rarely sights such reptiles as rattlesnakes, copperheads, coral snakes and water moccasins in the city.

Bird life abounds in Houston, which offers ideal nesting grounds for various types. The Edith L. Moore Nature Sanctuary in the western part of the city has 130 species, which one may view throughout the year, while a local bird club's checklist for birds in the Harris County area numbers nearly 350.

In addition to pigeons, house sparrows and starlings, some of the more common birds that claim

The Houston Zoo is an open door to the world of nature.

Houston as home throughout the year include cardinals, blue jays, mockingbirds, eastern meadowlarks, cattle egrets, red-winged blackbirds, loggerhead shrikes, barn owls, mourning doves, red-bellied woodpeckers, grackles and killdeers.

During summer, the Houston bird population increases when breeding birds, that winter in Central and South America, return to nest in the area. One of the most popular of these is the purple martin, for which many residents provide apartment birdhouses. Although the claim that each purple martin devours 2,000 mosquitoes a day is most likely an exaggeration, they do catch and eat numerous varieties of insects in flight. Moreover, their cheerful chattering pleases the ear.

The chimney swift, another Houston summer resident, takes refuge in many local fireplaces. While chicks cry loudly for food, their parents fly about, catching insects for their young. Nighthawks, on the other hand, prefer nesting on flat gravel roofs; their "penk" call is an evening sound familiar to many. The eastern kingbird, which emits a raucous noise while chasing a crow or a hawk from its nesting site, is more highly visible than another Houston summer breeder, the yellow-billed cuckoo. One might be able to observe yellow-crowned night herons, the only wading birds that nest in the city, in the higher limbs of tall oaks or pines. Green herons do not nest in residential areas, but frequent many of the small lakes and ponds throughout the city. The scissor-tailed flycatcher, a beautiful bird with salmon-pink sides and long streaming tails, is a common summer resident of Houston.

Still another bird that claims Houston as home during the warmer months is the fascinating ruby-throated hummingbird, difficult to find in its small lichen cup-shaped nest hidden in the branches of a tree. Other birds that are common summer visitors in the Houston area, include the great-crested flycatcher, wood duck and yellowthroat warbler.

PART II

THE PAST portrays the history of the city from the time of the settlement of Harrisburg, now a part of Houston, by John Harris in the early nineteenth century, through the founding of Houston by Augustus and John Allen in 1836, and up to the present. At one time the capital of the Republic of Texas, Houston's changing fortune through the nineteenth century and into the twentieth is described. Then comes a presentation of outstanding citizens who have contributed to the growth of the city and have left their lasting impression on it. Descriptions of the landmarks, monuments, the sites and sights, representing significant people, places and events in Houston's past, and present, follow.

HISTORY

Since the early nineteenth century Houston has undergone dramatic transformation. Its development goals were first set in 1836 by its founders, Augustus and John Allen, and from then on Houston pursued its great course throughout the nineteenth century and into the twentieth with such tenacious determination that any obstacles proved transitory.

For centuries before Europeans arrived in the area, numerous nomadic Indian tribes traversed the flat, semitropical region. Three Indian tribes—the Bidais, Karankawas and Orcoquisacs—sparsely inhabited the territory.

The Bidais left few lasting impressions of their culture. The Karankawas, who lived to the southeast near the Galveston coast, are remembered for their harassment of early settlers, among whom was the notorious eighteenth century French pirate Jean Lafitte. The seminomadic, rather primitive Orcoquisacs lived in the aftermath of the agricultural based civilization of the mound-building East Texas Caddo tribe. The Caddo word for "friendly," *tejas,* gave the state its name. The Orcoquisacs were a small tribe which roamed the lower San Jacinto and Trinity river valleys, fishing in family groups along the upper reaches of Galveston Bay. In winter time they settled into semipermanent villages along Spring Creek, in the northern part of present-day Harris County. There, the Orcoquisacs hunted bear, deer and buffalo, and sometimes cultivated maize.

EARLY EUROPEAN EXPLORATIONS

The bayous and flat lands became the pathways by which Spanish explorers, occasional French traders and Anglo frontier adventurers visited the area. Soon after Columbus "discovered" America, Spanish explorers ranged into the territory in the vicinity of present-day Houston. Among them were Captain Alonzo Alvarez de Pineda, who was the first to map

A mountainous Houston, painted by an artist who had never been there.

the Texas coast in 1519, and Alvar Nunez Cabeza de Vaca. The latter was captured by the Karankawa Indians in 1528, after his ship was wrecked on the Galveston coast. He escaped and fled westward into the interior, where he lived for some six years among the local natives, calling them the "cow" nation in reference to the herds of buffalo they followed. Thus began Spain's long hegemony over Texas, which was, until 1836, a part of Mexico. Spanish influence remains strong in Houston today.

In 1685, Rene Robert Cavelier, Sieur de la Salle, claimed all the lands west of the Mississippi River for King Louis XIV of France. La Salle built Fort Saint Louis near the site of present-day Port Lavaca, southwest of Houston. He camped at the headwaters of Cypress Creek in the greater Houston area in February 1687, and soon afterwards was murdered by members of his own party near Navasota to the northwest.

In the eastern part of Texas, competition between the French and Spanish characterized most of the eighteenth century. Trade routes, including the Spanish Atascosita Trail, which traversed what is now northern Harris County, stretched from Louisiana to the Rio Grande. However, neither the Spanish nor the French successfully introduced permanent settlements or gained firm control of the area.

ANGLO-AMERICAN COLONIZATION

In 1763, the Treaty of Paris marked the end of the French and Indian War and effectively eliminated the French presence from Texas. The more aggressive English soon replaced the French. In 1803, the United States obtained the Louisiana Purchase from Napoleon, and with it the French claim to all of the lands west of the Mississippi. Anglo-American adventurers and colonists soon arrived in Texas, notwithstanding the opposition of the Spaniards who did not recognize any American rights to those lands.

In the early 1820s, colonists began settling the land grants which Stephen Fuller Austin, the "Father of Texas," had secured. After Mexico gained independence from Spain in 1821, the Mexican government received the settlers warmly. Mexico was especially interested in establishing a buffer against invading Indians, particularly the feared Comanches from the north.

The original Texas colonizers, 297 families in all, became known as the prestigious "Old Three Hundred." Transforming the territory from a Spanish wilderness into an Anglo-American republic, some of the families chose to settle first in the present

RIGHT: *The glittering towers of the South's largest city complement the twilight sky.*

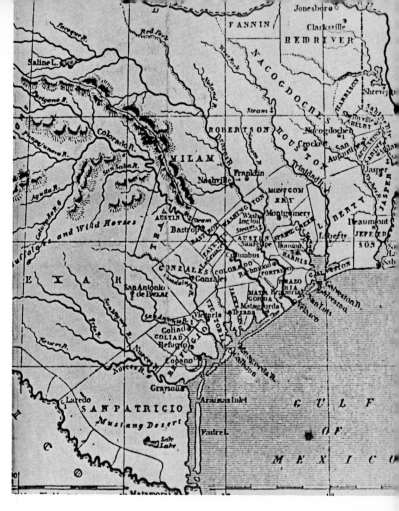

Harris County area. Among them was John Richardson Harris, grandson of the founder of Harrisburg, Pennsylvania. In 1826, Harris founded a settlement on the north side of Buffalo Bayou near its junction with Bray's Bayou, and called it Harrisburgh, later Harrisburg. In this first townsite, now known as Houston, Harris established a trading post and a sawmill.

The 1830s was a decade of great change in Texas. The Anglo-American settlers in the territory soon outnumbered the Mexicans, who became increasingly anxious about the growing Anglo presence and power. On April 6, 1830, the Mexican government annexed the territory to the Mexican state of Coahuila and prohibited both additional settlement of the area by colonizers from the United States and the importation of more slaves. Moreover, they imposed custom, duties and taxes, and stationed Mexican soldiers in Texas at the colonists' expense.

REVOLUTION AND TEXAS INDEPENDENCE

In 1833, the Anglo-American settlers' independence movement came into the open. By 1835 war with Mexico seemed inevitable. The Texans formed a provisional government at San Felipe in November and named General Sam Houston, former United States congressman and governor of Tennessee, as commander-in-chief of its army. In the middle of February, under their president, General Antonio Lopez de Santa Anna, the Mexicans besieged the fort of Alamo in San Antonio. The defenders' heroic stand in the face of overwhelming odds served to deepen the resolve of the other Texans. Meeting at Washington-on-the-Brazos on March 2, 1836, four days before the Alamo fell to Santa Anna's troops,

LEFT: *The* Broken Obelisk *by Barnett Newman, stands in the reflecting pool facing the Rothko Chapel entrance.*

Where buffalo and wild horses roamed in the new-born Republic of Texas (1836 - 1845).

the provisional government declared Texas independent. Fighting to the last man, such heroes as James Bowie and David Crockett went down with the Alamo. The ragged Texas army would later remember their feat in its battle cry.

An architect's vision of the Capitol Building of the Texas Republic.

The Capitol Hotel was very popular in horse and buggy days.

The temporary congress named David G. Burnet provisional president and established Harrisburg as the seat of government. Determined to crush the revolution, Santa Anna pursued the retreating Texas army. Intent on taking Harrisburg, Santa Anna marched to the town, arriving on April 14, 1836. But Burnet and the cabinet heard of the threat and fled to Galveston. Foiled, the Mexican general ordered the town of Harrisburg burned and continued eastward in pursuit. On April 20, 1836, after traveling 22 miles from Harrisburg, the Mexicans stopped on the peninsula created by the confluence of Buffalo Bayou and the San Jacinto River, opposite the camp of General Sam Houston and his Texans.

Houston, in the meantime, regrouped the Texas forces and positioned his outnumbered army on the peninsula. On April 20, the Mexicans and Texans fought a few minor skirmishes but, playing for time and opportunity, Houston avoided full-scale engagement. In the middle of the afternoon of the next day, as the overconfident Santa Anna enjoyed his siesta, Houston and 910 of his Texans stormed the 1,300 or more sleepy Mexicans in one of the epic battles of Texas history. With the battle cry "Remember the Alamo!" the Texans destroyed the Mexican army, killing half and taking the other half captive. The battle lasted only eighteen minutes. But, by the end of it, the ragged Texas army, composed of American expatriates, had won for Texas both independence and nationhood. In exchange for his freedom Santa Anna—the self-proclaimed "Napoleon of the West"—relinquished Mexico's claim to Texas. The Battle of San Jacinto, as it became known, led to the creation and independence of the Republic of Texas and, later to the treaty by which Texas joined the United States.

THE ALLEN BROTHERS AND THEIR DREAM TOWN

In the meantime, Augustus Allen and his brother John arrived in Galveston from New York in late 1831. Settling in Saint Augustine in 1832 and later in Nacogdoches, they engaged in a variety of promotional enterprises before arriving in the Harrisburg area.

Being shrewd businessmen, it did not take Augustus and John Allen long to realize the commercial potential of the area surrounding Buffalo Bayou. They were initially interested in several unavailable tracts of land, including Harrisburg, for the founding of a town. But the Harris estate was under litigation. Later after further investigation, the Allens learned that the bayou was navigable to a point further upstream and decided that the confluence of White Oak and Buffalo Bayous would make a good sport for a settlement.

In the summer of 1836, shortly after the Battle of San Jacinto, the Allens offered Mrs. Elizabeth Parrott $5,000 for a half league of the John Austin stake along Buffalo Bayou. The widow of John Austin, who was one of the "Old Three Hundred" colonists accompanying Stephen F. Austin, Mrs. Parrott readily accepted. Thus, on August 26, 1836, the Allens purchased some 6,000 acres of land on the southern bank of tree-lined, murky Buffalo Bayou, naming the site "Houston," in honor of the man who had become the hero of the new republic.

Gambling on the success of their new land venture, Augustus and John Allen believed that General Sam Houston, hero of the Battle of San Jacinto, was assured of election as first president of Texas. On August 30, 1836, the Allens announced the opening of their townsite, offering land for sale at one dollar per acre. Extolling Houston as the future "great interior commercial emporium of Texas," they advertised its merits, both real and anticipated, in the newspapers of Louisville, New Orleans, Washington and New York. Among the "exaggerated" descriptions was that of Houston as a thriving port city, propitiously located on Buffalo Bayou and "by nature" destined to be the republic's "future seat of government."

As expected, Texans elected Sam Houston their first president. Augustus Allen was elected to serve as the representative of Nacogdoches in the republic's first congress, which convened in October at Columbia, south of Houston. Offering his new "town" as the capital, Allen bolstered his proposal with promises of constructing a capitol building and providing land for government offices. His offer won congressional acceptance in the final resolution prior to adjournment in December. Houston, consisting of a few rough shelters and tents, became the new nation's capital.

In November 1836, Gail and Thomas Borden surveyed and mapped the original townsite, from Buffalo Bayou on the north to what is now Texas Avenue on the south, and from Crawford on the east to Bagby on the west. Gail Borden, who later achieved fame as the inventor of the process for condensing milk, was publisher of the *Telegraph and Texas Register,* the newspaper he founded in San Felipe in 1835 and moved to Houston in 1837. The Bordens plotted Texas Avenue, the western boundary of the Allens' townsite, 14 steers or 100 feet wide, in order to accommodate cattle drives. The Allen brothers, in turn, named many of the settlement's first broad streets (most were 80 feet wide) after early Texas settlers and heroes; several of those who fought in the Battle of San Jacinto chose to live in Houston City, as it was called.

Faced with the enormous task of building a capital city from scratch, the Allen brothers began three major building projects: the capitol, the county courthouse and a long row of buildings divided into stores and stalls. The block designated by the Allens for the county courthouse is today, as in the past, occupied by that institution.

To convince skeptics that Buffalo Bayou was navigable, the Allens offered the captain of the steamship *Laura M.* $1,000 to carry supplies and settlers from Galveston to Houston. Passing a few tents and rough shelters without realizing that that was the "prosperous" city of Houston, the captain continued on for about three more miles, until he was no longer able to navigate the vine-choked bayou and had to back his steamer down to "Allen's Landing" at the foot of Main and Congress streets. Although the last 16 miles of the journey from Harrisburg had taken three days, the captain completed the voyage, earning his incentive.

When the new republic's congress arrived in Houston in April 1837, the capitol was still incomplete, and only a few buildings had been erected. John James Audubon, the prominent naturalist, visited Houston at that time, studying and painting birds and other wildlife along the Gulf Coast. In a meeting with Sam Houston, Audubon expressed displeasure concerning the mud and the incomplete condition of the buildings. Thence, until the city paved its streets in the 1890s, Houstonians were called "mud turtles"— the latter part of the epithet surely being a misnomer if one considers the hectic pace of growth even in those early days.

EARLY HOUSTON

In June 1837, Houston was incorporated as a city with some 1,200 residents. It rapidly developed as a trade center for agricultural products, cotton, lumber and hides from the surrounding areas. Still, for some time to come, Buffalo Bayou constantly needed dredging, and railroads did not reach the town until the 1850s.

By the end of 1837, Houston had its first courthouse and jail. In 1838, John Carlos opened the city's first theater. In 1839, as the population of the city approached 3,000, the first public school was opened. Harrisburg County, established three years before, was renamed Harris County with Houston as county seat. The Allens' dream was fast becoming a reality.

Although he lived to see his town take its place as the national and local seat of government, John K. Allen died in 1838 of congestive fever. He was twenty-nine years old. The brilliant entrepreneur was spared the bitter disappointment that Houstonians were dealt by the 1839 congressional decision which moved the republic's seat of government to Austin in the Texas Hill Country, where the republic's congress met the following year. Heat, humidity, mosquitoes and other discomforts that plagued the legislators in addition to the absence of promised facilities in Houston, were cited as the reasons for the move.

Original plan of Houston, land of milk if not honey, as mapped by the Borden Brothers, inventors of the process for condensing milk.

THE **ORIGINAL PLAN** OF **HOUSTON**

The Harris County Court House proudly represents the law in Houston and Harris County.

Well into the 1840s, Houston looked like a frontier town, featuring characteristics of both the slower-paced South and the wild West. Besides these, the city had all the elements that later figured in its rise to pre-eminence in the state and in the country: hope, opportunity, ambition, enterprise, courage, innocence and youthful vitality.

Houston saw racial tension as well. Many of the early colonizers had built plantations and owned black slaves. Indeed, one of the underlying reasons for rebellion against Mexico was the outlawing, in 1830, of the importation of more slaves. The slave trade, active in Houston until the 1860s, contributed significantly to the initial settlement of East Texas.

The Indians, however, were friendly toward the whites; the Cherokees had conferred upon the republic's first president, and city's namesake, the title of "Honorary Chief." A few Cherokees lived on the north side of Houston, and occasionally did business at Kennedy's Trading Post.

In January 1840, at a time of economic crisis, a group of thriving businessmen established the Chamber of Commerce to help improve the business atmosphere. In 1841, a city ordinance officially created the Port of Houston, and the long task of improving the bayou for navigation began. By 1842, the Houston area population exceeded 4,700. Sam Houston, serving his second term as president of Texas, temporarily returned the seat of government to Houston that year, after Mexican troops invaded the republic and threatened the lawmakers in Austin. Meanwhile, receipts from the export of cotton continuously rose. Trade, rather than manufacturing, proved instrumental in the city's early growth.

Houston's city fathers built their city hall in the block that was designated as Congress Square on the original map; since the site of the capital was moved, the Allens never completed the planned government structures. Congress Square remained unbuilt and became a convenient spot at which farmers from the

surrounding areas sold their goods. People began calling the area Market Square, and it later served as the site of a succession of commercial enterprises.

Typical of the early successful merchants, Thomas William House rose from his beginning as a baker, who did some money lending as a sideline, to become a cotton magnate, banker and investor in railroads and public utilities. During the Civil War, he transported military equipment. Both he and contemporary William Marsh Rice emerged as millionaires by the time the Civil War ended. House and Rice contributed enormously to Houston's growth. Rice arrived in Houston in 1838 and became a partner in the commercial establishment of Rice and Nichols, as well as a founder of the Houston and Galveston Navigation Company. Renaming the firm the Houston Navigation Company, Rice acquired recognition as an early developer of Buffalo Bayou into a major shipping lane.

ANNEXATION, THE MEXICAN WAR AND STATEHOOD

With the 1840s came many changes in Texas generally and in Houston particularly. Sam Houston's second term as president of Texas ended in 1844 when the United States of America finally offered statehood to the republic. Although Texans had sought annexation since 1836, believing the future development of their country would be enhanced under United States' sovereignty, there were many in the United States Congress who opposed the annexation of a slave state. Nevertheless, on December 29, 1845, Texas became the twenty-eighth state of the Union.

Mexico promptly severed relations with the United States and, soon thereafter, the Mexican-American War broke out. Texans volunteered for military action in large numbers, and the increased traffic through the Port of Houston further contributed to the city's growth. When hostilities ended with the signing of the treaty of Guadalupe Hidalgo on February 2, 1848, Mexico yielded all its claims to the territory of Texas, part of nearly one million square miles of land it ceded to the United States. In addition to Texas, Mexico lost the territories that later became the states of New Mexico, Arizona, Nevada, California and Utah, as well as parts of present day Colorado, Wyoming, Kansas and Oklahoma.

In 1850, the United States took its first census covering Texas. Houston registered a population of 2,396 and Harris County, nearly double that figure, or 4,686. At a time when the entire population of Texas totaled 212,592, Houston accounted for what was merely a drop in the bucket—a little more than one percent.

Indeed, the city had just begun to surpass Harrisburg in prosperity. Farther downstream, at the Gulf of Mexico, Galveston ranked as the largest and wealthiest city in Texas, as well as the largest port. Competition and rivalry between Galveston and its aggressive neighbor, Houston, began in the 1840s. It characterized the relationship of the two cities during the remainder of the nineteenth century.

THE STRUGGLE FOR DOMINANCE

The decade of 1850 marked an era of significant economic growth in Houston. The city emerged as the regional center of rail transportation and of the cotton trade. Since Houston lay in the gulf coastal plain of Texas, where heavy rains could wipe out carriage roads, dependable rail transportation was a key factor in its economy's development. By 1860, 500 miles of rail track crisscrossed Texas; 350 of these miles and five railroad companies served Houston. Between 1854 and 1860, the volume of cotton shipped from Houston nearly tripled—from 39,923 to 115,010 bales annually. In addition to cotton, Houston exported wheat, cattle, rice and sugar. As an alternative to rail transportation, some city fathers began to promote water transportation and in 1858 Buffalo Bayou wharf fees were abolished.

Societies of music, art and philosophy sprang up as prosperity stimulated interest in culture and the arts. In 1854, free public education, as provided by

The general store owned by Thomas William House, supplied Houston with what it needed; first bread, then guns, and finally military equipment.

state law, came to Houston. The following year city ordinances instituted "blue laws" that closed bars, billiard parlors and bowling alleys on Sundays. Saloons, however, still outnumbered churches. By 1860, 4,845 people claimed Houston as their home; the population of the city had more than doubled in ten years.

The decade, however, was not without its setbacks. Sporadic epidemics of cholera and yellow fever plagued Houston. In 1853, Buffalo Bayou overflowed its banks and caused the first major flood in the city. Six years later, fires ravaged the central part of the

Allen's Station in the old Houston of frontier days.

city. But with a resiliency that became characteristic, Houston—and Houstonians—soon recovered.

THE CIVIL WAR AND RECONSTRUCTION

Recovery from plague, flood and fires came none too soon. What proved to be a more formidable setback, the War Between the States, now threatened Houston's progress. Although slavery had become a hotly debated national issue, it was only a secondary issue in Houston, where the question of secession was the major topic of debate. In 1859, Sam Houston left his United States Senate seat to become Texas' governor. Despite his opposition, the convention held on January 28, 1861, voted by a majority of 165 to 7 to withdraw from the Union. On March 16, Sam Houston was ousted from office when he refused to take the oath of allegiance to the Confederacy.

During the war, many of the city's young men joined the Confederate forces. Most served in local units such as the Confederate Guards, the Bayou City Guards, Turner's Rifles and Terry's Texas Rangers. Houston served as the military headquarters for the Confederate district of Texas, New Mexico and Arizona. When Federal troops occupied Galveston on October 4, 1862, Houston was inundated with refugees, many of whom chose to remain there after the war.

This was not the war's only repercussion for Houston. Union forces blockaded the entire Texas coast from the start of the hostilities. Some 1,600 Confederate forces under General John Bankhead Magruder were mobilized in Houston and recaptured Galveston Island on January 1, 1863. Although they held it until the end of the war, in 1865, and kept the port open, the vital shipping trade slowed to a trickle until it came to a standstill. Cut off from supplies and its port idle, most Houston residents and businesses suffered. Such goods as cotton were transported by rail and wagon to Mexican ports.

Throughout this period of hardship, Houstonians displayed their mettle in various ways. On September 8, 1803, Lieutenant Dick "the Kid" Dowling led a company of 42 men against a 15,000-man Union landing force at Sabine Pass. Capturing two of the four federal gunboats and a number of prisoners, in

The Main Street of Houston has progressed from a wide muddy road lined with wooden buildings to an asphalt and concrete ribbon surrounded by multi-story structures, as seen above, and at the top of pages 26, 28, 30, 32 and 34.

what proved to be the last major Union offensive in Texas, Dowling and his men prevented the Yankees from taking this strategic rail junction.

On June 19, 1865, Union General Gordon Granger announced the end of the war and proclaimed, from Galveston Island, the emancipation of Texas slaves. Thus originated the unique "Juneteenth" celebration in Texas. To prevent the outbreak of violence, the Federal government stationed troops in Houston as it did in many other towns. After a brief period of military rule, an unpopular Reconstruction government, denounced as carpetbaggers, was established in Texas.

Economic difficulties beset the state in the years immediately following the war, especially in areas such as Houston, which had openly supported the Confederate cause. Although slow, Houston's recovery followed a steady course. In the summer of 1867, the worst yellow fever epidemic in the city's history tragically interrupted the pace. Eventually, however, the enterprising spirit of the frontier persevered.

Soon, Houston's railroads were connected with the transcontinental system. By 1882, ten railway lines served the city, and it became one of the railway hubs of the South. With the formation of the Houston Board of Trade and the Cotton Exchange, the city emerged as a major center of commerce.

The port, as well as the railroads, received special attention from the city's leaders. In 1869, the Buffalo Bayou Ship Channel Company was created. Its purpose was to widen and deepen (to nine feet) the waterway, in anticipation of seafaring traffic. The following year the company (a private organization with some public support) succeeded in obtaining a congressional designation of Houston as a port of delivery, awarding it federal funds to finance an improvement project. By the late 1870s, the Buffalo Bayou Ship Channel Company deepened the draft to twelve feet, while widening the channel to 120 feet.

On March 30, 1870, Texas was readmitted to the Union, and in August of that year, Houston received a new city charter establishing eight city wards. But the city did not shed the restraints of the despised Reconstruction rule in Texas until 1873, when Texans elected a Democratic governor. In June 1873, Houston was reincorporated as a city, with a population of 9,400, and its earlier Republican charter was invalidated.

THE LAST QUARTER OF THE NINETEENTH CENTURY

Free from the imposed restraints of the postwar recovery period, Houston now embarked afresh on a new course of civic and economic development. Both of present-day major daily newspapers first set up shop in this period: the *Post* in 1880, with J. L. Watson at the helm, and the *Chronicle* in 1901, with Marcellus E. Foster, a former *Post* editor, as its publisher. In 1895, William Sydney Porter—who later achieved fame under his pen name of O. Henry—joined the *Post's* staff.

According to the United States census, the population of Houston in 1880 stood at 16,513. But by 1890, a thriving Houston claimed 27,557 in the decennial count. Two years later, the development of the area known as Houston Heights began across the Buffalo Bayou from the original Allen brothers' downtown Houston.

Between 1875 and 1900, the city registered several Texas firsts: the telephone was introduced in 1878, the electric streetcar in 1891 and, in 1897, the automobile—bearing with them the spawning of industry and much of the growth of twentieth century Houston.

And Houston began to reap returns from the fortunes made by some of its more prosperous

This oil well was one of hundreds pumping in Goose Creek, now part of Houston, in the early 1900 s.

citizens. In 1891, William Marsh Rice returned to Houston from New York City. He set up an initial $200,000 fund to establish an educational institution in Houston "for the advancement of literature, science and art." Events surrounding Rice's murder in 1900 delayed the fulfillment of his dream until 1911 and on the 75th anniversary of the Texas Declaration of Independence, the cornerstone of the institution's administration building was laid.

Now called Rice University, and referred to as the "Harvard of the South," the private Rice Institute ranked as the seventh wealthiest educational institution in the nation when it finally opened in 1912.

Houston claimed other benefactors during the late nineteenth century. In 1893, in one of his first philanthropic gestures, George H. Hermann donated a site near the embryonic Rice Institute for the charitable hospital that later bore his name. In 1898, a philanthropic gesture of a non-Houstonian, New York's Andrew Carnegie, reached the city in the form of a $50,000 endowment for a public library.

THE EARLY 1900s

A placid Houston stood on the threshold of the twentieth century—a progressive, small city of 45,000. It's economy, rooted in agriculture and distribution, had as yet no inkling of minerals and related manufacturing. When time came, though, its businessmen rose to the occasion in a manner typical of the spirit on which the early city thrived.

On the night of September eighth and ninth, in the first year of the new century, what became known as the Great Storm of 1900 devastated Galveston. Packing winds of more than 100 miles per hour, the violent hurricane sent fifteen-foot tidal waves crashing across the entire island, destroying most of what lay in its path. By the time the storm subsided, more than

Traffic was a problem in downtown Houston in 1929. Pictured here is the intersection of Franklin and Caroline streets.

5,000 people had died and thousands more were left homeless. This is still regarded today as the nation's worst natural disaster. In the aftermath of the hurricane, Thomas Edison visited the island to film one of his first newsreels.

Many of the storm's survivors either fled to or received aid in Houston, which escaped the brunt of the storm. Buffeted by winds only 60 miles per hour strong, Houston suffered mainly property damage. Galveston, at the time one of the wealthiest cities in the country and with a natural harbor that made it the commercial capital of America's Southwest frontier, was almost completely wiped out.

Galveston's misfortune provided the impetus for new growth in the Bayou City. Texas clearly had a real need for an inland port like Houston, safe from even the most destructive hurricanes. The following year, the first great gusher of oil in Texas erupted, further assuring Houston's role in replacing Galveston as the major Texas port.

Anthony Lucas' gusher at Spindletop, near Beaumont, ninety miles to Houston's northeast, erupted on January 11, 1901. Although it was not the

Members of the Houston Police Force in 1903, sporting moustaches.

first oil discovery in Texas, it ushered in the Texas oil boom and the petrochemical age, that changed the course of Houston's history. Spindletop's oil, as did oil from all the other gushers that followed, needed refining and distributing.

While Beaumont's establishment displayed a remarkable lack of interest in the task, Houstonians could not have responded to the opportunity more enthusiastically. Within a few months the city emerged as the refining and distribution center of Spindletop crude. By the end of the year, a refinery had been built in the Heights, and about 50 industrial plants in the city had converted to oil-fueled energy systems. In 1902, the Southwestern Oil Company was the largest independent oil refinery in the world. In 1905, oil was discovered closer to town, in the Humble oil field of northern Harris County, seventeen miles north of Houston. The following year, the big Goose Creek oil field in eastern Harris County came through. Both Humble and Goose Creek later yielded more than 100 million barrels of oil.

Related enterprises, such as natural gas companies and oil tool manufacturing, accompanied the developing oil industry. Enjoying its new found prosperity, Houston emerged as a "new South" town.

In 1905, Carrie Nation brought her crusade against sin to prosperous, naughty Houston, which was at the time conducting its own cleanup: in a radical and, one imagines, difficult ordinance to enforce, the city commissioners forbade men "to make goo-goo eyes" at, or otherwise flirt publicly with, ladies.

By 1906, some thirty oil companies and seven banks had opened offices in the city. Construction of the city's first "skyscrapers," buildings as high as eight stories, began downtown. In 1910, the census counted 78,800 Houstonians, as against about 39,000

The Union Station, opened in 1910, represented Houston's increased growth.

in Galveston (whose residents at present approach 70,000). Having finally surpassed Galveston, Houston did not fall behind again. Its population, in fact, continued to double in each succeeding decade to come.

At the end of 1911, the Houston-Galveston Electric Railway, known as the Interurban, made its first run. In January 1914, Houston made headlines as the first city in the South with a motor bus line. During the same year, the cotton market collapsed and the 51-mile-long, 100-foot-wide, 25-foot-deep ship channel opened. While the collapse of the cotton market did not affect Houston's economy to any great extent, the port proved extremely beneficial. The opening of the ship channel was made possible when the Federal government matched an equal amount of money raised locally for improvements, presaging the facility's role in the economies of both the United States and Houston. In August 1915, the arrival of the first ocean-going vessel at the Port of Houston via the Houston Ship Channel served to finally confirm the city's status as an international seaport. By 1919, authorities announced plans to deepen the channel's draft to a depth of thirty feet, while widening it to 150 feet. By 1928, Houston had its first airport, the Houston Municipal, or Main Street, Airport, and airmail service commenced as well. Improvement of transportation facilities aided the growth of the oil industry. By 1913, twelve oil companies were headquartered in Houston and, by the end of the 1920s, eight refineries were in operation.

Milestones in other aspects of city life accompanied Houston's economic growth. In 1913, a group of citizens formed the Houston Symphony Society; in 1924, the first art museum in Texas opened, and was later named the Museum of Fine Arts. The following year, George H. Hermann donated 285 acres of land to the city for the establishment of a park opposite Rice Institute, bearing his name. In 1925, the Hermann Hospital was inaugurated and remained one of the few to serve the area until the Texas Medical Center opened its doors in the 1940s.

During World War I, Houston's festering racial tension erupted in a violent confrontation between white citizens of the area and black soldiers stationed at Camp Logan, a U.S. military training base. In August 1917, black soldiers at the camp rioted, their resentment of the "Jim Crow" laws, then in force, exploding in fury. In the clash with policemen and white Houstonians, seventeen died (four policemen and thirteen blacks) and 22 were wounded. Later thirteen of the black soldiers were hanged and

World War I-era soldiers pridefully marching down Main Street from a nearby army camp, 1915.

numerous others received prison sentences of varying lengths; some of the terms were eventually commuted.

In 1924, Will and Mike Hogg, sons of former Texas governor James S. Hogg, arranged for the city to purchase the old Camp Logan land at cost. The result was the establishment of the 1,503-acre Memorial Park, located west of downtown Houston. Not only was Houston's public park space growing the city was also expanding. In 1918, the city consolidated with the Houston Heights development, launching what became a seemingly relentless and incessant pace in the city's expansion.

The city's population kept pace as well. In the census of 1920, Houston registered 138,276 citizens, an increase of 75 percent over the 1910 count. In the next few years, numerous future celebrities called the city their home, at least temporarily. Among these were Clark Gable, then a fledgling actor, and a young man from Central Texas, Lyndon Baines Johnson, who taught at the old Sam Houston High School. The runaway growth pattern characteristic of today's Houston took hold during the decade of the 1920s. By the year 1929, the population of the city exceeded 292,000, and at the same time, some 100,000 motor vehicles were registered.

The engine, gas tank, radiator and propeller of the Curtiss modified airplane, shown here in 1911 at the South Houston Airfield, were donated to the Smithsonian Institute in 1937.

Houston continued gaining national and international renown for its vast wealth and resources. Petroleum, livestock and natural gas were chief among them. Houstonians, proud of their town, never ceased efforts to promote it and enhance its prestige. Civic leader Jesse H. Jones was instrumental in convincing the organizers of the 1928 Democratic National Convention to meet in Houston. The first city in the South to host the national event since the War Between the States, Houston achieved widespread attention and a reputation as a hospitable place to visit.

DEPRESSION AND WORLD WAR II

In 1930, Houston replaced its northern cousin, Dallas, as the most populous city in Texas. Continually increasing numbers of people found Houston both a nice place to visit and an attractive town in which to settle, live and work.

Although there were shortages in both housing and work, Houston escaped the most adverse effects of the Great Depression, its economy displaying the resilience which has characterized it ever since. No banks failed in the dreadful aftermath of the depression: The major developer of the period, lumberman and financier Jesse Jones, persuaded city institutions to pool resources and thus keep weaker banks afloat. In 1930, the East Texas oil field, by far the biggest in the state, was discovered northeast of Houston; the production and refining of its petroleum provided employment to thousands.

In May 1932, Houston held its first Fat Stock Show, precursor of the immensely popular and internationally famous Houston Livestock Show and Rodeo. In June of that year, Houston Junior College, a community college founded in 1927, became the University of Houston; its first graduating class received its degrees in 1935. In 1933, another huge oil field, the Tomball field, was discovered in northern Harris County. Throughout the 1930s the volume of building in Houston increased considerably, as the city's economic development continued apace.

In a 1939 ruling, Houston won the right to control a 2,500 foot-wide strip of land along the ship channel for twenty miles from the city limits coupled with state laws granting cities nearly unrestricted authority to annex, Houston actively pursued a policy of growth.

This period saw the development of the Civic Center, an office and entertainment complex comprising not only existing and new buildings, but also the Sam Houston Coliseum (dedicated in November 1937) and the Music Hall (dedicated in April 1938).

Later, the Albert H. Thomas Convention and Exhibit Center (1967) and the Jesse H. Jones Hall for the Performing Arts (1968) joined the other structures; although officially not a part of the Oscar F. Holcombe Civic Center, the adjacent Nina Vance Alley Theatre (1969) is a nationally-acclaimed institution.

A unique Houston phenomenon, the absence of zoning laws, was particularly instrumental in facilitating the city's development. In the 1940 census, construction activity showed a feverish pace and a soaring increase in sales volume, while Houstonians numbered 384,514 and registered some 170,000 motor vehicles. That year a bus system replaced the streetcars, a sixty-year tradition.

Houstonians began to establish other city traditions. With World War II, and the increased dependence of the nation's economy and war effort on petroleum and its products, came the large-scale development of the petrochemical industry in the city. A vast industrial complex, complete with a continually expanding pipeline system, today exceeding 1,550 miles in length, grew along the Houston Ship Channel. This provided much of the impetus for the subsequent growth of the city. The third largest port after New York and Philadelphia at the outbreak of war, Houston ranked second after New York by 1948. Research and development evolved into a major industry.

The exploits of the fighting ship, the cruiser USS *Houston,* have seldom been equalled in the annals of Naval history. On January 7, 1927, a small

In this temporary structure, built for the 1928 Democratic National Convention in Houston, Franklin Delano Roosevelt nominated Al Smith for president of the United States.

group of Houston civic leaders formed the cruiser *Houston* Committee. The mayor of Houston, Oscar F. Holcombe, named Col. Thomas H. Ball, a former congressman, as its chairman and Commodore William A. Bernreider and Brig. Gen. Maurice Hirsch among its members. The committee induced the Secretary of the Navy to name a cruiser in honor of the City of Houston. The USS *Houston* was launched at Newport News, Virginia and commissioned on June 5, 1930. During her lifetime she served as the Presidential Flagship and the Flagship of seventeen admirals.

After the Pearl Harbor tragedy, the *Houston* (as the flagship of Adm. Thomas C. Hart), sailed from the Philippine Islands, under secret orders to raid and destroy Japanese naval units, transports and shipping in the China Sea. On that mission the *Houston* inflicted heavy damage and destruction to many ships and to vital communications of the enemy and fought in a succession of viciously fought battles against overwhelming odds.

Finally, in the Battle of Sundra Strait (sometimes referred to as the Battle of Java) in February 1942, the *Houston* engaged in violent combat. With turret blown to bits, decks strewn with the dead and dying, fires aboard, most guns destroyed and all ammunition exhausted, the ship went down. Over five hundred men were killed aboard the *Houston,* some two hundred drowned and some three hundred were captured by the Japanese.

Immediately after receiving the news of the fate of the cruiser *Houston,* the Secretary of the U.S. Navy, Col. Frank Knox, announced that a new ship, then under construction, would be named USS *Houston II.* A remarkable patriotic response occurred in Houston. On a call for volunteers to replace the men

of the cruiser *Houston* killed or captured in the battle, 1,432 men of Houston and its surrounding areas volunteered for service and 1,000 of these were enlisted. In addition, at a rally to provide funds for the new cruiser, over 85 million dollars were subscribed, sufficient to pay for the USS *Houston II*, with enough left over to pay for an aircraft carrier, later named the USS *San Jacinto*. The cruiser *Houston II*, following the valorous example of the first, was ordered to the Pacific and was later disabled in battle off Formosa.

A small bronze and marble historical marker at 1000 Main Street marks the site where the men of Houston and Texas volunteered to replace those lost on the first cruiser. A replica in miniature of the *Houston* is on display in the library of the University of Houston.

Development was not confined to industry and the economy. The Houston Zoological Gardens were established in 1941. The next year, voters authorized the sale of 134 acres of land adjacent to Hermann Park to the M.D. Anderson Foundation for the Texas Medical Center. The foundation was established in 1936 by Monroe D. Anderson of Anderson, Clayton and Company, international cotton brokers. Anderson was the moving force behind the idea of a major health care center in Houston. The M.D. Anderson foundation is still a major Houston philanthropic force. In 1943, the foundation successfully wooed the Baylor College of Medicine to the city from Dallas, where the college was founded in 1900. The only private medical school in Texas, Baylor was part of the Baptist-affiliated Baylor University until 1969.

At the end of 1944, the M.D. Anderson Foundation started the construction of the Texas Medical Center on the triangular site bounded by Fannin, Bellaire and the Hermann Hospital and Park. In 1945, it formed the Texas Medical Center Corporation to oversee development. In February 1946, the Texas Medical Center was formally dedicated.

POST WORLD WAR II

The years following World War II were characterized by enormous urban growth and prosperity in Houston. City engineers laid plans for the construction of radial arterials and the "loop" system of freeways. Work began on the projects, which were anticipated to provide comfortable road access from one part of town to another for a long time into the future. The planners, though, underestimated the volume of traffic the freeways were later expected to handle. Not many could have guessed at the numbers of automobiles and people that Houston would attract in the next thirty years.

Prominent among the structures erected downtown in the postwar construction surge was the magnificent Foley's building, which opened in 1947 and quickly

The end of World War I set Houston singing and the Rice Hotel was illuminated with victory lights.

became one of the most popular stores in Houston. Houston's steady parade of progress was not without levity and flamboyance. More fanfare accompanied the opening of oilman Glenn McCarthy's "63-shades-of-green" Shamrock Hotel on St. Patrick's Day 1949 than Houston had seen at any other opening celebration. Situated on a fifteen-acre parcel of land south of the downtown area, the hotel was later renamed the Shamrock Hilton.

In 1949, 268 oil fields operated within a 100-mile radius of Houston. That year, the city led the nation in postwar industrial expansion. In Texas, a state

Houstonians themselves were electrified by the new electric streetcar on its first trip down Texas Avenue, in front of the Rice Hotel.

whose population was eighty percent rural in 1900, the trend indicated a complete reversal. As the urban population approached eighty percent of the total, Houston led the march of burgeoning Texas centers. The city grew in area as well as population. In 1948, Houston doubled its size—73 square miles at the time—through the annexation of neighboring areas. It also ranked as the fastest growing city in the United States.

The city's growth included expansion of its educational facilities. Four institutions recorded milestones: Texas Southern University for Negroes, originally the Houston College for Negroes, became a state institution in 1947 and, in 1951, changed its name to Texas Southern University. The University of Saint Thomas, a Roman Catholic-affiliated private university, opened in 1947. In 1950, Rice Institute completed the 70,000-seat Rice Stadium, later one of the first homes of the young Houston Oilers football team. KUHT, the first educational television station in the United States, began broadcasting from the campus of the University of Houston in 1953. The city enjoyed other cultural firsts: in 1955, a group of citizens founded the Houston Ballet; the following year, the Houston Grand Opera gave its first performance.

The decade of the 1950s in Houston, coming as it did close on the heels of major industrial expansion, was not without its problems. Chief among them were the urban sprawl and transportation. The city took steps to alleviate them. In 1952, the Gulf Freeway was dedicated. In 1956, Houstonians approved a bond issue to facilitate expansion of the Port. At the same time, they supported widening the

Houston's own Shamrock Hilton, named for the "lucky clover," brings Houston "the luck of the Irish."

ship channel to 400 feet and deepening it to its present size of 40 feet. Houstonians gave little support, however, to the idea of improving the city's mass public transportation system, preferring instead the appropriation of funds for freeways. Bus ridership declined, continuing a trend initiated in the 1940s.

In response to an enormous increase in air traffic, the city improved its air links. In 1957, the Houston International Airport opened ten miles south of the central business district. Within a few years, however, it was rendered inadequate. Following a Civil Aeronautics Board ruling, which ended the Dallas monopoly on east-west air routes, construction began in 1961 on a new Houston Intercontinental Airport in northern Harris County. In 1967, the original Houston International Airport was renamed William P. Hobby Airport, to honor the former governor, publisher and philanthropist.

Annexation of neighboring areas again doubled the city's territory in 1956. This, coupled with a constant daily influx of newcomers, resulted in a large increase in the city's population by the time the 1960 census was taken. The decennial tally recorded 938,219 Houstonians, nearly twice as many as the 596,163 counted in 1950.

INTERNATIONAL CITY AND THE SPACE AGE

The 1960s signaled a period of further development in Houston, but the growth was not without attendant pain. Two widely divergent but related events of the decade's third year illustrated the range of contradictions inherent in Houston.

Rice Institute began admitting students of all races in 1962, and changed its name to Rice University. The university introduced tuition fees and, for the first time, became eligible to participate in federally funded programs. The same year, Houston became the center of the manned space explorations of the National Aeronautics and Space Administration (NASA) and received the sobriquet "Space City," a universal epithet to add to its list of nicknames. Later renamed the Lyndon Baines Johnson Space Center, the United States Manned Spacecraft Center thrust Houston into the international limelight, surrounding the city with the dream-like aura that typifies space travel. Houston became the symbol, an initial outpost for man's forays into space and the gate to the final frontier.

NASA's selection of Houston as home of the astronauts precipitated an influx of both scientists and related industries from throughout the world to the city. Economic diversification, largely initiated in the 1940s, when the ship channel industrial complex developed, proceeded in earnest. International trade and the engineering and construction industry came to the fore as well. In 1962, the World Trade Building opened—one of the first of its kind in the United States.

Throughout the 1960s, Houston consistently ranked third or fourth in the nation in annual dollar value of construction. By the late 1970s, it invariably began ranking first. Tall skyscrapers, ten times as tall as the ones that went up in the early days of the century, began defining Houston's skyline, dramatically rising above the green, flat, expansive terrain. The towering buildings mirrored the energy and enterprise of its people.

Builders and developers were among the busiest groups in Houston. In 1963, with the completion of several large buildings downtown, office space in the city increased by forty percent; foremost among these was Cullen Center. In April 1965, the first enclosed sports stadium in the world, the Harris County Domed Stadium, or Astrodome, opened seven miles southwest of downtown and was immediately claimed by Houstonians to be the "Eighth Wonder of the World." The following year, the Astrohall and, in 1968, the Astroworld opened, marking the completion of the Astrodomain. In 1967, construction began downtown on One Shell Plaza which, at fifty stories, was the tallest building west of the Mississippi River.

Among numerous other construction projects were those completing the Civic Center components, as well as Allen's Landing Park and Old Market Square. The latter two attempted to revive the oldest section of the city while creating a place of entertainment and enjoyment. Another reflection of the city's response to contemporary lifestyle, the new Miller Outdoor Theatre in Hermann Park, was built in 1968. In 1975, the unique Pennzoil Place, consisting of two huge trapezoidal towers designed by architect Philip M. Johnson, was erected and stands as a testimony to creative modernism.

In the 1960s, though, commuters increasingly dominated downtown. City centers of activity extended outside the central business district. Houstonians' love affair with their automobiles resulted in the frenzied construction of residential subdivisions, commercial strips and shopping centers alongside the loops, arteries and radials of the increasingly complex network of freeways. In 1969, within the so called "Magic Circle" area of southwestern Houston, on Interstate Loop 610, Galleria I opened. An immensely successful shopping-entertainment-dining complex, it preceded by eight years the opening of the adjacent Galleria II. Balconied high-rise offices punctuate the complex, a project of the prolific Houston developer Gerald D. Hines, and transmit an ambience of space-age futurism. In 1976, Kenneth Schnitzer's Century Development Corporation completed Greenway Plaza, another multiuse complex between the Southwest Freeway and Richmond Avenue in Southwest Houston.

Simultaneously, city benefactors did not ignore culture. The de Menil family commissioned the mystical, interdenominational Rothko Chapel, con-

Houston, as shown here, continues to grow both upward and outward beyond its present limits.

taining fourteen abstract oil canvasses of the late artist whom the chapel honors with its name. In 1966, longtime Houston doyenne, Miss Ima Hogg, donated her family's mansion, Bayou Bend, to the Museum of Fine Arts. Sitting on fourteen acres, Bayou Bend houses one of the foremost collections of early American decorative arts in the country. In 1972, the Contemporary Arts Museum moved into its new home on Montrose. January 1976, saw the opening of the Central Library facility of the city's public library system. At the mid-1970s, Houston boasted of at least eighty museums and art galleries.

Environmental interests were not overlooked, either. One program, in particular, resulted in the elimination of pollution in the ship channel to the extent that fish reappeared there after a twenty-year absence. With the largest concentration of scientists in the southwest this achievement seemed only fitting for Houston.

Amid all these advances, vestiges of Houston's frontier heritage remained, adding provincial color and contrast to a place of modern progress. The Texas legislature legalized the sale of liquor by the drink, for instance, in 1970, but Houstonians did not eliminate the need for "brown bagging" until 1975. Texas law still prohibits another modern vice, pari-mutual gambling; hence the affluent Houstonian's occasional journey to Louisiana, Las Vegas or to the Mexican border towns.

Nevertheless, throughout the 1970s word of Houston's tolerance and sophistication continued to spread. In 1973, the city hosted the first national

The Central Library, now physically accessible to the whole city, is the central "brain" of extensive research services.

convention of the newly organized National Women's Political Caucus—the first national feminist meeting since 1848.

The city attracted corporate decision-makers in droves. Between 1970 and 1980, more than 200 companies moved to call Houston home. Statistics show that office space had increased 172 percent during that time. Like the thousands of individuals who relocate in Houston monthly, contributing to its rise to fifth largest city in the United States, businesses are undoubtedly attracted by the city's weather, friendliness, lower taxes and unemployment, availability of labor and lower costs of construction and living.

During the 1970s, the economy, city boundaries and population have expanded and diversified. In 1979, Houston's city council representation was changed by federal order and the number of council members increased from eight to fourteen, in an attempt to give minorities a better opportunity to participate in local government.

It is estimated that as many as 6,000 persons per month come to join the ranks of Houstonians. While the census counted 1,232,802 residents in 1970, as the 1980s began the city's population is approaching two million. As many as one million more live in the greater metropolitan area. Thus, the city accounts for nearly one-seventh of the total population of Texas, itself the third most populous state in the country.

The average age of Houstonians, a young lot, is 28. Houstonians are attracted to their city for many of the same reasons that influenced its founding fathers to settle in the area; opportunity, hope and freedom from restrictions are chief among them. Growing at the fastest rate of all major cities, Houston is a world metropolis, not merely an American, Southwestern, or Texan city. Indeed, some fifty nations are represented in the growing ranks of its consular corps, which is the largest in the South and Southwest, and fifth largest in the United States.

A stimulating city of diversity and paradox, Houston is characterized by boundless energy and youthful vitality, tolerance and exuberance blended with its distinctive air of humor and good nature. Research and development and international commerce and cultural progress and consistent growth together best symbolize the destiny of the City of the Future. In them lies the future of Houston, the City of Destiny.

GREAT HOUSTONIANS

Many have contributed to Houston's development and growth from a small settlement on the bank of the Buffalo Bayou to the international metropolis that it is today. As a crossroads in the commercial highways of the world, Houston has been the home of a variety of people with the Midas touch.

These are the people we have called **Great Houstonians,** luminaries in such diverse fields as agriculture and banking, real estate and transportation, construction and medicine, oil and politics, investment and the arts. The following few are representative of the many individuals who have left their mark on Houston, urging it ever onward to its inevitable destiny.

Earliest among Houston's greats are the city's founders, the Allen brothers. They envisioned a thriving metropolis in a place full of lush vegetation where no man had settled before. **AUGUSTUS CHAPMAN ALLEN** was born on July 4, 1806, in Canasareaugh, New York, and **JOHN KIRBY ALLEN** was born in 1810 in Orville, near Syracuse, New York, to Sarah (Chapman) and Roland Allen.

Suffering from poor health since childhood, Augustus immersed himself in intellectual pursuits. At the age of seventeen, he graduated from a polytechnic institute in Chittenango, New York, where he later became a professor of mathematics. He resigned from the world of academia in 1827, in order to take the position of bookkeeper with the H. and H. Canfield Company in New York City.

His brother John had a knack for work and business even as a child. At the age of seven, he began to work in a hotel. Three years later, he was a store clerk and, at the age of sixteen, became a porter in a hat shop enterprise in Chittenango. Soon afterwards he joined Augustus in New York City, where the two brothers bought stock in the Canfield Company, marking the first enterprise of the fraternal entrepreneurs.

John Allen

In the winter of 1831-1832, Augustus and John Allen moved to Texas, arriving first in Galveston and soon thereafter moving to the small town of Saint Augustine. In 1833, they joined a group of land speculators in Nacogdoches and involved themselves in a variety of enterprises, including the procurement and sale of land certificates. Instead of joining the army when the revolution against Mexico began in 1835, the Allen brothers personally equipped and armed a vessel, called the *Brutus,* and set out to protect the Texas coast and to transport troops and supplies. Following increasing objections to their operations as civilians who were not members of the Texas armed forces, and rumors

that they were privateering, the Allens, in January, 1836, sold the ship at cost to the new Texas government and the *Brutus* became the second vessel in the fledgling Texas navy.

So, speculating on what to do, the brothers came across some land that they thought truly promising. Financed by an inheritance received by Augustus' wife, Charlotte, on August 26, 1836, the brothers purchased 6,600 acres along the Buffalo Bayou for $5,000, for the purpose of establishing a new city. At the suggestion of Charlotte, they named their townsite for the hero of the time, General Sam Houston.

Augustus Allen

John Allen, a delegate to the first congress, succeeded in having Houston named as the capital of the Republic of Texas. This act gave the city the big boost it needed in its first years of initial development. John Allen died of congestive fever on August 15, 1838. Since he had not married and did not leave a will his estate was entrusted to his parents and when they died in 1841, the other remaining Allen brothers took over.

In 1843, Augustus terminated his business relations with his brothers, mainly because he was unhappy with the management of the Allen properties. During the 1840s he began dealings with the president of Mexico, Benito Juarez. His health failing, Augustus transferred the bulk of his various enterprises to Charlotte. Later, in 1850, they separated, pledging to keep the details of their differences forever secret. Augustus left Houston permanently, never to return to the city he founded. Charlotte, however, remained in Houston until her death in 1895.

In 1852, Augustus Allen was appointed United States consul in the Pacific port of Tehuantepec in southern Mexico and later took a similar position in the port of Minotitlan, in 1858, where he worked to establish a trade route or canal, through Mexico. He also developed an extensive shipping business before becoming critically ill in 1864. He went to Washington, D.C. to resign his consulships and died there of pneumonia on June 11, 1864, just before his fifty-eighth birthday. He was buried in New York. Houston's Allen Parkway, Allen Center as well as Allen's Landing Park, all immortalize the name of the city's founders.

GENERAL SAMUEL HOUSTON, the Texas national hero and the namesake of the Allens' new town, was born on March 2, 1793, in Rockbridge County, Virginia, to an officer of the Revolutionary War and his wife. After the

Sam Houston

death of her planter husband, Houston's mother moved with her nine children to Blount County, Virginia. There young Sam met and developed a strong friendship with the neighboring Indian tribe, the Cherokees, a relationship he maintained and nurtured for the rest of his life.

In the War of 1812, Houston served under General Andrew Jackson, and earned his lifelong friendship. In Alabama, at the Battle of Horseshoe Bend against the Creek Indians, Houston displayed the courage that became his hallmark. There he received wounds in his right shoulder which never entirely healed.

Tall, handsome and ambitious, Houston returned after the war and settled in Lebanon, Tennessee, just outside of Nashville, where he studied law and established a practice. At the age of thirty, in 1823, he was elected to serve as a United States congressman. Four years later, he was elected governor of Tennessee. Shortly thereafter, Houston married a seventeen-year-old beauty, Eliza Allen, a Tennessee heiress.

After three months, however, Eliza left him and Houston, disillusioned, resigned as governor. For a period of time he returned to Arkansas to live among his friends, the Cherokees. Later they conferred upon the "Raven," as they called Houston, the title of honorary chief.

Houston arrived in Texas on December 2, 1832, determined—and destined, some say—for greatness. On March 2, 1836, the Texas Convention, of which Houston was a member, adopted a Declaration of Independence at Washington-on-the-Brazos. As it happened, Texans celebrate their Independence Day on the anniversary of Sam Houston's birthday.

Serving as commander-in-chief and general of the Texas army, Houston soundly defeated the troops of Mexican president General Antonio Lopez de Santa Anna at the famous Battle of San Jacinto on April 21, 1836, gaining independence for the new republic. Wounded in his ankle, Houston journeyed to New Orleans to recover. There he met Margaret Lee of Alabama, and four years later he married her.

Having returned to Texas, Houston was elected as the president of the newly independent Republic of Texas on September 5, 1836, holding that office until 1838. In May of the following year, with the government settled in the new city of Houston, he made political headway by obtaining recognition of the new republic from the United States.

From 1841 to 1844 he served a second term as president of the republic and pushed to have Texas admitted to the Union. When this was accomplished in 1845, and Texas became the twenty-eighth state, Houston

and Thomas J. Rusk were elected as the first United States senators from Texas. Houston influenced congress to establish, in 1854, a 1,280-acre reservation for Indians northeast of Houston. The Alabama and Coushatta tribes still live there today.

Houston left the Senate after his election as the seventh governor of Texas in 1859. When Texas voted to secede from the Union, Houston voiced his opposition, refusing to lead the state in such a move. He was consequently removed from the governorship in March, 1861.

Houston retired to his farm near Huntsville and died of pneumonia on July 26, 1863, at the age of seventy, still respected although in disfavor. His last words were, "Texas, Texas, Margaret!" A state university in Huntsville, a national forest in southeast Texas, as well as numerous places, buildings and establishments have been named in his honor.

Saloon-keeper, soldier and Confederate folk hero, **LIEUTENANT RICHARD WILLIAM DOWLING,** known as "Dick the Kid" to his buddies, was born in Tuam, Galloway County, Ireland in 1838. One of Mary and William Dowling's seven children, Dowling arrived in New Orleans at the age of ten to visit relatives, accompanied by his eleven-year-old sister Honora. Later, the rest of the family arrived in New Orleans. When Dowling's parents died in a cholera epidemic, the children moved first to Galveston and later to Houston. On Thanksgiving Day, November 30, 1857, at the age of 19, Dowling married Elizabeth Anne Odlum.

In 1860, Dowling opened the popular "Bank of Bacchus" Saloon at the corner of Houston's Main and Congress streets. During the war, Dowling closed his saloon and enlisted to defend the Confederacy. He was made a first lieutenant in the Davis Guards, a Texas homeguard outfit consisting entirely of Irish stevedores. Dowling first saw action as an artillery officer on one of Confederate General John Bankhead Magruder's "cotton clad" vessels which recaptured Galveston Island on January 1, 1863 from Union occupation.

On September 8, 1863, while commanding the Davis Guards defending the strategic Sabine Pass, Dowling and his band of 42 routed a Union flotilla consisting of five gunboats, 22 vessels and some 15,000 men, part of General Franklin's army sent to establish a blockade on the Texas coast. The Guards captured two gunboats and 350 prisoners. Dowling's victory was credited with halting the advance of Union troops to the Texas mainland. Dowling became a folk hero. His heroism at the Battle of Sabine Pass was the subject of popular poems *Lt. Richard Dowling* and songs.

After the war Dowling re-opened "The Bank of

Bacchus," and continued to operate it successfully until his untimely death from yellow fever in 1867. He was not yet thirty years of age. A statue commemorates his heroic stand at Sabine Pass and a street in Houston is named in his honor.

Like Dick Dowling, **EMMA SEELYE** was a combat veteran of the Civil War. Disguised as a man under the name of Frank Thompson, she enlisted in Company F of the Second Michigan Infantry of the Grand Army of the Republic. The only woman to enlist in that army, Seelye served with distinction for two years and was decorated for bravery, masquerading as a man all along. She served until 1863, when she had contracted malaria and feared detection. Settling in Houston, she published her memoirs in a book entitled *The Nurse and the Spy*. The book about her adventures in the army became a best seller and sold some 175,000 copies. It also revealed her deception and her disability pension was withdrawn, although eventually it was restored by an Act of Congress. Seelye donated much of the profit from her book to Houston hospitals before she died in 1898.

About the time Sam Houston was completing his first term as president, **WILLIAM MARSH RICE** arrived in Houston. Rice was born in Springfield, Massachusetts on March 14, 1816 to Patty (Hall) and David Rice. His father, a skilled mechanic at the government gun plant in Springfield, had invented the Rice Musket.

The eldest of ten children, Rice attended public schools in Springfield as well as the Wesleyan Academy in nearby Wilbraham. After working for a year as a clerk in a grocery store, he operated his own country store, bought for him by his father. Within two years, Rice accumulated some $2,700 in profit and left New England to make his fortune in the new nation of Texas.

He arrived in Houston almost penniless, after losing most of his belongings at sea. An industrious, ambitious man, Rice was undaunted and began to work as a store clerk. Within a few years, he had recouped his losses, entered into a partnership with Ebenezer B. Nichols and opened a general merchandise store, which they named "Rice and Nichols, Exporters, Importers and Wholesale Grocers."

Among other ventures, Rice, like Nichols, became involved in transportation. He founded the Houston and Galveston Navigation Company, which later became the Houston Navigation Company, and was instrumental in the development of the Buffalo Bayou Ship Channel.

On July 4, 1850, Rice married eighteen-year-old Margaret C. Bremond. In 1853, they purchased a home, built by Nichols some three years earlier, located at the corner of San Jacinto and Congress streets, opposite Courthouse Square.

Mrs. Rice died on August 16, 1863. It is believed that following the funeral service in their home, Rice never returned to live in it. Instead he departed for Mexico and

little is known of this period of his life. It is known, however, that Rice left Texas as a wealthy man, for, by the time the Civil War broke out, his fortune was estimated at about three-quarters of a million dollars.

From the 1860s to the 1890s, Rice lived in New York and New Jersey. In 1885, he bought the Capitol Hotel at Texas and Main streets. Following his death in 1900, a deed executed by Rice and his second wife, Elizabeth Baldwin, was filed by the trustees of Rice Institute. The deed gave the hotel property title to the institute and stipulated that any hotel on the site should be called the Rice Hotel. That is why the seventeen-story structure built on that site in 1912 by Jesse Jones bears that name.

In 1891, Rice established an initial endowment of $200,000 for the Rice Institute. His intention, he said, was to give the new institution a firm financial foundation, and he stated: "Texas received me when I was penniless, without friends or even acquaintances, and now in the evening of my life, I recognize my obligation to her and to her children. I wish now to leave to the boys and girls struggling for a place in the sun the fortune I have been able to accumulate."

Lengthy litigation initiated by his second wife's relatives after her death in 1896 delayed the realization of Rice's dreams. His own murder four years later further delayed the plan.

The murder of Rice on September 23, 1900 in his New York City apartment was one of the most widely publicized crimes in the nation's history. A sensational trial revealed that he was killed by Charles Jones, his valet, who used chloroform to ensure that Rice, approaching his eighty-fifth birthday, would not wake up from his sleep. The courts later found that Albert P. Patrick, attorney for Mrs. Rice's relatives, conspired with the valet to kill Rice and, by using a fake, so-called "New York will," sought to become the primary beneficiary of his fortune. The truth came to light, and since Rice left the bulk of his vast estate to the William M. Rice Institute for the Advancement of Literature, Science and Art, his dream was fulfilled. By the time the institute opened in 1912, the endowment had grown to seven million dollars and, at its inception, Rice Institute was among the wealthiest universities in the United States.

DR. EDGAR ODELL LOVETT was the first president of the institute established by William Marsh Rice. Lovett was born in Shreve, Wayne County, Ohio on April 14, 1871, to Maria Elizabeth (Sprent) and Zephania Lovett. In 1890 he received a Bachelor of Arts degree from Bethany College in West Virginia and, after teaching mathematics there for two years he left for the University of Virginia, where he became an instructor in mathematics and astronomy. In 1895, he received both Master of Arts and Doctor of Philosophy degrees from that university.

Dr. Edgar Lovett

In 1897, Dr. Lovett married Mary Allen Hale of Kentucky, and the Lovetts soon thereafter departed for a tour of the leading European educational institutions. He received M.A. and Ph.D. degrees from the Universities of Christiana, Norway, and Leipzig, Germany. Upon his return to the United States, Dr. Lovett joined the faculty of Princeton University as an instructor in mathematics. In 1907, while teaching at Princeton and serving as chairman of that institution's Department of Astronomy, Dr. Lovett was unanimously selected to be the first president of the as-yet-to-be established Rice Institute.

Dr. Lovett and his wife arrived in Houston in 1909. His first task was to organize the faculty of the institute, which opened in 1912 with an enrollment of 77 students. Dr. Lovett served as president of Rice for some 34 years, from the time of its opening until he retired on March 1, 1946. He was largely responsible, through his selection and recruitment of the institution's faculty, for Rice's record of achievement and for the maintenance of its high scholastic standards. Under his direction Rice became known as the "Harvard of the South."

In 1946, Dr. Lovett was given the title of President Emeritus. The following year, the administration building was named Lovett Hall in his honor. He continued to serve on the board of trustees in an advisory capacity. Before he died on August 13, 1957, at the age of 86, Dr. Lovett received honorary Doctor of Laws degrees from three universities including Drake in Des Moines, Tulane in New Orleans, and Baylor in Waco. He was also a member and commander of the French Legion of Honor.

The parents of **GEORGE HENRY HERMANN,** another prolific Houstonian philanthropist, arrived in the city to seek their fortune in 1838. With only five dollars in hand they established one of the first bakeries on Houston's Main Street, after Hermann's mother had pawned her jewels to purchase flour and sugar. Shortly before Hermann's birth, his father expanded his activities to the dairy business.

The youngest of four sons of Verina (Fanny) Michels and John Hermann of Davos, Switzerland, George was born on August 6, 1843 in a two-story house at Smith and Walker streets. He was given the name of an older brother who had accidentally shot himself and died three years before.

In the fall of 1861, at the age of eighteen, Hermann joined the 26th Texas Cavalry serving in the Confederate Army until it was disbanded on May 15, 1865. In the meantime in 1862, his father died and his mother died a year later.

George Hermann

After the war, Hermann became involved in the cattle business, rising from stock-keeper and cattle driver to a partnership in a brokerage firm. Returning to Houston in

1872, he entered into business with W. J. and Julius J. Settegast, and started selling land as well as cattle.

In 1884, Hermann began dealing exclusively in real estate. Among his many transactions was the trading of a team of horses and a buggy for a tract of land in northern Harris County. When the big Humble field was discovered in 1904 he found that the tract lay at the center of the oil producing field.

Hermann proceeded to amass a huge fortune. At the time of his death, his estate was worth several million dollars. Despite his wealth, he lived frugally and chose to bestow much of his fortune on the people of Houston. He donated ten acres of land in what was then the South End of Houston, for the establishment of a charitable hospital. On June 6, 1914, Hermann donated an adjacent 285 acres of land for a park opposite Rice Institute. Two other notable donations were a parcel of land to the Houston Art League for the founding of a museum, which became the Museum of Fine Arts, and Hermann Square at the site of his childhood home in front of City Hall. He donated this small park, dedicated to his mother, with the stipulation that Houstonians be able to sleep in it overnight, "undisturbed by the forces of law and order."

Four months after providing land for the larger Hermann Park, on October 21, 1914, he died at Johns Hopkins Hospital in Baltimore, Maryland. The park, which contains the Houston Zoo, was opened in 1920. Four years later, the art museum, the first in Texas, was dedicated. Hermann Hospital began operating in the area where the Medical Center was later built. Today, both the old and the new Hermann hospitals, as well as the Hermann Professional Building, are memorials to Hermann's philanthrophy.

Known for his skill in behind-the-scenes diplomacy and for his role in negotiating peace terms at the end of World War I, **COLONEL EDWARD MANDELL HOUSE** was born in Houston on July 26, 1858, to Mary Elizabeth (Shearn) and Thomas William House. His father was a prosperous banker with large holdings of sugar cane and cotton lands. A frail child, House was educated in the Northeast at Hopkins Grammar School in New Haven, Connecticut, and at Cornell University, which he entered in 1877. He returned to Texas upon the death of his father in 1880.

Col. Edward House

House became involved in state politics during the 1892 reelection bid of Governor James S. Hogg. Winning reelection in a stunning upset victory, Governor Hogg declared House an honorary colonel in the state militia.

Regarded by his friends as the epitome of an ideal Southern gentleman, Colonel House was credited with securing the elections of Governors Hogg, Charles A.

Culberson (1895-1899), Joseph D. Sayers (1899-1903) and S. W. Lanham (1903-1907). On the national scene, he was a pivotal figure in the election and administration of President Woodrow Wilson, who assigned him the responsibility for selecting the cabinet, which included three Texans. His role in the Vienna Congress, called to negotiate the peace terms at the conclusion of World War I, earned him the respect and admiration of leaders of several European countries. Several of these countries have erected statues of Colonel House in recognition of his actions.

Often described as a power broker and as the founder of the modern Democratic party of Texas, Colonel House avoided holding or accepting public office himself. He believed that doing so would have interfered with his effectiveness and freedom. Colonel House died on March 28, 1938 at the age of 79.

Gov. (Jim) Hogg

GOVERNOR JAMES STEPHEN (JIM) HOGG, in whose 1892 reelection bid House wielded considerable influence, was the first native-born governor of Texas, serving as the nineteenth governor of the state from 1891-1895. Hogg was born on March 24, 1851 near Rusk in Cherokee County, one of five children of Lucanda and Joseph Louis Hogg, an attorney and brigadier general in the army. His formal education was limited; he attended a private school for a short time and was tutored at home until the advent of the Civil War. In 1862, when Hogg was eleven years old, his father died and his mother died in the following year. Hogg, his two brothers and two sisters had to attend to the family plantation.

In 1866, Hogg attended school in Alabama. Upon his return to Texas, he began working with Andrew Jackson's newspaper in Cherokee County, while continuing his self-education. The family estate was soon sold to pay taxes and Hogg went to work for the local sheriff. Incurring the ire of outlaws, he was followed over the Cherokee County line and shot in the back. He soon recovered, however, and from 1871 to 1873 worked at various newspapers in East Texas. In 1873, he became a justice of the peace in Quitman, Wood County. Two years later he received his license to practice law and married Sarah Ann (Sallie) Stinson.

In 1876, Hogg suffered his only defeat in running for an elective office in Texas at the hands of state legislator John Griffith. Two years later, Hogg was elected county attorney in Wood County. Between 1880 and 1884, when he began the private practice of law in Tyler, he served as district attorney in the old seventh district, earning a reputation as the most aggressive and successful district attorney in the state. In that office he became the first Texas Democrat to win the black vote. In 1886, Hogg was elected as Democratic Attorney General of Texas, and served from 1887 to 1891, during the two terms of Governor L. S. Ross. He supported new legislation benefiting public schools and enforced laws regulating monopolies, especially railroads. He was known as a proponent of the free market system and he helped write the second state antitrust law to protect the public from monopolistic interests.

Hogg also supported the establishment of a Railroad Commission. With a platform emphasizing antimonopoly legislation, Hogg was elected governor of Texas in 1890. In 1891, the Railroad Commission of Texas was established. Other legislation supported by the reform governor included the passage of the alien land law, intended to limit ownership of land by foreign corporations to the benefit of Texans.

Hogg's reelection bid of 1892 was hotly contested. Since his policies aroused bitter opposition as well as strong support Texans reelected him by a narrow margin over his closest opponent, fellow Democrat George W. Clark. The margin was 55,000 votes. In his second term, Hogg continued to support public schools at both lower and higher levels of education and personally labored to attract investment capital to Texas from the East Coast. After his second term expired in 1895, and the death of his wife later the same year, Hogg returned to private law practice.

In debt when he left office, Hogg proceeded to build his Austin law practice and invest in land. He also continued to promote reforms in Texas and at several public appearances at the turn of the century, proposed the prohibition of free paths for railroads and of public funds for lobbyists. "Let us have Texas," he said, "the empire state, governed by the people. . . ."

With James Swayne and three others, Hogg formed the Hogg-Swayne Syndicate, which purchased 15 acres of land near Beaumont in the Spindletop oil field. Later, the syndicate merged with the Texas Fuel Company, headed by J. S. Cullinan, to form the Texas Company, which became Texaco, Inc.

Following his return from a trip to England, Hogg left his law practice in Austin and moved to Houston, where he joined in the law firm Hogg, Watkins and Jones. Injured in a rail accident, Hogg retired to the Varner-Hogg Plantation north of West Columbia in Brazoria County—a plantation begun in 1824 by Martin Varner, one of Stephen F. Austin's "Old Three Hundred" colonists. In 1918, oil was discovered on the estate.

Hogg held modern political views. He supported legislation granting easy access to public records for all, as well as the elimination of insolvent Texas companies, and laws against corruption in general.

Hogg died on March 3, 1906 shortly before he reached his fifty-fourth birthday. His interest in public welfare was instilled in his children. Jim Hogg County in South Texas, created in 1913, was named in his honor. In addition, two state historical parks were dedicated as memorials to him: the 177-acre Jim Hogg State Park in Cherokee County, donated by the City of Rusk in 1941, and the 26-acre Governor Hogg State Park in Wood County. An historical site, the Governor Hogg State Park contains a museum housing items that belonged to him.

John Kirby

Like Jim Hogg, **JOHN HENRY KIRBY** has a state forest reserve named for him. Lawyer, lumberman, oil man and "Father of Industrial Texas," John Kirby was born on November 16, 1860,in Tyler County, Texas, to Sarah (Payne) and John Thomas Kirby. His only formal education was at Southwestern University in Georgetown, Texas, which he attended for a time until his funds were exhausted.

Kirby became a clerk in the Woodville, Texas law office of Samuel Bronson Cooper, a senator in the Texas legislature. Between 1882 and 1884, he served as a clerk in the Senate.On November 14, 1883, Kirby married Lelia Stewart of Woodville.

He studied law privately and in 1885, Kirby was admitted to the Texas bar. After impressively representing Eastern landowners in a case, he became general manager of two of the largest timber companies in Texas, the Texas and Louisiana Land and Lumber Company and the Texas Pine Land Association. He moved to Houston in 1890,and joined the Houston law firm of Hobby and Lanier. Always interested in marketing and developing the timber of southeast Texas, Kirby initiated the construction of the Gulf, Beaumont and Kansas City Railroad. This railroad, which later became a part of the Santa Fe Railroad system, ran between the Neches and Sabine rivers. Kirby also invested in timberland and, in 1896, constructed his first sawmill at Silsbee, Texas.

The Kirby Lumber Company was established on July 5, 1901 to manufacture and transport lumber. At its peak, between 1910 and 1920, Kirby Lumber had some 16,500 employees and included twelve operating mills and five logging camps. In the early 1900s, Kirby became president of Southwestern Oil Company of Houston and in 1920, founded the Kirby Petroleum Company.

A member and officer of several lumber trade and government organizations, Kirby was elected twice to the Texas House of Representatives. In 1923, he received an honorary law degree from Lincoln Memorial University in Cumberland Gap, Tennessee. In 1929, he donated part of what is today the 626-acre John Henry Kirby State Forest. Located in Tyler County in southeastern Texas, it is the smallest state forest in Texas. Kirby died shortly before reaching his eightieth birthday, on November 9, 1940.

Inventor **HOWARD ROBARD HUGHES, SR.** became involved in the oil industry while it was still in its infancy. Hughes revolutionized the process of drilling for oil with his invention of the first rotary rock bit.

Born in Lancaster, Missouri, on September 9, 1869, to Jean Amelia (Summerlin) and Felix Turner Hughes, the young Hughes spent his boyhood in Keokuk, Iowa, where his father maintained a successful law practice. After studying law at Harvard University and the University of Iowa, Hughes returned briefly to Keokuk to join his father's law firm. He left, however, to engage in zinc and lead mining in Joplin, Missouri. In 1901, just a short time afterwards, news broke of the Lucas Gusher at Spindletop south of Beaumont. Scores of oil lease hunters, including Hughes, flocked to Texas.

Around 1906, Hughes became interested in finding a solution to the problem of drilling through hard rock formations and began experimenting. While working in 1908 in Oil City, Louisiana with his business associate, Walter Sharp, Hughes produced a small wooden model of a roller-type bit with cone-shaped tooth cutters. The following year, he successfully tested the first rotary rock bit in an oil well at the huge Goose Creek field, just east of Houston. Since it was the first cone-type rock bit featuring rolling cutters, capable of drilling faster and more efficiently, he formed, with Walter Sharp, the Sharp-Hughes Tool Company to manufacture and market his new bit and tool joints.

Hughes is credited with the invention of numerous other time and money saving drilling devices. With his operation headquartered in Houston, his early advances in rotary drilling technology focused attention on the city as the world's leading manufacturer of drilling equipment and tool joints. After Sharp's death in 1912, Hughes bought Sharp's share of the business. and in 1915 renamed the firm the Hughes Tool Company.

Hughes died on January 14, 1924, at the age of 54, leaving the bulk of his million dollar estate to **HOWARD ROBARD HUGHES, JR.** an eighteen-year-old student at Rice Institute. The heir to Hughes' fortune became an aviator, moviemaker, entrepreneur and reclusive billionaire before his death in April 1976. Although he sold Hughes Tool Company, Howard Robard Hughes,Jr. became an American household name for generations to come.

Niels Esperson

NIELS PETER ESPERSON, like Hughes, was another immigrant to Texas shortly after the birth of the oil industry. An oil man and financier, Esperson was born in Ronne, Denmark, on June 3, 1857, to Julia Anne Marie (Funk) and Herman Esperson. Educated in public schools, Esperson graduated from high school at an early age. He arrived in New York City, in 1872, at the age of fifteen and journeyed to San Francisco, reaching that city with only five dollars in his pocket. Esperson worked on a ranch while studying English and geology. In 1889, he moved to El Reno, Oklahoma and opened a real estate office. There he met Mellie Keenan and married her four years later.

On hearing news of a gold strike near Cripple Creek, Colorado, in 1895, Esperson joined the scramble for mining rights in the area. Not only did he fail to find gold but he contracted tuberculosis and nearly died. Later the Espersons moved to East Texas.

In 1904, Esperson began drilling in the Humble oil field in northern Harris County. After many dry wells, he finally struck oil and found some 200 producing wells in the course of two years. Subsequently he developed other Gulf Coast oil fields and formed a company, which he named The Invincible Oil Company, a name symbolizing his enduring spirit.

Along with his numerous oil-related endeavors, Esperson was instrumental in planning and financing the construction of the Houston Ship Channel. He headquartered several of his various commercial enterprises in Houston. Among these were the Reed Roller Bit Company, Blue Ridge Development Company, Guardian Trust Company, Mid-Continent Clay Company, Houston Mill and Elevator Company, Rio Grande Gulf Corporation, Gulf Coast Rice Mills and the Grant Locomotive Company. Esperson remained a resident of Houston until his death from a heart attack at the age of 65 on October 21, 1922.

After Esperson's death, his wife, **MELLIE KEENAN ESPERSON,** assumed the management and planning responsibilities of his many businesses. One of her early construction projects, the million dollar Majestic Theater, opened in 1923. An accomplished business woman and administrator in her own right, Mellie was born in Manhattan, Kansas around 1870, and was reared and educated in Oklahoma. Although her husband's initial business ventures were failures, Mellie believed in him and encouraged him in all his endeavors.

Three years after her husband's death, Mellie marrried Harry Ewing Stewart, the *Post-Dispatch* advertising manager. She remained however, in control of the Esperson interests. She planned and built the 32-story Niels Esperson Building in memory of her husband. At the time of its completion in 1927, five years after his death, it was the tallest building in Texas and third tallest in the United States. In 1934, Mellie and Harry Stewart were divorced, after he moved to Dallas. In 1941, she completed the Mellie Esperson Building next to the one named after her husband. Although she died without revealing her age, it is believed that she was about 75 years old at the time of her death.

Mellie Esperson

The legacy of **JOSEPH STEPHEN CULLINAN** reached beyond that of other Houston greats. Born in Sharon, Pennsylvania, to Mary and John Francis Cullinan, he began working as a refiner in the Pennsylvania oil fields at an early age. Six years before he moved to Texas in 1897, Cullinan married Lucy Halm.

Arriving in Corsicana, Cullinan organized the first pipeline and refining company in Texas, J. S. Cullinan and Company. Later it became the Magnolia Petroleum Company. To increase the consumption of oil, at a time when the automobile industry was still in its infancy, Cullinan introduced two new applications of petroleum: as fuel for locomotives and as a dust settler on streets.

In 1901, Cullinan moved to Beaumont, Texas. In March, with the support of such investors as the Hogg-Swayne Syndicate, with former governor James S. Hogg a

Joseph Cullinan

principal, he established the Texas Fuel Company for the purchase and transfer of oil from the Spindletop field. In March 1902, Cullinan formed the Texas Company, for the storage and transportation of oil, and marketed its products under the brand name Texaco.

Soon Cullinan formed many subsidiaries to deal in petroleum products. In 1905, he acquired new oil field leases, including one at the Humble field in northern Harris County. He constructed refineries at Port Arthur and Port Neches and initiated an international marketing program. By 1908, Cullinan relocated the Texas Company headquarters to Houston.

Cullinan served as president of the Texas Company from 1903 to 1913, the year the company's headquarters moved to New York. From there it continued diversifying and expanding, both nationally and internationally and, by 1929, it operated refineries in six Texas cities. It was well on its way to becoming the energy giant it is today.

J. S. Cullinan died at the age of 76 in Palo Alto, California. In 1959, some 22 years later, the name of his Texas Company was officially changed to Texaco, Inc. Although Texaco is still headquartered in New York, Cullinan's concentration of the company's operations in Houston at the turn of the century, initiated a trend which resulted in the city's preeminence as a center for the oil industry. The twenty-story Petroleum Building which Cullinan built in downtown Houston in the early 1900s, is among the legacies of his endeavors.

GOVERNOR ROSS SHAW STERLING was a pioneer oil man and the founder of a company, which was a forerunner of one of today's huge energy corporations.

Sterling was born February 11, 1875 on a small farm near Anahuac, Texas to Mary Jane (Bryan) and Benjamin Franklin Sterling, a captain in the Confederate Army. He attended public school in Anahuac and on October 10, 1898, at the age of 23, married Maud Abbie Gage. Sterling began his career as a farmer and captain of a small schooner before entering the oil industry in 1903. The first of his successes came when he hit a gusher at Sour Lake. By 1910 he had two other wells and, with Walter W. Fondren, Sr., organized the old Humble Oil Company. It in turn became the parent company of the Humble Oil Corporation and in 1973, the Exxon Corporation.

Sterling served as president of the Humble Company until he sold his interests in 1925. The same year, he bought the Houston *Post,* merging it with the Houston *Dispatch* when he acquired the latter newspaper in 1926. In 1925, Sterling also became involved in real estate development in Houston and its vicinity. Among his projects were the residential Rossmoyne addition in Houston, where he built the Sterling Mansion, and the 22-story *Post-Dispatch* Building. Sterling entered the political arena as well when Governor Dan Moody (1927-1931) appointed him chairman of the Texas Highway Commission, which was only sporadically effective since its formation in 1917. Sterling, however, established a consistent highway program.

On January 20, 1931, Sterling was sworn in as governor of Texas after defeating the former governor (1925-1927) Miriam A. "Ma" Ferguson in the first and second Democratic primaries. His administration lasted only two years. On January 17, 1933, Ma Ferguson returned for her second term in the governor's mansion in Austin. A major problem arose during Sterling's term: unrestricted production in the huge new East Texas field drove prices down causing a depression in the oil industry. To reduce production, Governor Sterling declared a drilling curfew in four East Texas counties and ordered the National Guard to enforce it. While the Texas courts declared his move unconstitutional, he succeeded in assigning the Texas Railroad Commission its first regulatory authority over oil field drilling.

After Ma Ferguson defeated Sterling in his bid for a second term, Sterling returned to the oil business in Houston. He formed another oil company, the Sterling Oil and Refining Company, and served as its president from 1933 until he retired in 1946. A member of the Houston Port Commission from its inception, Sterling was also an original member of the board of trustees of the Hermann Hospital Estate. He also made various gifts to civic causes. Among these were Sterling's bay home in La Porte, given to the Houston Optimist Club for a boys'

Gov. Ross Sterling

home in memory of his son who died as a youth, and a wooded camp overlooking Galveston Bay, donated to the South Texas YMCA. Governor Sterling died in Houston at the age of 74.

Sterling's partner in the Humble Oil Company, **WALTER W. FONDREN, SR.,** arrived in Houston from Beaumont with his wife in 1904. In 1911, he and Sterling organized the Humble Oil Company with an initial capital of $75,000.

Because of his extensive knowledge of drilling, Fondren served as director and vice-president in charge of field operations while Sterling handled management and financial affairs.

Fondren was born on June 6, 1877 in Union City, Tennessee, to Thomas Fondren, a farmer, and his wife. After the death of his parents in Arkansas, where the family had moved in 1883, Fondren moved to Texas at the age of seventeen where he began working in the Corsicana oil fields in 1899, just at the beginning of the oil boom.

Fondren's career, like Cullinan's, paralleled the growth of the oil industry in Texas. In 1901, he moved from Corsicana to Beaumont and became an independent driller at the nearby Spindletop field. Later   *Walter Fondren, Sr.* he became a drilling contractor and independent oil operator, at a time when oil men were developing the coastal fields. On Valentine's Day, February 14, 1903, Fondren married Ella Cochrum in Corsicana.

Until he retired in 1933, Fondren served as vice-president of Humble Oil, thereafter forming the Fondren Oil Company. He also served as a vice-president and director of the National Bank of Commerce. In 1934, during the depression, Fondren accepted the position of district director of the Federal Housing Administration in charge of the recovery programs in 41 area counties. He was a director of the Seaboard Life Insurance Company and a national director of the derrick equipment standardizing for the American Petroleum Institute. In addition, he served as a member of the board of the Houston Methodist Hospital.

A leading layman in the Southern Methodist Episcopal Church, Fondren, throughout his life, worked for charitable causes and contributed to educational programs. In 1920, he was elected a trustee of Southern Methodist University in Dallas. Fondren died suddenly on January 6, 1939 in San Antonio, Texas, at the age of 61, while attending a Methodist Church meeting as a lay representative from Houston. His wife, Ella, continued his philanthropic endeavors. In 1946, she donated funds to Rice Institute for a new library. In 1968, the Fondren-Sterling and Ella F. and Walter W. Fondren buildings of Houston's Methodist Hospital opened as additional legacies of the Fondren philanthropy.

WILLIAM PETTUS HOBBY, editor, publisher and twenty-sixth governor of Texas, was born March 26, 1878 in Moscow, Texas, one of six children of Eudora Adeline (Pettus) and Edwin E. Hobby. He moved to Houston with his family when he was fifteen and, in 1895, began working for the Houston *Post* as a circulation clerk, later becoming a business writer. In addition he became involved in politics and, with others, founded the Young Men's

Democratic Club of Houston. In 1904, fellow party members elected him Secretary of the Democratic State Executive Committee. Meanwhile at the *Post*, he rose to the position of city editor before leaving the Houston newspaper in 1907 to manage the Beaumont *Enterprise*. A part owner of that paper, Hobby soon bought the *Enterprise* outright.

In 1914 and again in 1916, Texans elected Hobby as lieutenant governor of the state. On August 25, 1917, at the age of 39, Hobby became the youngest man to hold the office of governor when in a special session, the Senate impeached Governor James E. "Pa" Ferguson in his second two-year term. In 1918, Hobby soundly defeated Ferguson, and continued to serve in the governor's office for four years, until January 18, 1921.

William Hobby

Hobby's administration is remembered for the increased state support of public schools, and the passage of laws providing aid to farmers. He appointed the first State Highway Commission in 1917, and established the oil and gas division of the Railroad Commission. Educational milestones included stronger compulsory school attendance laws, free textbooks for public schools and increased aid to rural schools as well as increased general school apportionment.

In March 1918, Hobby called a special session of the Texas legislature to enact women's suffrage laws in Texas. Later, the State Supreme Court upheld this act. Thus women were able to vote in Texas' July, 1918 primary, nearly a year before Texas became the first state in the South and the ninth in the Union to adopt the Nineteenth Amendment to the U.S. Constitution.

Instrumental in obtaining loans for farmers affected by severe droughts in 1917 to 1918 in middle West Texas, Hobby's administration also signed into law legislation establishing a quarantine against the pink bollworm, and initiating payments to farmers whose cotton crops suffered damage from the pest.

After his terms as governor, Hobby returned to the Beaumont *Enterprise*, purchasing in addition the Beaumont *Journal*. In 1924, he became president of the Houston *Post-Dispatch*, continuing in that position after Ross S. Sterling sold the paper to J. E. Josey in 1931. In 1929, Hobby's first wife, Willie Cooper, died. Two years later, he married the local Houston beauty, Oveta Culp.

In 1939, Hobby purchased the Houston *Post*. Under his guidance it grew, both in circulation and in prestige. Radio station *KPRC* and television station *KPRC-TV*, were also part of the Houston Post Company. In 1955, Hobby became board chairman of the Houston Post.

Hobby died in Houston on June 7, 1964, at the age of 86. Three years after his death, the old Houston International Airport, located seven miles south of downtown, was renamed Hobby Airport in his honor.

Many great Houstonians, **MONROE DUNAWAY ANDERSON** and his partner William Lockhart Clayton, chief among them, derived their wealth from cotton. Banker, cotton merchant and prominent Houston philanthropist, M.D. Anderson was born in Jackson, Tennessee in June 1873.

In 1904, Anderson joined with his brother, F.E. Anderson, and Will Clayton to organize a cotton merchandising firm in Oklahoma City with a capital investment of $9,000. The following year, Clayton's brother Ben joined the firm. Anderson, Clayton and Company, as the enterprise became known, opened a branch office in Houston in 1907, and Anderson moved to the city to manage its operations. In 1916, the Andersons and Will Clayton relocated the headquarters of the firm to the Houston Cotton Exchange Building to utilize the Port of Houston's newly expanded facilities. Worth two million dollars at the time of the move, Anderson, Clayton and Company continued to grow until it became the largest firm of its kind in the world.

Anderson was one of Houston's greatest philanthropists. In 1936, he created the M. D. Anderson Foundation for "charitable, scientific or educational purposes in Texas . . . the benefit of mankind and . . . the advancement of human welfare." Anderson willed the bulk of his estate to the foundation, the primary force behind the financing and construction of the renowned Texas Medical Center.

The main goal of M. D. Anderson's gifts was for the establishment, support and maintenance of hospitals and institutions of medical and scientific research. A bachelor, Anderson died of a stroke at his Houston home on August 6, 1939 at the age of 66. The M. D. Anderson Hospital and Tumor Institute of the University of Texas Cancer Center, established nearly thirty years after his death, ranks among the most outstanding of his legacies. The M. D. Anderson Memorial Library at the University of Houston is another.

Monroe Anderson

WILL CLAYTON, Anderson's partner, often referred to as "Mr. Cotton," was born on February 7, 1880 in Tupelo, Mississippi to James Monroe Clayton and his wife. After his cotton farm failed in 1886, Clayton's father moved the family to Jackson, Tennessee, where Clayton became acquainted with the Andersons.

Although Clayton attended public schools in Jackson, he quit at the age of thirteen after completing the seventh grade. By studying shorthand at night, he became a deputy clerk and public stenographer and, in 1895, secretary to Jerome Hill of the Cotton Ginners Compress Company of St. Louis, Missouri. Thus began his long and successful career in the cotton business.

The following year, Clayton moved with Mr. Hill to New York City as an employee of the American Cotton Company. While in New York, he studied French, economics, politics and geography and, in 1904, became an assistant general manager of the firm.

On August 1, 1904, Clayton and the Anderson brothers formed the cotton merchandising firm Anderson, Clayton and Company in Oklahoma City. Instrumental in the growth of the firm into an international corporation, Clayton later became known as "the greatest cotton merchant in the world."

Will Clayton

Eventually, Anderson, Clayton and Company maintained branch offices in such cotton-producing lands as Egypt and South America and boasted sales offices on five continents.

In 1940, Clayton took a leave of absence from the company and turned his attention to national affairs. Starting as an unsalaried official in Governor Nelson Rockefeller's office for the coordination of inter-American affairs, Clayton later served as Deputy Federal Loan Administrator, Assistant Secretary of Commerce and War Property Administrator before becoming Undersecretary of State for Economic Affairs in December 1943. His greatest achievement in government was the creation of the European Recovery Program, better known as the Marshall Plan.

Although Clayton left his post as Assistant Secretary of State in October 1947 and returned to Houston, to continue as chairman of the board of Anderson, Clayton and Company, he did remain active in international affairs. In 1948, he served as chairman of the United States delegation to the United Nations conference on trade and employment held in Havana, Cuba. A long-time advocate of unrestricted world trade as an antidote to communism, Clayton enthusiastically supported the establishment of the European Common Market and, as vice-chairman of the Atlantic Union Committee, promoted free economic exchange among all democracies.

After retiring as head of Anderson, Clayton and Company in 1950, Clayton became involved in a number of civic causes in Houston. He began to focus attention on slums and the concept of replacing them with low cost housing projects. In addition, Clayton supported a program

promoting international student exchange. One of his last bequests was a $350,000 grant to the Johns Hopkins University School for Advanced International Studies in Washington, D.C. He died in Houston on February 8, 1966 at the age of 86.

Financier, banker, lumberman, civic leader and federal administrator, six-foot-six-inch **JESSE HOLMAN JONES** was a contemporary of Clayton's who also made an impact both locally and nationally. Jones was born on April 5, 1874 in Robertson County, Tennessee to Laura Anna (Holman) and William Hasque Jones, a successful farmer and tobacco exporter. In 1883, his father moved the family to Dallas, Texas where, in the early 1890s, Jones began to work in the lumber firm of his uncle.

Between 1895 and 1905, Jones rose to the position of manager of the Dallas office and then to general manager of the entire company, moving to Houston in 1898 after the death of his uncle. He later established the South Texas Lumber Company and, in August 1904, the Jesse H. Jones Lumber Company. The same year, he was awarded the contract to furnish the lumber for the Texas Building at the St. Louis Louisiana Purchase Exposition.

Houston became the center of Jones' various enterprises. He also expanded into banking, real estate and the development and construction of commercial buildings. From 1910 to 1930, the initial "skyscraper" era in Houston, he was the major developer in the city, involved in the erection of most of Houston's major office buildings along Main Street. Among the twenty or so buildings he constructed were the Kirby, Commerce, Milam, Rusk, Mason, Electric and C & I Life Insurance buildings.

In December 1920, Jones married Mary Gibbs of Mexia, Texas. He bought and published the Houston *Chronicle* and became president of the National Bank of Commerce, the forerunner of Texas Commerce Bank, and of the Bankers Mortgage Company.

Through a large party contribution, and by financing a new convention hall, Jones assured the selection of the city as the site of the 1928 Democratic National Convention. After Franklin Roosevelt nominated Alfred E. Smith as a candidate for president, it was common to hear the question, "How can you be any more Democratic than Smith and Jones?"

Jesse Jones

During the Great Depression, Jones called Houston's leading bankers together and persuaded them to accept a plan to prevent smaller city banks from failing. Since the beneficial effect of his leadership extended beyond the limits of the city and state, Jones' actions brought him national recognition. In 1932, President Herbert C. Hoover appointed him to the Board of the Reconstruction Finance Corporation and the following year, President Franklin D. Roosevelt named Jones chairman of the board of that institution, a position he held until 1939. Roosevelt also appointed him to the board of the Export-Import Bank (1936 to 1943), and to the posts of administrator of the Federal Loan Agency (1939 to 1945) and Secretary of Commerce (1940 to 1945). He supervised the New Deal lending programs and, although his New Deal colleagues considered that many of his policies were too conservative for their taste, he protected hundreds of individual banks, railroads and industrial plants from financial failure. Considered a controversial figure within the administration, Jones nevertheless exerted considerable influence as an intermediary between the administration and the business community.

He did not neglect local affairs, even while involved in the higher echelons of federal government. He was director-general of the Texas Centennial celebration, held in 1936. In April 1937, at ceremonies held at the San Jacinto Battleground, he sealed the cornerstone of the San Jacinto Monument, the tallest masonry monument in the United States. In recognition of his service to the state of Texas and to the nation, the state legislature commissioned an official portrait of Jones, unveiled in 1935 in the state capitol in Austin. He served as chairman of the Texas committee for the 1939 New York World's Fair and for the San Francisco Golden Gate Exposition.

In 1940, Jones was greatly disappointed when he failed to gain the nomination as the Democratic Party's vice-presidential candidate. From then on he became increasingly supportive of anti-Roosevelt political factions. In January 1945, President Roosevelt asked Jones to resign as Secretary of Commerce and from the Federal Loan Agency as well. Although Roosevelt offered him other posts, Jones refused them and later withheld the Houston *Chronicle's* editorial support from Democratic Party nominees in the election years 1948 and 1952.

Before he died in Houston on June 1, 1956, at the age of 82, he and his wife established a charitable foundation called Houston Endowment, Inc. His name is immortalized in the Houston Civic Center's Jesse H. Jones Hall for the Performing Arts, which opened in 1968, and the Jesse H. Jones Library at the Texas Medical Center in Houston.

Like Jones, his contemporary, **HUGH ROY CULLEN,** oil man, "King of the Wildcatters" and philanthropist, loomed large on the Houston scene. Born on July 3, 1881 in Denton County, Texas to Louise (Beck) and Cicero Cullen, a farmer, he was the grandson of Texas legislator Ezekiel W. Cullen, who advocated the establishment of the Texas public school system.

His formal education in the San Antonio public schools was limited to a few years. Cullen began to work for a cotton broker when he was sixteen years old. Like

Anderson and Will Clayton, Cullen entered the cotton business and also began to deal in real estate. On December 29, 1903, he married Lillie Cranz in Schulenberg. They had four daughters and a son. In 1911, they arrived in Houston.

Hugh Cullen

While still involved in cotton, Cullen began his association with the oil industry as a lease hunter for James Cheek, the developer of Magnolia Park and the builder of the M and M Building. In 1918, Cullen became an independent oil driller. Perfecting the method of drilling deep wells, he was extremely successful in finding oil in fields hitherto considered unproductive. Among his major oil strikes in southeastern Texas were those at the Pierce Junction, Rabbs's Ridge, Blue Ridge, Humble, Thompson and Tom O'Connor fields. A part owner of the South Texas Petroleum Company, he later formed his own oil firm, the Quintana Petroleum Company, which is still operated by his heirs from Cullen Center.

Cullen was particularly proud of his Humble oil discovery because he had to overcome a heavy shale problem. Another of his major strikes was at Blue Ridge. J. M. West, Sr. had offered to invest three million dollars for Cullen to drill there, proposing to give him a one-fourth share in any oil he found. Cullen turned West down and insisted that they invest equally. Several gushers were subsequently struck. While West sold his interest to the Humble Oil and Refining Company for twenty million dollars, Cullen developed the rich Tom O'Connor field with his profits. Since then, his Quintana Petroleum Company has been one of the major producers of oil in Texas.

In 1936, the University of Pittsburgh awarded him an honorary doctoral degree for his achievements in the oil industry. An advocate of states' rights, Cullen opposed many of the 1930s' New Deal measures. In Texas, he actively supported W. Lee O'Daniel for governor in 1938 and 1940, and O'Daniel's successful bid for a United States Senate seat in 1941. In 1939, Cullen served as vice-president of the Texas World Fair Commission.

An early backer of the University of Houston, Cullen donated more than 11 million dollars to the institution for various projects, and served as chairman of its board of regents. In addition, he contributed an equal sum to health care projects in the city. In 1947, with an initial endowment of some 160 million dollars, he established the Cullen Foundation, which continues to benefit education and medical research in Houston.

In 1945, Cullen received honorary degrees first from Baylor University and, two years later, the University of Houston in recognition of his achievements in the oil industry and of his interest in education. Cullen served as director of the Boy Scouts of America and became an honorary member of the American Hospital Association as well as a member of the Sons of the Republic of Texas.

By 1955, it was estimated that Hugh and Lillie Cullen had given away some 90 percent of their fortune to charitable causes. The major beneficiaries, the University of Houston and the Texas Medical Center, honored Cullen by naming key buildings for him. Texas Southern University, Baylor Medical College, the Houston Symphony and the Houston Ship Channel were other recipients of the Cullen philanthropy. Hugh Roy Cullen died in Houston on July 4, 1957 at the age of 76.

Julia Bedford Ideson

While other great Houstonians made good in business and politics, women in Houston made advances in culture and the arts. Largely credited with developing the Houston public library system into the institution it is today, **JULIA BEDFORD IDESON** was born on July 15, 1880, in Hastings, Nebraska, to Rosalie (Beasman) and John Castree Ideson. She attended Hastings public schools until 1891, when her father moved the family to Houston. After graduating from Houston public schools, she entered the University of Texas at Austin as a member of the first class to study library science at that institution.

After graduation from college in 1903, Ideson became city librarian in charge of the new Houston Lyceum and Carnegie Library. Dedicated on March 2, 1904, the library resulted from Andrew Carnegie's $50,000 gift to Houston in 1898. Serving as president of the Texas Library Association from 1910-1911, Ideson took a leave of absence from her duties at the Houston library and spent the year of 1913 in Paris, France, as secretary of the American Art Students' Club. Upon her return to Houston, she became involved in the third Liberty Loan Drive for World War I bonds as a member of the Harris County Women's Committee. Ideson also organized the library at the United States Army's Camp Logan, later volunteering for library work overseas. In 1919, the American Library Association assigned her to Camp Pontenezeon in Brest, France.

After the end of World War I, Ideson launched a campaign to broaden the funding base for the Houston public library system. Joined by the library board, the newspapers and civic groups, Ideson, in 1921, secured the passage of a city ordinance earmarking a percentage of city taxes for library purposes. In October 1926, a new central library building replacing the outgrown Lyceum opened in downtown Houston at Smith and McKinney.

From 1932 to 1934, Ideson served as president of the Southwestern Library Association and, in 1932, became the first Houston woman to be listed in *Who's Who,* a compendium of leaders of American thought and accomplishment. She also edited volume numbers two and four of the *Handbook*

of Texas Libraries and, while still chief librarian of the Houston public library system, directed the opening of six branches and a bookmobile.

Some six years after her death on her sixty-fifth birthday in 1945, the central library building was renamed in her honor to commemorate Ideson's long years of service to the library system. The Spanish Renaissance Revival-style Julia Ideson Building, replaced by a new, modern central library building dedicated in January 1976, was renovated and reopened on November 4, 1979 to house the Texas Room and its extensive collection of materials relating to Houston and the state.

Many of the gifts of **ANNETTE FINNIGAN,** suffragette, art patron and philanthropist, benefited Houston's public library system while Ideson was still its head.

Born in 1873 in West Columbia, Texas, Finnigan, in 1876, moved with her family to Houston, where her father, Captain John C. Finnigan, established a successful hide business.

Finnigan attended Houston public schools and Wellesley College in Massachusetts. As a young woman, she spent much of her time in New York City, where her father's business took the family. In 1905, the family returned to Houston.

After her father's death in 1909, Finnigan assumed active management of his business interests. She also became active in the leading social cause of the time—equal voting rights for women —working with the suffrage movement in Houston and throughout Texas. She and her sisters, Elizabeth and Katherine, contributed to the early organization of the Houston Suffrage League, and helped organize a 1913 suffragette march in Houston led by Angelina Pankhurst. In 1914, the state Suffrage League elected Finnigan president. During the winter of 1915, she devoted her time to lobbying in Austin for the passage of an equal suffrage bill by the Texas legislature. It was effected three years later. She also served as president of the Woman's Political Union.

Annette Finnigan

After a serious illness in 1916, Finnigan adopted a less strenuous lifestyle. She became interested in world travel and in collecting works of art, rare books and antiques. In 1931, she began donating gifts to the Houston Museum of Fine Arts and the Houston Public Library. Among the first of these was a textile collection from India, Iran and the Middle East. Other gifts to the museum included ancient Greek vases and funerary items, examples of medieval Spanish sculpture and decorative arts and a collection of rare laces. She also donated to the library 65 rare books and items, dating from the twelfth through the seventeenth centuries: two twelfth century manuscripts, *Ambrose* and the

Venerable Bede's *Commentary on Tobias* from part of the collection which also includes Oriental scrolls and reproductions of the Codex Aureus and Codex Alexandrinus, as well as some sixteenth century works on Petrarch, Erasmus, Caesar and Dante. One of her last gifts to the City of Houston was an 18 acre site in the Fifth Ward, the North End of Houston at the time, for a "Negro park," a symbol of her concern for blacks at a time when public facilities were segregated.

Although she was a resident of New York City for the last 25 years of her life, Finnigan considered Houston her home. After her death in 1940 at the age of 67 her ashes were buried in the family plot in Houston.

These women were not alone in unselfish service to Houston during the first half of the twentieth century. Black physician, civic leader and the son of former slaves, **BENJAMIN JESSE COVINGTON** figured prominently in establishing the first city hospital for blacks. Covington was born "in the sixth year of freedom" on his family's farm near Marlin, Texas. Because the farm home burned down when he was a child, destroying family records kept in a Bible, he did not know his birth date.

Covington spent his early childhood on the farm, planting, chopping and picking cotton. He attended public school near Marlin and in 1886, at the age of 15 or 16, he enrolled at Hearne Baptist Academy. Supporting himself through college as a janitor and bell ringer, he graduated in 1892 and then taught for a short time at a country school near Marlin. He soon left the post, however, because of the animosity of some members of the community who felt that his teacher's salary of $75 per month, plus some $25 in private tutoring fees, was more than a black should earn.

In 1894, Covington moved to Houston to work as a bookkeeper for a half-brother. The following year, he entered Meharry Medical College in Nashville, Tennessee. Once again working his way through school, he graduated as a physician in 1900. He returned to practice medicine in Wharton, Texas, having earlier worked there as a doctor with a temporary permit. Subsequently he moved to Yoakum where he met and married Jennie Belle Murphy, with whom he later had a daughter.

On June 18, 1903, the day preceding the Juneteenth celebration, Dr. Covington moved his practice permanently to Houston. Because of his skill and dedication, it grew rapidly. Soon his 10-bed hospital on Canal Street could not adequately meet the demand. He began planning for a larger hospital for blacks about 1910, but was interrupted by World War I. During the influenza epidemic of World War I, Dr. Covington developed a formula for the cure of the flu. Learning of his discovery, the local United States Army medical corps requested and secured his formula.

In 1911, Dr. Covington built a two-story, fifteen-room house at Dowling and Hadley streets. It was here that he and his wife entertained such black dignitaries as Booker T. Washington and Marian Anderson.

Involved in the reorganization of the Lone Star Medical Association after his graduation from medical school, Dr. Covington served as secretary-treasurer for ten years before members elected him president in 1920. Some five years later, he and four other Houston doctors established the Houston Negro Hospital, a forerunner of the present Riverside General Hospital.

Throughout his life, Dr. Covington exhibited a deep concern for community health and welfare. Active in a number of civic associations as well as a leading member of the Antioch Baptist Church, he was honored by such organizations as the Omega Fraternity and the Business and Professional Men's Club of Houston. Some 10 years before his death at the age of 90 or 91 the Masonic Lodge, of which he was a long-time member, established a medical school scholarship in his name in recognition of his 50 years of professional service. Dr. Covington practiced medicine until he died on July 21, 1961 in Houston.

Throughout the twentieth century, however, there were those who contributed to Houston's reputation as the "city of wealth." Few so colorfully projected the image of a "millionaire" as did **JAMES MARION WEST, JR.,** known as "Silver Dollar Jim," an attorney, oil man, cattle rancher and eccentric.

"Silver Dollar Jim" West was born on September 26, 1903 in San Antonio, Texas to Jessie Dudlin and James Marion West, Sr. When West was two years old, his father moved the family to Houston and later made a fortune in cattle ranching and in the lumber industry. Young Jim West attended the old Houston Central High School and Southwestern University in Georgetown, Texas, later studying law at the University of Texas Law School in Austin.

"Silver Dollar Jim" typified the spirit of the so called "eccentric Texas millionaire," if anyone did. He tipped only with silver dollars—often 20 or 25 at a time. For his own amusement he would toss a handful of them on the floor of a restaurant and watch while waitresses scrambled for them. To entertain guests at swimming parties, "Silver Dollar Jim" would drop a number of the coins into the pool to observe other guests diving for them.

His standard tip for doormen at the Shamrock Hotel, whenever they delivered one of his 40 Cadillacs to the front door, was three silver dollars. When the color blue took his fancy, he had all his personal and business cars so painted.

His eccentricity was not limited to silver dollars nor to the color blue. West loved radio. He owned a radio station and had as many as eight antennae on innumerable personal cars. He was very interested in law enforcement and was especially supportive of the Houston Police Department. West assisted the force in various ways: he placed his powerful radio receiver at the disposal of the Houston police; he attended police conferences and was known to cruise with their patrols and held a Texas Ranger's Commission. West died on December 18, 1957 at the age of 54.

Another of Texas' great oil men, who rose from relative to obscurity the top of their profession, was **ROBERT EVERETT (R. E. BOB) SMITH**. He was born on August 28, 1894 in Greenville, Texas to Robert Davis Smith and his wife. In 1905, Smith's father took the 11-year old boy with him to visit the Spindletop oil field, where the elder Smith had bought some land. The boy was fascinated and indeed, a few years later Bob Smith became a field worker for the Texas Company and the Gulf Company in the booming East Texas oil fields. In 1911, he graduated from Humble High School and, for the next 10 years, played semi-professional baseball in the area.

An independent, red-headed man with a penchant for wearing white suits in his later years, Smith became, in 1920, a drilling contractor and owned 36 producing oil wells in East Texas as well. In 1925, he moved to Houston. The city became headquarters for his various enterprises, which soon included ranching, real estate and, eventually, philanthropy.

Smith was an intuitive man with little formal education. For years, his oil company functioned with no geologists— Smith knew by instinct, and by observation of surface indications, where oil was, and he discovered it himself. His holdings and interests extended far beyond the boundaries of Houston and Texas. In 1952, he became part owner of the Philadelphia Athletics major league baseball team, and later was instrumental in Houston's acquisition of a major league baseball franchise. While his partner, Roy Hofheinz, provided the promotional skills, Smith provided the money, in 1962, for acquiring a National League franchise team—the Houston Colt .45's, now the Astros. Smith served as chairman of the board for the Houston Sports Association and strongly supported the two bond issues totaling $31 million for the construction of the Harris County Domed Stadium (the Astrodome).

By 1964, Smith owned some 11,000 acres of land in Harris County, including a 4.5 mile-wide tract in southwest Houston and parcels in north Houston, all amounting to about two percent of the entire undeveloped acreage in Houston. In addition, he owned some 25,000 acres of ranch land throughout Texas and Oklahoma on which he raised more than 10,000 heads of various types of cattle, thoroughbred and quarter horses. At the time of his death, he was the third largest individual landholder in Harris County.

Smith served on the boards of numerous civic, religious and educational institutions. Among the positions he held were chairman of the Houston Housing Authority, member of the National Conference of Christians and Jews, and trustee of Methodist Hospital, Southern Methodist University in Dallas, Southwestern University in Georgetown, Texas and Lon Morris College in Jacksonville, Texas.

A quiet philanthropist, Smith donated both land and money to the Texas Methodist Conference and the University of Texas Medical Branch at Galveston, among others. He received honorary doctor of law degrees from Southwestern University, Pepperdine University and Texas Wesleyan College.

Smith died at his River Oaks home on November 29, 1973 at the age of 79. Among the memorials to the Houston oil man is an oil derrick in downtown Kilgore in northeast Texas and the gymnasium, named in his honor, at Lon Morris College in Jacksonville, Cherokee County, East Texas.

Another great Houstonian remembered for his civic and cultural legacies, is **OSCAR FITZALLEN HOLCOMBE,** mayor of Houston for a total of 22 years. Born on December 1, 1888 in Mobile, Alabama to Sarah King (Harrell) and Robert Slough Holcombe, a lawyer, he moved in 1891, with his family to San Antonio, Texas. In 1899, Holcombe's father died, and the 10-year-old boy went to work to supplement the family income by selling newspapers. Four years later, he left school to work full time.

Oscar Holcombe

Arriving in Houston in 1907 at the age of 18, Holcombe, like Jesse Jones, began working in an uncle's lumber company. Within a year he became assistant manager and, after working for a short time as a salesman for a door company, entered the construction business in 1912. In May of the same year, he married Mamie Gray Miller. Among the first contracts were construction projects for the Houston public schools.

In 1921, at the age of 32 Holcombe entered his first race for mayor of Houston. He promised reorganization of city departments, the paving of streets, the building of new schools and better business administration. Houstonians elected him mayor in April 1921. He was reelected in 1923, 1925 and 1927.

Because he was prematurely gray, Everett Collier, an editor of the Houston *Chronicle,* nicknamed him "the Old Gray Fox."

Holcombe's early administrations were marked by the widening of streets and the paving of both residential and commercial thoroughfares, the improvement of sewage systems by the extension of water and sewer mains and the construction of such public buildings as the municipal auditorium, farmers' market and branch libraries. The passage of a state law creating the navigation district, including all of Harris County and not the city of Houston alone and thereby distributing taxes more fairly ranked among the most significant achievements of his tenure. Holcombe also created the new municipal offices of city manager and public service commissioner as well as the city planning commission. In addition, he established the Houston Independent School District.

Holcombe served as mayor from 1921 to 1929, and then returned to the construction business until 1933, when he was elected again. Serving until 1937, he later returned to complete several other terms as mayor, from 1939 to 1944, 1947 to 1953 and 1956 to 1958, for a total of eleven years. Holcombe lost his last bid for reelection in 1958 to Lewis Cutrer, primarily due to his stand against integration of public swimming pools because it would "prevent bloodshed and violence." The city of Houston pursued its policy of annexation during his terms of office and its area increased from 34.4 to 352 square miles.

Holcombe died of pneumonia on June 18, 1968 in Houston, at the age of 79. The Houston Civic Center, named the Oscar F. Holcombe Civic Center in his honor, is among the tributes to his years of service to the city.

An exhibit hall within the Oscar F. Holcombe Civic Center Complex bears the name of Congressman **ALBERT THOMAS,** a member of the United States House of Representatives from 1936 until his death 30 years later. Thomas was instrumental in securing the location of the United States National Aeronautics and Space Administration (NASA) Manned Spacecraft Center, now the Lyndon B. Johnson Space Center in Houston in 1961.

Born in Nacogdoches, Texas on April 12, 1898 to Lonnie (Langston) and James Thomas, he graduated from Rice Institute in 1920 with a Bachelor of Arts degree. During World War I, he served in the army as a second lieutenant.

In 1922, Thomas married Lera Millard of Nacogdoches. Earning a Bachelor of Laws degree from the University of Texas in 1926, Thomas was admitted to the Texas bar the following year. He served as Nacogdoches County attorney until 1930, when he moved to Houston to become assistant United States attorney. In 1936, Thomas was elec-

Albert Thomas

ted to the United States House of Representatives as a Democrat from the eighth congressional district. In 1949, he became chairman of the House subcommittee on independent office appropriations. He also served on the subcommittee on defense appropriations and on the joint committee on Texas House delegation.

When the Humble Oil Company discovered oil on about half of the 30,000-acre West Ranch, the company donated some 1,000 acres of the ranch land to Rice Institute. In turn, Herman Brown, a trustee of Rice University, offered the tract to the United States government on behalf of the institute as the site for NASA's Manned Spacecraft Center. Vice-President Lyndon B. Johnson, then chairman of the Space Council, and Thomas, a member of the NASA board, played leading roles in the eventual acceptance of Rice University's offer.

In November 1963, President John F. Kennedy, who had persuaded Thomas to continue in office and not to retire, and Vice-President Lyndon B. Johnson, honored Thomas at a testimonial dinner in Houston. In 1964, Thomas was named chairman of the House Democratic caucus.

By the time of his death on February 15, 1966, at the age of 67 Thomas ranked eleventh in seniority in the House. Houston elected his wife Lera to complete his term. Some time after he died, the Albert Thomas Convention and Exhibit Center in Houston was named in his honor.

The activities of **MISS IMA HOGG,** known as the "First Lady of Texas" benefited another section of the

Oscar F. Holcombe Civic Center. Miss Ima was born on July 10, 1882 in Mineola, Texas, the only daughter of Sarah Ann (Stinson) and Governor James Stephen Hogg. Her father named her after the heroine in a long epic poem written by her uncle, Thomas Elisha Hogg.

In 1891, Miss Ima and her brothers Will, Tom and Mike with their father moved into the Texas Governor's Mansion in Austin upon his inauguration as the nineteenth governor of the state. They remained there until the end of his second term in 1895. Among other qualities, Governor Hogg instilled in his four children a deep concern for the citizens of Texas.

Between 1899 and 1901, Miss Ima attended the University of Texas at Austin, which had opened in 1883, and thereafter moved to New York City to study music. She was very close to her father and was with him when he died in Houston in March 1906. After his death, she continued to study piano both in the United States and in Germany and, in 1909, moved to Houston to teach. She was one of the organizers of the Houston Symphony Society when it was formed in 1913 and served as its second president from 1917 to 1921.

In 1918, the Hogg family developed their West Columbia oil field, south of Houston, and their wealth increased substantially. Like her brothers, Miss Ima used her share for the benefit of the public. Among her endowments was one for the founding of the Houston Child Guidance Center, an innovative institution in the field of child psychology. In addition, she helped carry out her brother Will's legacy after he died in 1930. One of his bequests resulted in the creation, in 1940, of the Hogg Foundation for Mental Health at his alma mater, the University of Texas at Austin.

From 1943 to 1949, Miss Ima served on the Houston School Board. Between 1946 and 1956, she served 10 more years as president of the Houston Symphony Society. Involved with the symphony throughout her life, Miss Ima was instrumental in attracting several world famous conductors. In 1948, she became the first woman president of the Philosophical Society of Texas. She was also active in the League of Women Voters, Texas Welfare Association, Texas State Historical Association and Daughters of the Republic of Texas.

Miss Ima Hogg

Miss Ima was avidly interested in the history of the state of Texas. In the 1950s, she restored her father's 66-acre plantation north of West Columbia in Brazoria County. The home itself was built around 1824. In 1956, the site became the Varner-Hogg Plantation State Park and Miss Ima deeded the property to the state.

She also became involved in activities outside the state of Texas. In 1960, President Dwight D. Eisenhower appointed Miss Ima to the advisory committee on the arts for the National Cultural Center in Washington, D.C., which later became the Kennedy Center for the Performing Arts. In 1962, she was appointed by Mrs. John F. Kennedy as advisor to the White House's Fine Arts Committee.

In 1963, Miss Ima became the first woman to receive the University of Texas Distinguished Alumnus Award. In the same year, she purchased some 131 acres of historic tracts of land in Winedale, Fayette County, Texas. and supervised extensive restoration of the properties. Two years later she donated the land and the buildings to the University of Texas at Austin; they became the Winedale Museum, an outdoor museum and study center. She later donated some five acres of land to the 26-acre Governor Hogg State Park, a Wood County historical site named for her father.

Miss Ima was an active supporter of the Houston Museum of Fine Arts, to which she donated many significant works of art, including several Remingtons. An avid collector of early Texas furniture as well, Miss Ima made an outstanding contribution to the museum in 1966 when she donated the Hoggs' 15-acre River Oaks estate, Bayou Bend. Built in 1929, it houses one of the finest collections of early Americana, seventeenth to nineteenth century decorative arts and the second largest collection of American antiques in the nation. At the same time, she established a $750,000 securities endowment for the maintenance of the mansion and the surrounding formal gardens.

In October of the same year, Miss Ima was honored at the twentieth annual awards banquet of the National Trust for Historic Preservation, held in Philadelphia. Recipient of the seventh annual Louise du Pont Crowninshield Award, established in 1960, Miss Ima and her work in Texas restoration were nationally recognized. Accepting the award, Miss Ima expressed the philosophy that motivated her philanthropic and cultural contributions in these words:

"Texas, an empire in itself geographically and historically, sometimes seems to be regarded as remote or alien to the rest of our nation. I hope in a modest way Bayou Bend and these other memorials may serve as a bridge to bring us closer to the heart of an American heritage that unites us."

Held somewhat in awe by those who knew her for her many contributions to the cultural life of Houston, Miss Ima once spoke to a young matron who had come to take her for a Sunday drive. "Many people assume," she said, "that if one has plenty of money, one's situation is ideal. They forget that I have no husband, no children and no close relatives in Houston. On Sundays the servants are off and if you had not called, I would have been alone all day in that empty house." Miss Ima's young fiancé was killed in World War I and after the war she had spent some weeks in Gurdjieff's sanatorium in Fontainbleu, where Katherine Mansfield wrote several of her well-known books.

In June 1968, the University of Texas bestowed the prestigious Santa Rita Award on Miss Ima, the first person to receive it, for her activity in higher education. The highest honor bestowed on an individual by the university, the institution named the award for the first oil well to produce on land owned by the university in West Texas, on May 23, 1923.

While visiting London, Miss Ima died on August 19, 1975 at the age of 93. The major beneficiary of her will was the Ima Hogg Foundation.

Nina Vance

The work of **NINA VANCE,** on the cultural scene both at the local and the national levels, benefited the vital institution that complements Houston's Civic Center. Artistic director and founder of the Nina Vance Alley Theatre, Mrs. Vance was born on October 22, 1914 in Yoakum, Texas, and attended Texas Christian University, Columbia University and the American Academy of Dramatic Arts. In 1947, Vance mailed 214 penny post cards, invitations to artists and potential sponsors to join in forming a theater-in-the-round, to be located off a Houston alley. The result was the Alley Theatre.

Although it began modestly, as an 84-seat theater, the Alley is now one of the nation's leading regional repertory theaters, showing new as well as classical productions. It is also one of the three oldest resident theaters in the United States. In 1968, the Alley Theatre moved into its present home, adjacent to the Oscar F. Holcombe Civic Center, at the corner of Texas and Louisiana.

Nina Vance's tenure at the Alley brought her both professional and personal recognition. In 1958, the English Speaking Union sponsored Mrs. Vance in touring British repertory theaters. The following year, the Ford Foundation awarded her a director's grant. In 1960, President Kennedy invited Vance to serve on the advisory committee of the **proposed National Cultural Center, now the Kennedy Center for the Performing Arts. Secretary of State Dean Rusk** appointed her to two terms on the United States Commission on International Education and Cultural Affairs, the only woman to so serve. Vance was one of seven American directors who observed contemporary Soviet theater in Moscow, while touring the U.S.S.R. at the invitation of the Soviet Ministry of Culture and the United States Department of State. As a result of this trip, *Echelon*, a Russian play, was recreated in the United States in 1977 under the direction of Galina Volchek, its original director. Vance received numerous other awards, including the Matrix Award of Theta Phi, the Outstanding Alumni Award of Texas Southern University and the Houston Y.W.C.A. Woman of the Year Award. After a long illness, Vance died on February 18, 1980 at the age of 66 in Houston. The Alley Theatre was renamed The Nina Vance Alley Theatre in her honor.

LANDMARKS AND MONUMENTS

Houston is a young, bustling city. Its history has yet to take its appropriate place in most people's consciousness. Yet its past and present are well reflected in its landmarks and monuments. They tell the story of the city's early bid for capital honors, its later development as a leading center of local commerce to its present status as a national and international center of business and industry, education, medicine, the arts, space travel and research.

OLD HOUSTON

For two years, in 1837-1839, Houston was the capital of the Republic of Texas. The capitol building located at what is now 917 Texas Avenue, was a two-story, simple, unadorned, frontier-style frame structure. After the government was moved to Austin, the capitol was remodeled and became the Capitol Hotel. Here, in 1858, Anson Jones, the last president of the Republic of Texas, committed suicide. J. L. Barnes acquired the Capitol Hotel in the 1870s, demolished it in 1882 and replaced it with a new Capitol Hotel, designed by A. Groesbeck. William M. Rice bought the hotel in 1885 and renamed it the Rice Hotel. In 1912, Jesse Jones erected the present building of the Rice Hotel, now listed on the National Register for Historic Places.

The Scanlan Building, at 405 Main Street, occupies the site of what used to be the Executive Mansion. It was a private one-and-a-half story home with dormer windows, built by Francis R. Lubbock in 1837. That same year the Republic of Texas bought the house for use as the Executive Mansion. Two presidents, Sam Houston and Mirabeau Lamar, lived there during their terms of office.

Market Square, bounded by Preston, Milam, Travis and Congress streets, was originally designed as the commercial hub of the city. The Kennedy Trading Post, also known as the Kennedy Bakery after the bakery business that the family maintained on the premises for a long time, is located there. Listed on the National Register for Historic Places the Kennedy Trading Post was built in 1847 by Nathaniel Kellum, one of Houston's early developers. The building is believed to be the oldest public two-story frame building in the city and now houses a bar named La Carafe. At the bar entrance an historical marker proclaims that Sam Houston once slept there.

The older buildings in the downtown area, dating from the late 1800s to the 1900s, are monuments to the diverse activity of early Houstonians. These buildings housed hotels, railroad stations, banks, retail outlets, manufacturing and (at the turn of the century) oil, gas and related industries. In March of 1880, former President Ulysses Grant came to Houston aboard the first train to arrive at the new Union Station on Crawford Avenue; Geronimo, Chief of the Apaches, in 1894 passed through this station on a Federal train as a prisoner. The original Union Station was replaced later by one designed and built by Warren and Wetmore, the architects who designed New York's Grand Central Station. The Sheppard Building, at 219 Main Street, built in 1883, is an imposing Victorian structure, named for B. A. Sheppard who, along with T. W. House, introduced banking to Houston in the 1850s. The old Troy Laundry Building, at 910 Prairie, dates from 1882 and features Romanesque arches displayed under an embellished metal cornice.

Cotton played a major role in the economy of nineteenth and early twentieth century Houston and the center of the trade was the old Cotton Exchange Building. Situated on Travis and Commerce, the Cotton Exchange Building was completed in 1884. This Renaissance Revival style building was made of red Philadelphia pressed brick faced with Texas

An old house beautifully restored, located in the Sixth Ward, Houston's oldest neighborhood.

San Felipe Cottage originally on Old Stage Coach Trail (now West Dallas) bought by the Joseph Meyer family and donated to The Heritage Society.

limestone. The building was originally topped by a bale of cotton, made of zinc; this was later removed. Currently it is used as an office building. The Sweeney, Coombs and Frederick Building, on Main and Congress, was built in 1899. The building originally housed a jeweler's shop and has been restored by Harris County and entered on the National Register for Historic Places.

By the turn of the century, the two- and three-story structures in the downtown area were giving way to taller buildings. Among the tallest structures dating from this period were the 11-story Scanlan Building; the Texas Company's Building, a 13-story structure at 1111 Rusk, and the 13-story Union National Bank Building.

CHURCHES

The Allen brothers deeded land to the Reverend Mr. Littleton Fowler, the Methodist pioneer minister who served as chaplain to the Senate of the Republic of Texas. In 1844, the first church, a Methodist Episcopal, was built on that site. In 1867, the original church was replaced by a new one with a new name, Shearn Methodist Episcopal Church South. In 1883, yet another building replaced the 1867 structure and was renamed the Charles Shearn Memorial Church. Because of the rapid business growth of the area, the parish decided that the location was not suitable for a church any more, sold the land in 1907, and in 1910 built a new church at Main and Clay, where it still stands today, renamed the First Methodist Church.

The Church of Annunciation, built in 1868 at the corner of Texas Avenue and Crawford, is the oldest

existing church building in the city. It was designed in Romanesque style and was made of limestone and cement plaster with brown trim. Inside the church are marble altars, statues and stained glass windows; a fresco decorates the sanctuary dome.

Standing in the shadow of the sprawling Allen Center complex on Robin Street is the Antioch Missionary Baptist Church, the oldest black church in the city. It was founded in 1875 by freed slaves, with the Reverend Mr. Jack Yates as its first pastor. Dr. Benjamin Covington, one of the earliest black physicians in Houston, was a parishioner of this church.

Christ Episcopal Church, the oldest congregation in Houston, organized in 1839, is located at the Christ Church Cathedral at the corner of Texas Avenue and Fannin. Built in 1893, the cathedral was designed by Silas McBeen in the style of the medieval Gothic architecture; it features exquisite stained glass windows. The church walls are covered with ivy, brought from the walls of Westminster Abbey in England.

MANSIONS AND HOMES

During the late nineteenth century and the early part of the twentieth century, affluent Houstonians built large mansions and fine homes throughout the city. Some have survived and are still used as residences or serve other purposes. Main Street was lined with mansions, all of which have since given way to office buildings. The Henry Fox house, the last mansion on Main Street, occupied the site of the present Exxon Building. The Waldo Mansion, on 202 Westmoreland Avenue, is the oldest occupied house in Houston. Built in 1885 at the intersection of Caroline and Rusk Streets, it was moved to its present site in 1905. Other mansions which have been restored include the John Kirby Mansion, designed by James Ruskin and built in 1928. The Kirby Mansion became the headquarters of the Red Cross and is currently owned by Gulf States Oil Corporation.

Home of the Pillot family, who provided food for thought from their bookstore and nourishment for the body from their grocery store.

The T.P. Lee house was built in 1910 and was purchased by the Basilian Fathers of Toronto in 1946 to serve as the first building of the new University of St. Thomas. The old Howard Hughes l. ne on 3921 Yoakum has also been incorporated into St. Thomas University. The W. W. Fondren, Sr. house, built in 1923, is one of the last mansions remaining on Montrose Avenue, once Houston's most elegant thoroughfare. Close by are the Waldo Mansion and No. 435 Hawthorne, where the late Lyndon B. Johnson lived when he taught at Old Sam Houston High School in the 1920s. It is still owned by the Johnson family.

One of the historic communities in Houston is the Old Sixth Ward, better known as the Sabine Historic District. It is bounded by Washington and Union, Houston and Capitol streets and the Glenwood Cemetery. The district has the largest collection of intact wood frame Victorian homes in the city, dating from the late 1800s to the early 1900s and is listed on the National Register for Historic Places. Another historic district is the Broadacres neighborhood, in the South Main section of Houston, featuring homes built between 1923 and 1930. The district has applied for listing on the National Register for Historic Places.

Woodland Heights is a late nineteenth Century community containing Colonial Cuban and Greek Revival style homes. Travis School, which opened in 1890 as a one-room country school, is located in this area. Among its alumni are Texas Senator John Tower and the novelist William Goyen.

THE MODERN SKYLINE

Rising above the flat prairie terrain, the towering skyline of Houston is a symbol of the city's energy and enterprise. Beginning in the 1920s, the old skyscrapers have symbolized industrial development, the growth of financial institutions and expansion of the city's international commercial base. Among these are the Humble Building at 1224 Main Street, built in 1921; The Petroleum Building, 1314 Texas Avenue, built in 1927; the Niels Esperson Building, 808 Travis Street, built in 1927; and the Gulf Building, at 712 Main Street, built in 1929. The Federal Land Bank Building, located at 430 Lamar Street, of Spanish Renaissance Revival style, 1928, has been remodeled twice, the last time in 1978.

After World War II the central business district changed as taller multipurpose building complexes became more numerous. Notable among these are the trapezoidal Pennzoil Towers, Allen Center, Houston Center, Cullen Center and the 50-story One Shell Plaza building, which is one of the largest reinforced concrete structures ever built. While the Cullen Center, the Allen Center and the Shell Plaza complexes provide mostly office space, the Houston Center, which is now in its first phase of development,

The red brick home designed by James Ruskin for John Henry Kirby, Houston's own lumber baron, housed the Red Cross Headquarters and is now the comfortable office of Gulf State Oil Corporation.

will also have housing, hotels, theaters and shopping facilities.

New additions to the downtown skyline include the Texas Commerce Tower and The Allied Bank Plaza, the tallest buildings in the United States outside of New York and Chicago. Architect I. M. Pei has designed the 75-story Texas Commerce Tower, under construction at the intersection of Texas and Travis, which, upon completion in 1981, will be the tallest building in Houston as well as in the Southwest. The Allied Bank Plaza structure will be just 28 1/2 feet shorter. The 55-story First International Plaza, at Dallas and Smith, is scheduled to be completed in the latter part of 1980.

The 30-story Hyatt Regency Hotel, located at the intersection of Louisiana and Dallas, is famous for its exterior elevators and the Spindletop, a revolving restaurant situated on its roof.

Other business districts around the city feature equally imposing architecture. Glenn H. McCarthy spurred development of the area farther south on Main Street when he bought 15 acres of land at the intersection of Holcombe Boulevard and South Main, where he built the Shamrock Hotel, a massive structure with a green roof inaugurated in 1949 with a still unmatched fanfare. Other developments outside the downtown area have altered the skyline in the midst of residential neighborhoods of the city. The Galleria, designed by Hellmuth, Obata and Kassabaum of St. Louis, with an eye on Milan's famous old Galleria Vittoria Emmanuele, contains shopping malls, theaters, hotels and restaurants. Greenway Plaza is more office oriented, boasting several skyscrapers as well as a sports arena, The Summit, a shopping mall and a hotel.

THE PEDESTRIAN "TUNNELS"

Where other cities have restricted automobile traffic in some central business districts in order to give pedestrians easy access to facilities, Houston uses a system of privately constructed underground access ways for pedestrians' comfort. Dubbed by Houstonians "the Tunnels," the brightly lighted subterranean walkway system connect clusters of buildings in the downtown area as well as in other parts of town, containing shops and restaurants and providing easy access to others. The main "tunnel" system totals approximately 2.8 miles in length and connects about 50 buildings and parking facilities. The largest continuous section interconnects 15 major office buildings, retail establishments, hotels and parking facilities in the heart of downtown Houston.

Houston has its underground tunnel system, a possible salvation in case of fire or enemy attack — or even traffic difficulties.

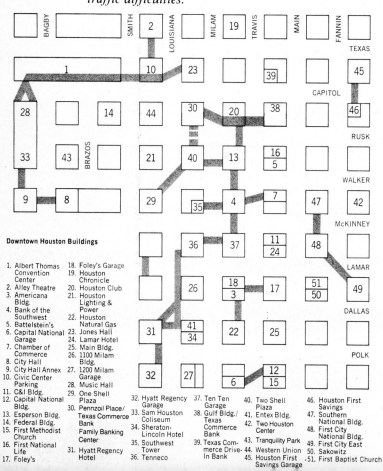

City Hall and the Oscar Holcombe Civic Center buildings are linked together in a separate tunnel system. Starting from Jones Hall to the Nina Vance Alley Theatre, it makes it possible for a pedestrian to walk to City Hall, City Hall Annex, the Music Hall, Sam Houston Coliseum, Albert Thomas Convention Center and the Tranquility underground garage without being exposed to the weather. Two separate tunnel systems serve the county buildings in the city. The first one links the Criminal Courts Building with the Family Law Center. The other connects the County Administration building with other county facilities.

PARKS AND MONUMENTS

Parks are abundant throughout the city. The 545-acre Hermann Park, which contains the zoo and public recreational facilities, was named for George Hermann, an affluent Houstonian who, in 1914, donated the land for the park. Located in it is the log house headquarters of the Daughters of the Republic of Texas, San Jacinto Chapter. Reminiscent of the early log houses in Houston, the stones for the fireplace come from historic old homes throughout Texas. In another part of the park stands a statue of General Sam Houston, which was unveiled in August, 1925. Besides this, it was George Hermann who also donated land in the present City Hall area for a public square. The one stipulation he made was that anybody who might wish to do so could sleep there "undisturbed by the forces of law and order."

Memorial Park is the largest public park in Houston, stretching over a thousand acres. The park contains the Houston Arboretum and botanical gardens and numerous recreational facilities.

Tranquility Park, designed by Charles Tapley and dedicated on the tenth anniversary of the first lunar landing, is a tribute to man's achievements in space travel. Neil Armstrong's words, transmitted from the moon, "Houston. Tranquility base here. The *Eagle* has landed," are written in many languages on plaques placed at the entrance to the park. The mounds and depressions on the parks surface represent the cratered lunar surface.

Named for the founders of Houston, the Allen brothers, Allen's Landing Park is situated on Buffalo Bayou at Main Street. This is where the Allens first set foot in the area that would become the city of Houston and where they built their original trading post. Undertaken as a Bicentennial Project by the city, Allen's Landing is a historical theme park.

The grave of John Kirby Allen, who died shortly after helping found the city, lies in Founders' Cemetery, on West Dallas and Valentine. The cemetery was renovated in 1936 by the State of Texas as part of the state's centennial celebrations. Anson Jones, the last president of the Republic of Texas; Thomas Lubbock, commander of the Terry Rangers; James

Downtown Houston Buildings

1. Albert Thomas Convention Center
2. Alley Theatre
3. Americana Bldg.
4. Bank of the Southwest
5. Battelstein's
6. Capital National Garage
7. Chamber of Commerce
8. City Hall
9. City Hall Annex
10. Civic Center Parking
11. C&I Bldg.
12. Capital National Bldg.
13. Esperson Bldg.
14. Federal Bldg.
15. First Methodist Church
16. First National Life
17. Foley's
18. Foley's Garage
19. Houston Chronicle
20. Houston Club
21. Houston Lighting & Power
22. Houston Natural Gas
23. Jones Hall
24. Lamar Hotel
25. Main Bldg.
26. 1100 Milam Bldg.
27. 1200 Milam Garage
28. Music Hall
29. One Shell Plaza
30. Pennzoil Place/Texas Commerce Bank Family Banking Center
31. Hyatt Regency Hotel
32. Hyatt Regency Garage
33. Sam Houston Coliseum
34. Sheraton-Lincoln Hotel
35. Southwest Tower
36. Tenneco
37. Ten Ten Garage
38. Gulf Bldg./Texas Commerce Bank
39. Texas Commerce Drive-In Bank
40. Two Shell Plaza
41. Entex Bldg.
42. Two Houston Center
43. Tranquility Park
44. Western Union
45. Houston First Savings Garage
46. Houston First Savings
47. Southern National Bldg.
48. First City National Bldg.
49. First City East
50. Sakowitz
51. First Baptist Church

A statue of Sam Houston whose dreams of Texas' possibilities still encourage Houstonians to go forward, stands near the entrance to Hermann Park at Main Street.

Holman, one of the early mayors of Houston and Howard R. Hughes, Jr., the reclusive billionaire can be found in Glenwood Cemetery, one of the oldest graveyards in town.

CIVIC AND CULTURAL LANDMARKS

Only a few of the old civic buildings exist today. The Julia Ideson Library Building, named for the long-time Houston librarian, was erected in 1926 as part of the planned civic center. It is the only building of a proposed complex that was erected. Designed by Cram & Ferguson, the Ideson Building has been constructed in Spanish Renaissance style. The historical room of the building houses collections of Texas history and the Circle M Collection, donated by Salvation Army Major E. T. Milsaps. Adjoining the Ideson Building is the octagonal shaped new Houston Public Library, completed in 1976. The Library contains over three and one half million books and documents. It is linked to the Ideson Building by a pedestrian tunnel.

Next to the public library stands Houston City Hall. Completed in 1939, the structure was designed by Joseph Finger and built by the Public Works Administration using white fossilized limestone. The ceiling murals were painted by Daniel MacMorris and depict the themes of industry, law, culture and administration.

Within a short walking distance, in the heart of downtown Houston, is the Oscar F. Holcombe Civic Center, the site of trade shows, sporting events,

operas, ballets, conventions and other events. A $40 million complex of four magnificent exhibition buildings, the Civic Center is close to major hotels, theaters, specialty shops, department stores, restaurants, clubs and office buildings. Included in the complex are the Jesse H. Jones Hall for the Performing Arts, the Sam Houston Coliseum, the Music Hall and the Albert Thomas Convention Center. Jesse Jones Hall, which opened in 1966, stands on the site of the old Houston Auditorium. The Houston Endowment, Inc., a charitable fund set up by Jones himself, provided the funds for erecting the hall, with a seating capacity of up to 3,000, in memory of Jesse Jones' life of service to the nation and to the city. In the lobby of Jones Hall is a sculpture by Richard Lippold. Called Gemini II, it is an artistic rendition of the spirit of the Space Age made of 2,300 polished aluminum rods held in place by 90,000 feet of goldplated wire, creating an illusion of shimmering rays in space flight. The elegant teakwood panelling of Jones Hall achieves the ultimate in theater-concert hall design.

Named for the long-time Houston Congressman, the Albert Thomas Convention and Exhibition Center

The Julia Ideson Library, named for Houston's best-loved librarian, has its own underground tunnel to the Houston Public Library and Research Center.

has 127,500 square feet of exhibition space, 40,000 square feet of meeting rooms and parking for 2,000 cars. It serves as a complete, flexible meeting place for the nation's business leaders, as well as a magnificent showplace for the products of various industries. It is also the home of the National Space Hall of Fame.

Opposite Jones Hall stands the Nina Vance Alley Theatre, built in 1969. It is the home of the repertory theater founded and directed by the late Nina Vance. One of the finest residential professional theaters in the U. S., the Alley features an 800-seat multispace stage and a 300-seat arena.

Other theaters are found outside the downtown area. The Tower Theater opened originally in 1936 and was converted to a live theater in 1979. It opened its doors with the stage performance of the Texas based play *The Best Little Whorehouse in Texas,* which achieved national acclaim on Broadway.

Miller Outdoor Theatre in Hermann Park, recently renovated, is an open-air theater which features professional and amateur productions.

The Houston Museum of Natural Science, in Hermann Park, contains numerous exhibits, including the Milsaps collection of coins and the Westheimer group of minerals. The Burke Baker Planetarium, opened in 1964, is a unit of the museum.

The Museum of Fine Arts, designed by William Ward Watkin, was completed in 1924 and features a wide range of exhibits including the Beck collection of French impressionists; Venetto's *Portrait of a Man;* Tintoretto's baroque exercise, *Tancred Baptizing Clorinda,* painted around 1582; and Umlauf's *The Fishers* and *The Pieta.*

Bayou Bend, the home of the Hogg family at 2940 Lazy Lane, was donated by Miss Ima Hogg to the Museum of Fine Arts in 1966. It houses Miss Hogg's

Known as the Old Cherry Home, this classic Southern frame structure is now designated a Houston landmark.

collection of seventeenth to nineteenth century decorative arts and period rooms.

Named for the late painter Mark Rothko, the Rothko Chapel is a small octagonal building commissioned by the de Menil family as an ecumenical chapel. Fourteen huge abstract canvasses by Rothko hang in the chapel, illuminated by a single skylight. The resulting effect is subdued and mysterious. Outside the chapel stands Barnett Newman's sculpture, the *Broken Obelisk,* also commissioned by the de Menils.

Opened in 1899 as the first city park, the 20-acre Sam Houston Park is now an outdoor museum containing a permanent exhibition of old Houston homes. The project is sponsored by the Harris County Heritage Society. Nathaniel Kellum's house, a plantation-style house built in 1847, is the oldest brick home in Houston. In 1850, Kellum moved from Houston, selling his home to Abram W. Noble. During the 1850s, Mrs. Zerviah M. Noble and her daughter, Catherine A. Kelly, operated one of Houston's first private schools in the Kellum-Noble house. A second restored home in the park is the San Felipe Cottage, a typical Texas cottage of the 1870s.

Another park feature is the Long Row reconstruction, a replica of Houston's first shopping strip. Part of the city's bid to become the capital of the Texas Republic, the Long Row construction was hastily put together in 1837. The Long Row housed, among others, R. C. Barry & Company, tailors; A. McGowen, tin, sheet, iron and copperware vendor; Cooke & Ewing, druggists and Dick Dowling's Bank of Bacchus saloon. The original structure burned down in 1860.

The Nichols-Rice-Cherry house was originally built in 1850 in a Greek Revival style, for Ebenezer B. Nichols, a native of Cooperstown, New York. William M. Rice owned the house between 1851 and 1863 and Mrs. Emma Cherry saved it from demolition in 1897. In 1957, it was presented to the park by Gus Wortham, an insurance executive.

The lumber of the Pillot House, built in 1868 and moved from McKinney Avenue to the park, was chosen by Eugene Pillot, one of the early developers in Houston. It is a mid-Victorian structure with some significant features, including what is considered to be the first inside kitchen in a Houston home.

Other structures in the park include the Old Place, a log cabin built by John W. Williams (an Austin colonist) on the banks of Clear Creek about 1824, which is the oldest structure in Harris County; St. John Church, an Evangelical Lutheran Church, built in 1891; the *Spirit of the Confederacy* statue placed in the park by the Daughters of the Confederacy; and the Sam Houston Park Bandstand, a replica of the original turn-of-the-century "Houston City Park" bandstand.

EDUCATIONAL INSTITUTIONS

Rice University is Houston's most architecturally distinguished place of learning. Spanish eclectic in style, the buildings are surrounded by formal gardens. The 300-acre landscaped campus, with red roofed buildings and courts surrounded by oak and cypress trees, is located in the South Main area. Modeled after the collegiate system of old English universities, Rice attracted a wide range of scholars, among them Julian Huxley, the noted biologist and evolution theorist, who taught at Rice in 1913. The original building, Lovett Hall (now the administration building), reflects old world charm in its Mediterranean lines. In the center of the Quadrangle, which Lovett Hall looks upon, is the statue of William Marsh Rice. Rice's ashes are buried at the base of the statue.

The University of Houston, the largest university in the city, is built on 330 acres south of the Gulf Freeway. It started as a junior college of the Houston Independent School District in 1927 and achieved university status in 1934. Local Houston philanthropists have aided the growth of the university. The names of its schools and buildings—the Cullen School of Engineering, the Nina Cullinan Hall, the Hilton School of Hotel Management and the M.D. Anderson Memorial Library—indicate the sources of generous gifts. The eight story M.D. Anderson Memorial Library has a carillon on its roof. The seven story General Classroom Building stands in an ornamental sunken garden. The University of Houston's downtown college is housed in the old Merchants and Manufacturers Building (the M & M Building), designed by Giesecke and Harris. The ten story structure, dedicated in 1930, was patterned after a similar Chicago building of the 1920s.

Texas Southern University is located on 58 acres at Wheeler Street. The archives of the old Negro College for Men, which it succeeded, are in the vaults of the college library. Former Congresswoman Barbara Jordan is an alumna of the school.

POINTS OF INTEREST

Houston is renowned throughout the world as the home of the Texas Medical Center, the Lyndon Johnson Space Center, the Astrodome, the third largest port in the United States and the San Jacinto Monument. The Texas Medical Center has one of the finest concentrations of medical facilities in the world located in one area. It includes 20 major health institutions, among them two medical schools, a dental school, two nursing schools and seven hospitals. Two of the world's leading heart surgeons are found here: Dr. Michael DeBakey is affiliated with Methodist Hospital and Dr. Denton Cooley operates at St. Lukes Hospital. The Texas Medical Center is a monument to human achievement, knowledge and ingenuity.

The battleship Texas, *landlocked now and another reminder of Houston's glorious past, looks toward the San Jacinto Monument.*

Located on NASA road, in the Clear Lake area of Houston, is the Lyndon B. Johnson Space Center, from which the nation's space missions are controlled. The space center has made Houston synonymous with the nation's space achievements. It was from the space center that man's first moon landing was directed. The Center contains the facilities for selection and training of astronauts, and for design, development and testing of manned spacecrafts. On display on the grounds of the center are replicas of the various spacecraft developed by the U.S. space program. The Center is composed of many buildings, among them are the Project Management Building, the Flight Crew Training Laboratory and the Technical Service Office Building.

The multipurpose Astrodomain achieved a lot of firsts, both nationally and worldwide, when it was opened in 1965. The complex includes the Astrodome, a domed stadium; Astroworld, an amusement park; and hotel and convention facilities. Hailed as the "Eighth Wonder," the Astrodome is the first domed stadium ever constructed. Built at the cost of 38 million dollars, the 208-foot tall domed stadium was erected on drained marsh land. It featured the first synthetic turf and the first indoor baseball game was played on it before a crowd that included President Lyndon Johnson and Texas Governor John Connally on April 9, 1965.

The Port of Houston has been one of the busiest ports of call for national and international ships ever since its completion in 1914. The ship channel extends from the Turning Basin down Buffalo Bayou through Galveston Bay to the Gulf of Mexico. Along the Turning Basin and the channel stretches an extensive network of oil pipelines, refineries and cotton compresses. The Port of Houston is one of the few ports that handle containerized cargo.

The San Jacinto Monument and Museum are located on the San Jacinto Battleground. The edifice was erected as a tribute to the Texas army which, led by General Sam Houston, defeated the Mexicans in 1836. Atop the monument—the tallest masonry structure in the world, fifteen feet taller than the Washington Monument—carved in stone is the Lone Star of Texas.

The sun dial, on the main axis of the monument, about 200 yards west of the reflection pool, was erected by the San Jacinto Chapter of the Daughters of the Republic of Texas. The San Jacinto Museum of History exhibits memorabilia of the Daughters of the Republic of Texas and documents pertaining to the Texas Veterans Association, which held its first convention in Houston on May 13-15, 1873. The membership consisted of citizens, soldiers and seamen who lived or served in Texas between 1820 and 1845. Moored near the battleground since San Jacinto Day, 1948, is the USS *Texas,* also known as the *Battleship Texas,* survivor of the dreadnaught class

The San Jacinto Monument commemorates the Battle of San Jacinto and houses cherished reminders of that historic occasion.

and a veteran of two world wars and many campaigns. The state of Texas saved its namesake battleship from the scrap heap and turned it into an interesting and useful historical monument. The *Battleship Texas* is open to visitors year-round and contains a museum of documents and memorabilia of its long service in the U.S. Navy.

PART III

THE ECONOMY traces in detail the emergence of the city of Houston as an economic giant. It offers an account of the growth of the city's economy from its beginning, highlighting the development of the key sectors, such as oil and gas, argriculture and others. It then continues with a presentation of banking and financial institutions, utilities, labor relations and port facilities as aspects of the fine economic climate. Then follows an analysis of the city's diversified economy. Houston's role as an international center for energy, commerce and industry is discussed. Also covered are the bustling retail and wholesale trade, the services and manufacturing facilities. NASA and the Texas Medical Center are shown as examples of research and development activities which attract medical, scientific and engineering talent from throughout the world to the bustling city of Houston.

BUSINESS AND INDUSTRY

Houston has a robust economy with a remarkably diverse economic base. Today it is the energy capital of America and a world focal point for energy research. Renowned for its expertise in science, medicine, engineering and technology, the city is also a major center for international trade, banking and commerce. Houston, with its surrounding area, is one of the nation's vital manufacturing regions, and the city is a national leader in construction and wholesale trade, with a rapidly expanding retail market. A capital of agriculture since its early days when cotton was king, Houston's impressive transportation capabilities combine to make it also a modern agribusiness center.

Perhaps the key element in Houston's continually growing and historically sound economy has been a consistently positive attitude towards the free enterprise system. This desirable business climate has stimulated the expansion of economic activities.

Houston's strength lies in its adaptability in a changing economy. It is an economic leader, as will be seen, because new layers of economic activities have expanded the scope of Houston's economy without displacing existing pursuits.

The Tenneco Chemicals Plant, a modern alchemist, produces chemical building blocks for Houston's industry, including hydrocarbon chemicals, stabilizers, synthetic and organic chemicals.

ECONOMIC HISTORY

The city's development from a small backwater settlement into a prosperous metropolis of international significance took place within the relatively short period of 140 years. Its economic history helps explain why Houston is the city of destiny.

It has been said that Houston is a flourishing trade center today because of its fortunate location. John and Augustus Allen, the enterprising pioneers, chose this spot in 1836 because it was the navigation point closest to the already established settlement of San Felipe de Austin on the Brazos, which Stephen F. Austin had established as the first Anglo-American community in Texas.

Most of Houston's original settlers came on small boats up the bayou, which connected the city with Galveston Bay and the Gulf of Mexico. The first steamship, the 85-foot long *Laura M.* sailed up Buffalo Bayou in January of 1837, demonstrating that the city could indeed develop into an inland port.

Houston's first economic crisis came three years after its founding, when New Orleans' suppliers cut off Houston merchants' credit, and the Republic of Texas currency dropped to one-quarter and then to one-tenth the value of the U.S. dollar. Simultaneously, the capital was moved from Houston to Austin, another threat to the city's economic stability. As if these setbacks were not enough, an epidemic of yellow fever swept through the city, wiping out one tenth of the population.

Despite these problems, Houston slowly began to recover during the 1840s, emerging as the commercial center for nearby towns. Important to Houston's future economic development was the treaty by which the Republic of Texas became, in 1846, a part of the United States. This made Houston more accessible to the flow of capital and people. Houston built warehouses and stored cotton during the 1850s, as its brokers continue to do today. The city established, in addition, a strong agricultural and lumber trade. Houston's first rail link was laid in 1853, a turning point in the city's development as a national marketing center.

The War Between the States had an adverse effect on Houston's economy. The war effort and the consequent dislocation of people disrupted the city's economy. As a result, the postwar Reconstruction period brought economic hardships to Texas. But the financial losses suffered during the war and its aftermath subsided sufficiently to allow Houston's economy to grow again.

Major products were cotton, lumber and cattle. The Port of Houston served to aid and diversify the lumber industry, since pine and hardwood were transported by way of the ship channel. As the amount of marine traffic to the East Coast increased, the channel was expanded to an average 12 foot depth by Commander Charles Morgan, who obtained a federal grant for the project. Morgan later stretched a chain across the channel at Morgan's Point and charged all comers a toll. Following Morgan's death in 1892, the United States government paid his heirs $92,888 for the rights to the channel and the toll restriction was removed. Eventually, the channel was deepened to 17.5 feet.

Until the turn of the century, Houston's economy

A vista of the Houston Ship Channel, including, at top, the Turning Basin.

A bird's eye view of the famed National Aeronautics and Space Administration Lyndon B. Johnson Space Center, spread over a 1,620-acre site 22 miles southeast of downtown.

Pressurized storage tanks that contain liquids are part of the refinery, seen in background. Located in the eastern part of Houston near the ship channel.

was largely based on agriculture and ranching. Besides cotton, cattle and timber, rice growing and fishing gained significance. All, however, were overshadowed when oil was discovered at Spindletop in 1901. The development of this potent natural resource then became the most significant layer of Houston's economy. "Houston" and "Texas" became synonymous with "oil." As oil revolutionized social structures and priorities at home and abroad, it served to propel the United States toward economic and political leadership in the world.

Two major events contributed to Houston's economic advancement. On September eighth and ninth, 1900, a tidal wave and hurricane struck Galveston Island. Thousands lost their lives and hardly a building on the entire island remained standing. Galveston never wholly recovered. The aftermath of this disaster served to revitalize efforts to set up Houston as a major port. Unlike Galveston, the Port of Houston is located inland and is largely immune to such disasters. Congress then invested more money in waterway improvements. The Texas legislature established the Harris County-Houston Ship Channel Navigation District, today called the

Port of Houston Authority, and in November 1914, President Woodrow Wilson pushed a button in Washington, D.C., which fired a cannon in Houston and officially opened the then 25-foot deep ship channel. The Port of Houston became increasingly a major factor in the city's economic development.

The other event that worked in Houston's favor was when the United States turned to Houston for the oil and fuel needed for the World War I effort. By this time, Houston had an expanded port facility capable of handling vital overseas shipments. The first deep water vessel, in fact, arrived at the Port of Houston in August, 1915, and the first refinery was set up along the ship channel in 1918. The growth of the automobile industry—the largest manufacturing industry of all time—led to increased demands for oil. The oil industry expanded its incredible production capacity to fill the automobile's insatiable maw.

The 1920s were, for Houston, an era of prosperity. The port and railroads expanded, cotton revenues reached new heights, and new construction altered the city's skyline. However, the Great Depression, beginning in October 1929, tried Houston's economic strength. Although business activities declined throughout the nation, Houston's economy was relatively stable, and not one bank failed. Industry became an important part of the economy in the

RIGHT: *The U.S. space explorer pointing skyward at NASA's Lyndon B. Johnson Space Center.*

Flight controllers at work in Building 30, Mission Control, NASA's communications center, during a manned flight of the U.S. space program.

plant flourished in the area, and a third important layer was added to Houston's complex economy. World War II pushed the Port of Houston to ever-greater expansion. The city became the center of the explosive development in the petrochemical industry, which used oil products to manufacture such vital materials as synthetic rubber. The industry continued to expand and went on to include plastics, besides oil tools and equipment. Food processing (coffee and rice) and high-technology industries added another dimension to Houston's economy during this period.

In the post-war period the Texas Medical Center became a reality, elevating Houston to international prominence in the field of medicine. The National Aeronautics and Space Administration chose Houston for its Manned Spacecraft Center, and the center was completed in the 1960s. Houston became "Space City," as the world looked through its eyes out to the stars. Engineering, that bridge between science and practicality, became a more significant activity in and around the city.

The 1960s saw a dramatic increase of construction and the establishment of divisional and service headquarters by some of the nation's largest corporations in Houston. The huge companies represented in Houston include Shell, Tenneco, Pennzoil,

1930s, although agriculture and oil remained the leading sectors in the city's successful economy.

The 1940s brought greater diversification. The continued growth of the oil industry induced major process industries to locate along the banks of the ship channel. Cement plants, a paper mill and a steel

The magnificent Texas Medical Center as seen from above. It is renowned throughout the world as one of the most advanced health facilities.

COMPARATIVE COST OF LIVING (Fall 1979)

METROPOLITAN AREA	INTERMEDIATE BUDGET	RELATIVE INDEX*
Boston	$24,381	119
New York	23,856	116
Washington	22,206	108
San Francisco	21,478	105
Philadelphia	21,436	104
Minneapolis	21,426	104
Cleveland	20,868	102
Detroit	20,821	101
Seattle	20,719	101
Chicago	20,564	100
URBAN AVERAGE	**20,517**	**100**
Denver	20,468	100
San Diego	20,088	98
St. Louis	19,963	97
Pittsburgh	19,890	97
Los Angeles	19,871	97
Kansas City	19,618	96
HOUSTON	**19,025**	**93**
Atlanta	18,821	92
Dallas	18,301	89

Source: U.S. Department of Labor   Copyright© 1980 Unibook, Inc.
* % of U.S. Urban Average

Anderson Clayton and Company and Cooper Industries. Among the service industries in Houston by this time were Brown and Root, American General, Texas Eastern, El Paso and Sysco. Exxon, Texaco, Kellogg, Fluor and Bechtel represent some of the major divisional headquarters in the city. U.S. Steel is also located in Houston.

Houston today is not only the oil capital of America but it is also the world's energy capital, with leaders in research and development shaping its future.

As the city's economy continued to diversify, it became increasingly more international. Foreign trade grew to almost one-half of the Port of Houston's total tonnage by the 1970s.

The city has incorporated an impressive series of economic activities into a multifaceted and thriving economy. It is true that Houston has had outstanding opportunities for economic enlargement but another vital factor in the success of the Houston economy is its business climate.

ECONOMIC CLIMATE

Houston's attitude, spatial arrangements, labor resources and the established infrastructure characterize the city as a progressive and youthful community for investors.

Houston's central business district is a vibrant area in an age when many city centers are in decay. At the same time, business sites are found in pockets all over the city, a result of Houston's conscious decision to remain unzoned and not to restrict business activity. While other major cities specify where business locations begin and end, and where residential sites start and stop, Houston permits development of business, industry and residential areas side-by-side. Both state and city governments have always maintained an aggressively pro-business attitude.

Houston consumers generally find shopping centers, gasoline stations, banks and restaurants within easy reach, a convenience from a geographical standpoint. Major multiblock developments are located throughout the city, as are office and industrial parks. The truck, sea and rail capabilities of the Port of Houston have concentrated a great number of heavy industries in the port area. Though there is a lack of zoning in Houston, almost every neighborhood has deed restrictions to restrict indiscriminate land use and to avoid infiltration of businesses in essentially residential neighborhoods.

Support of the future expansion of the city's economic base, is provided by the state law which

TOTAL EMPLOYMENT —
HOUSTON METROPOLITAN AREA

1970 - 1979 — Increase: 58%

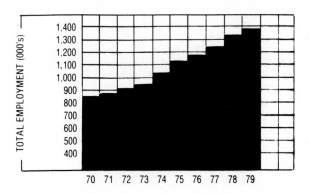

Source: Texas Employment Commission   Copyright© 1980 Unibook, Inc.

DISTRIBUTION OF HOUSTON NON-AGRICULTURAL EMPLOYMENT, BY INDUSTRY (March 1980)

	%	Total Employed	000's
		0 50 100 150 200 250	
Manufacturing	16.58		230,900
Retail Trade	15.31		213,300
Contract Construction	10.14		141,200
Medical & Professional Services	9.55		133,000
Business & Personal Services	9.54		132,900
Wholesale Trade	8.53		118,800
Local Government	8.24		114,800
Finance, Insurance & Real Estate	6.04		84,200
Mining	5.06		70,500
Transportation & Allied Services	4.35		60,600
State Government	2.11		29,400
Utilities	1.52		21,200
Communications	1.36		19,000
Federal Government	1.36		19,000
Agricultural Services	0.31		4,300
Total	**100.00**		**1,393,100**

Source: *Houston Labor Market Review*. Texas Employment Commission
NOTE: Data include Houston Met. Area.

gives the City of Houston annexation authority and extraterritorial jurisdiction throughout the growing unincorporated areas surrounding the city. This arrangement works to insure the city's strength and vitality.

Houston's labor environment is certainly favorable to management and a strong argument can be made

A Goodyear chemical plant supervisor carefully tests the specific gravity of liquid latex. This is an early stage of synthetic rubber production, following the addition of coagulants.

that it is also beneficial to individual workers as well. Organized labor is limited and only 13 percent of the Texas labor force is unionized, proportionately smaller than in any other major industrialized state. Mass picketing and secondary boycotts, strikes and picketing are illegal in Texas, a state which upholds the right-to-work principle. Further, the closed shop and the union shop are prohibited by Texas law. Unemployment insurance taxes paid by employers in Texas are among the lowest in the United States, as are total welfare payments per capita. The policy of encouragement toward business has proved to be highly beneficial to the individual worker, since Houston's unemployment rate usually has been half to two-thirds of the national average.

Houston's per capita income ranked fourth among the nation's 20 largest metropolitan areas in 1978. According to the Bureau of Labor Statistics report, *Autumn 1979 Urban Family Budgets*, Houston's annual cost of living ranked third lowest among 25 metropolitan areas surveyed for upper, intermediate and lower-level income families. Relatively high wages and relatively low costs combine to make Houston the envy of other large urban areas.

Houston's employment rolls have increased by more than 50 percent during the 1970s while many other metropolitan areas have experienced declining growth.

The city's ever growing demand for manpower, especially technical and clerical workers, cannot be fully met locally; consequently, qualified people are being sought from other parts of the United States and the world.

INTERNATIONAL ACTIVITY

Since 1976, the number of foreign-owned companies located in Houston has more than doubled. Approximately one-third of the manufacturers in the Houston area have foreign dealings. English companies (105 of them) make up more than one-quarter of foreign-owned firms in Houston, while there are 80 Japanese, 48 German and 40 French firms. It is estimated that foreign firms provide around 20,000 jobs for Houstonians. Some of the large foreign companies operating in Houston are Aramco Services Company, Davy International, Inc., Denka Chemical Corporation, Elder International, Hycel, Inc., Kirby Building Systems, Inc., Mobay Chemical Company, Olsen, Inc. and Soltex Polymer Corporation.

In addition to the firms, there are 14 foreign trade, investment and tourist offices in Houston. In April 1980, Rumania became the first Eastern Bloc nation to open a permanent trade office in Houston. Fifty foreign consulates reside in the city, including the first U.S. Consulate opened by the People's Republic of China in the fall of 1979.

So vitally important is Houston's technology and expertise in the search for energy that an important relationship has developed between the oil-rich Middle Eastern nations and Houston, earning the city the title "Middle Eastern capital of the U.S." In fact, Houston handles more than half of the $7 billion annual U.S. trade with the Middle East.

Energy is not the only attraction for foreign businesses. Major foreign steel companies and banks have branches operating out of Houston. Two major foreign steel companies have their U.S. headquarters in Houston—British Steel Corporation, Inc., of the United Kingdom, and Mannesmann Pipe and Steel Corporation of Germany. One of the primary imports handled by the Port of Houston is foreign steel.

There were 46 foreign bank offices in Houston in 1980. Foreign banks use their Houston offices to negotiate business transactions, although they are not allowed to conduct other usual banking activities.

International activity in Houston has had a significant influence on the entire community. There has been a large increase in Houston's foreign

Ships from around the globe, big and small, pass through the Port of Houston.

The oil industry's Annual Offshore Technical Conference hosts many elaborate exhibitions.

population, giving it a unique cosmopolitan flavor. A wide variety of foreign food restaurants, cultures and languages have been introduced to Houston, numerous foreign students attend the city's universities, retail stores draw thousands of shoppers from abroad and the Texas Medical Center is a mecca for patients from around the world.

Foreigners in Houston have invested large sums in unimproved property and in residential, commercial and industrial developments. As Houston attracts such foreign capital, its contributions to the nation's balance of payments grow even further.

Houston's international importance is recognized by foreign heads of state as well. The list of state visitors in Houston includes China's Vice Premier Deng Xiao ping, Britain's Prince Charles, France's President Valery Giscard d'Estaing, Egypt's President Anwar el-Sadat, Jordan's King Hussein, Saudi Arabia's Prince Saud Al-Faisal, New Zealand's Prime Minister Robert A. Muldoon and Sweden's King Carl XVI Gustaf among others.

In the last decade Houston has seen a tremendous increase in air travel. As the Southwest's international air hub, with two major airports, Houston Intercontinental Airport and William P. Hobby Airport. These airports, which recorded over 12,000,000 domestic passenger arrivals and departures in 1979, had 1,006,286 international arrivals and departures in the same year. Air freight companies provide Houston with direct all-cargo services to Europe, the Middle East, East Asia, the Caribbean and South America. Growth has been so great in airport traffic that both airports are undergoing expansion, and the capacity of the Houston Intercontinental Airport will be more than doubled when present construction work is completed.

While foreign activity in Houston has been proliferating, Houstonians have also been increasingly active in foreign lands. There are 2,700 Houston companies which maintain offices or facilities in 107 foreign countries throughout the world, with major exports being agricultural products, petroleum equipment and chemicals. Houston's largest bank—First City National—has offices in Singapore, London, Tokyo and Nassau. The city's second largest bank—Texas Commerce—is represented in Hong Kong, London, Bahrain, Mexico City, Tokyo, Caracas and Nassau. A total of eight Houston banks have international departments and several have offices or representatives in other nations, or close ties with foreign banks and financial institutions.

The important ingredient in Houston's international presence is its sophisticated Port facilities,

RIGHT: *Brown & Root's mammoth Greens Bayou Marine Fabrication Facility, where permanent offshore drilling and production platforms are manufactured for the petroleum industry.*

BELOW: *The Port of Houston's mammoth crane and unloading facilities, here unloading a big vessel from Wilmington, Delaware.*

ABOVE: *Public exhibits at the Johnson Space Center auditorium building feature the spacesuits of America's manned space program.* BELOW: *The lunar roving vehicle test module.*

which help the city play a dynamic role in international commerce.

PORT OF HOUSTON

The Port of Houston is today the third largest in the nation in total tonnage behind the ports of New York and New Orleans. The port's total cargo tonnage was 122,400,000 in 1979 and 5,500 ships called. Approximately 80 percent of the ships using the port are foreign vessels, coming from more than fifty nations, making Houston's port second only to New York in total foreign trade.

Most foreign ships using the port are registered under the flags of Liberia, Greece, Great Britain, Panama and Norway. With five grain elevators, the Port of Houston is the world's leading wheat exporting port and it has more tidewater grain storage than any other U.S. port. The chief port in an area rich with raw and semi-raw materials, Houston's terminals handle such major products as cotton, flour, livestock, oil field machinery, timber, oil and petrochemicals. Authorities predict that by December, 1980 the port should be taking in 1.4 million barrels of oil daily.

Today, the Port of Houston's principal exports are oil field and construction machinery, wheat, iron and steel, corn and cereals. Principal imports include crude petroleum, iron ore, automobiles, crude minerals, molasses and organic chemicals.

The port's ten largest trading partners in 1979, in terms of dollar value and total tonnage were:

PORT OF HOUSTON TOP TEN TRADING PARTNERS		
	Dollar Value	Total Tonnage
1 Saudi Arabia	$1,956,000,000	14,107,982
2 Japan	1,685,000,000	3,200,272
3 Mexico	1,240,000,000	6,532,873
4 W. Germany	1,031,000,000	677,322
5 United Kingdom	800,000,000	1,274,279
6 Soviet Union	775,000,000	4,573,274
7 The Netherlands	690,000,000	821,525
8 Brazil	679,000,000	3,151,239
9 Venezuela	644,000,000	1,151,903
10 Nigeria	624,000,000	4,258,225

SOURCE: Houston Chamber of Commerce   Copyright© 1980 Unibook, Inc.

Houston: City of Destiny displays its refineries, its manufacturers, its grain elevators and its storage facilities.

The Port itself consists of the ship channel with a depth of 40 feet in most places and a minimum width of 400 feet. The ship channel is lined with numerous docks and several industrial parks adjoin it.

The Turning Basin, located four miles east of Houston's central business district, is the first of three port divisions. It provides turnaround room for freighters in a broad 36-foot-deep waterway and is the ultimate destination for grain, cargo and conventional-sized container ships. The Bayport Division is a deep draft water area consisting of a three-mile-long, 40-foot-deep channel designed for large chemical and petroleum tankers. Finally, Barbours Cut Terminal, situated at the entrance to Galveston Bay, 25 miles east of the Turning Basin, was built for lighter aboard ship (LASH) container and roll-on/roll-off vessels. The port's Vessel Traffic System, operated by the United States Coast Guard, protects ships using the narrow waterways.

Houston's sophisticated port facilities and its large industrial complex have spawned a modern and well-maintained network of railroad services. Six large railroad systems operate in Houston, while some 30 others have offline offices there.

The excellent freeway network tying Houston with the rest of the nation makes intercity and interstate movement of goods a smooth proposition. Easy access to industrial and consumer markets from Houston's midcontinent location allow the supplier and manufacturer maximum site location alternatives. A great number of specialized carriers operate from Houston as well, such as 14 tank truck lines and

A four-story storage tank undergoes routine maintenance. The tank houses butadiene, a raw material used to produce synthetic rubber.

oilfield equipment haulers. More than 200 local delivery trucking firms operate in the 33-city local delivery zone.

BANKS

Rapid expansion of the banking market, particularly of international banking, has been a major result of Houston's economic growth. Harris County's 161 banks reported a record of $21.2 billion in total deposits at the end of December 1979. The county's 39 savings and loan associations showed deposits totaling $5.2 billion at the end of the same period. Houston banks which recorded more than $500 million each in total deposits are:

FULL-SERVICE BANKS	DEPOSITS
First City National Bank of Houston	$4,783,904,00
Texas Commerce Bank	4,112,822,000
Bank of the Southwest	1,422,098,000
Allied Bank of Texas	943,869,000
Houston National Bank	825,168,000
First International Bank	564,073,000

SAVINGS AND LOAN	
Gibraltar	1,082,212,000
Houston First American	984,731,000
University	692, 843,000

Bank debits to individual accounts, widely considered a major indicator of the level of aggregate business activity, totaled $756 billion in 1979, a jump of $287 billion from 1978 totals.

UTILITIES

Another favorable characteristic of Houston's economy, which provides an inducement for business and families to relocate there, is its low utility costs. Houston's utility rates are among the lowest in the nation. The Houston Lighting and Power Company, the sixth largest investor-owned, tax-paying electrical utility company in the nation, serves Houston with rates that enable families to pay less for their electric service than residents of other Texas cities.

Natural gas is supplied by Entex, Inc., which serves over half a million Houstonians. Since the city has one of the nation's largest concentrations of natural gas resources, its natural gas ranks among the lowest-priced sources of energy in the United States.

One telephone company, Southwestern Bell, provides telephone communications for Houston while there are five other independent telephone exchanges in outlying areas. Calls within Houston and to a large portion of its suburbs are toll-free, and new service usually requires a one-time deposit.

Houston's city government provides water, sewer and free garbage pick-up service. Water is supplied at reasonable rates by the city to residential and industrial users. The city has provided water sources adequate to meet residential and industrial demand as projected

RIGHT: *An island unto itself, here we see an offshore oil rig in the Gulf of Mexico. Such a rig may house a work crew for several weeks and has its own helicopter landing pad.*

for the next fifty years, by establishing great reservoirs in Lake Houston, Lake Conroe and Lake Livingston, all north of the city.

Neither Houston nor Texas has a corporate or a personal income tax. A franchise tax is levied on companies operating in Texas in the amount of $4.25 per $1,000 capital and profits. A six percent sales tax is levied on the sale of all goods except groceries and medicine.

ENERGY

The oil and gas industry and the city of Houston have a long history of close association. More than half of the nation's basic petrochemical manufacturing capacity and nearly half of the nation's capacity for first stage derivatives are found in the Houston region. Houston's unique pipeline system makes possible the efficient transfer of fuel, feedstock and chemical products among more than 150 chemical plants, refineries, gasoline processing plants and salt domes. Houston's product pipelines have been continuously expanding and extend more than 1,550 miles (2,495 kilometers).

The energy industry is Houston's single largest economic sector. In 1978, the crude oil capacity of Houston and Texas Gulf Coast petroleum refining was over four million barrels of refined products per day. National oil and gas companies have continued to center their activities in Houston, which is the location of corporate headquarters or management offices of 34 of the 35 largest American oil companies,

as well as some 400 smaller oil firms. In addition, about a quarter of the nation's oil and gas pipeline companies are based in Houston. Exxon USA moved its main operations to Houston in 1960, when it was still known as the Standard Oil Company of New Jersey, and Shell Oil Company followed in 1970. Other major oil companies with headquarters or major divisions in Houston include Texaco USA, Tenneco, Mobil, Pennzoil, Conoco and Gulf.

Many energy-related companies have established refineries along the Port of Houston's Ship Channel, thereby contributing significantly to the region's industrial productivity. The largest energy-related companies based in Houston (1979 figures) are:

	REVENUES	EARNINGS
1) Shell Oil	$14,546,000,000	$1,126,000,000
2) Tenneco	11,200,000,000	571,500,000
3) The Coastal Corp.	4,289,000,000	100,500,000
4) United Energy Res.	3,133,654,000	111,687,000
5) El Paso Co.	3,088,556,000	138,134,000
6) Texas Eastern	2,944,168,000	180,551,000
7) Pennzoil	2,051,693,000	238,518,000

(Exxon is not included on this list because its headquarters are located in New York.)

The following graph presents an index to recent value added by manufacture within the competitive and growing Sun Belt Region.

Value Added by Manufacture ($MILLIONS)

METROPOLITAN AREA	1977*	RANK	1976*	RANK	1972	RANK	ANNUAL % CHANGE 76-77	ANNUAL % CHANGE 72-77
Houston-Galveston	8,415	1	7,567	1	4,973	1	11.2	11.1
Dallas-Fort Worth	6,374	2	5,747	2	4,029	2	10.9	9.6
Louisville	4,433	3	4,210	3	3,134	3	5.3	7.2
Atlanta	3,686	4	3,476	4	2,437	4	6.0	8.6
Combined Miami-Ft. Lauderdale	2,370	5	2,079	5	1,619	5	14.0	7.9
Phoenix	2,319	6	2,068	6	1,393	6	12.1	7.9
Memphis	2,204	7	1,922	7	1,346	7	14.7	10.4
Birmingham	1,808	8	1,602	8	1,119	8	12.9	10.1
Tampa-St. Petersburg	1,439	9	1,290	9	956	10	11.6	8.5
New Orleans	1,358	10	1,249	10	1,008	9	8.7	6.1
Oklahoma City	1,108	11	977	11	765	11	13.4	7.7
San Antonio	730	12	638	12	458	12	14.4	9.8

Source: *1972 Census of Manufactures*, U.S. Department of Commerce
*Estimated by Texas Commerce Bancshares Economics Division

Many equipment manufacturers and suppliers, marine service contractors and seismic exploration and drilling companies are based in Houston. Among these are Cameron Iron Works, Schlumberger, Hughes Tool Company, Reed, AMF Tuboscope, Dresser Industries and TRW Mission.

Ancillary petroleum industry activities have contributed to Houston's economy as much as has the oil and gas industry. Brown and Root, Pullman-Kellogg, Raymond International, Bechtel and Fluor are among the major energy-related engineering and construction companies found in the city.

The future of the oil and petrochemical industry in Houston remains bright as long as oil, gas and coal are the world's primary fuel sources. Further, new worldwide trade prospects in oil are favorable. Houston is looking forward to, and is developing, alternative sources of energy to protect its status in manufacturing and industry. To that end, nuclear power plants are under construction and lignite deposits are being developed to ensure the continued economic and individual requirements of the area.

The beauty of the oil industry: one of many oil refineries in Houston's intricate and extensive petroleum and petrochemical complexes.

The Houston-Gulf Coast petroleum and petrochemical complex is also the site of about 60 percent of the U.S. petrochemical industry. The region also produces 80 percent of the nation's synthetic rubber. The Goodyear Tire and Rubber Company is one of the rubber affiliates located in Houston.

MANUFACTURING AND INDUSTRY

Houston is a major industrial and manufacturing center of products other than those related to oil, gas and petrochemicals. With 1,300 plants with 20 or more employees, Harris County, in which Houston is located, ranked fourth largest in industrialized areas in the U.S. in 1978. It registered shipments totaling $23 billion dollars. The main income producing manufacturing groups are chemicals and allied products, food and related products, non-electrical machinery and fabricated metals.

Distribution of Houston Manufacturing Employment (March 1980)

	% OF TOTAL	0 10 20 30 40 50 60	NUMBER EMPLOYED
Machinery (Non-electrical)	23.73		54.800
Fabricated Metals	15.03		34,700
Chemicals & Allied Products	14.77		34,100
Printing & Publishing	6.58		15,200
Petroleum Refining	6.11		14,100
Electrical Machinery & Equipment	5.63		13,000
Food & Related Products	5.59		12,900
Primary Metals	5.50		12,700
Stone, Clay & Glass	3.81		8,800
Miscellaneous Non-durable Goods	3.38		7,800
Miscellaneous Durable Goods	3.07		7,100
Transportation Equipment	2.69		6,200
Paper & Allied Products	1.82		4,200
Lumber & Wood Products	0.99		2,300
Furniture & Fixtures	0.65		1,500
Textile & Apparel	0.65		1,500
Total	**100.00**		**230,900**

Source: *Houston Labor Market Review*, Texas Employment Commission
NOTE: Data include Houston SMSA only.

Copyright© 1980 Unibook, Inc.

WHOLESALE AND RETAIL TRADE

Houston ranks as the leading industrial marketing center in the Southwest. Wholesale trade accounted for $12.8 billion in sales in the Houston-Galveston area in 1972, and it paid the wages for 8.2 percent of the region's employees in the same year.

Retail sales figures rank the Houston area fourth among the nation's major metropolitan areas in sales, with retail sales expanding 137.7 percent between 1973 and 1978. Total retail sales figures amounted to $10,214,278. The Harris County area already has over 200 malls and shopping centers with more than 50,000 square feet each, 12 of these exceed

Houston is one of the nation's key industrial centers. A machine tool operator at Cameron Ironworks uses a programmed drill press with an indexing table.

750,000 square feet and five exceed 1 million square feet. At least six more malls, each between 800,000 and 1,200,000 square feet in area, are planned for completion by 1985. In 1979, total department store sales increased by seven percent.

AGRICULTURE

Once the backbone of the Houston economy, agriculture still plays a significant role. Surrounded by a 20-county coastal prairie region, in which agriculture predominates, Houston is a major international "agribusiness" center. Agricultural income in Harris County increased some 128 percent between 1970 and 1979. Houston has the facilities for agricultural commodity marketing, processing, packaging and distribution. More than half of the export tonnage shipped from the Port of Houston is composed of agricultural products. The city is the largest supplier of agricultural chemicals, fertilizers and fuels in this nation.

The 100-mile radius around Houston accounts for 28 percent of the total U.S. production of rice. Soybeans were the largest agricultural income producing crop in 1979. Agricultural leaders that year, in terms of revenues, were:

Construction booming in downtown Houston. The Capitol National Bank reaches up in the foreground. Behind it, the First International Bank Building nears completion.

Soybeans	$14,900,000
Beef	12,900,000
Rice	11,900,000
Nursery crops	11,400,000
Horses	6,000,000
Timber	4,000,000

CONSTRUCTION

Houston and Harris County led the nation's construction industry during 1979, with $2.6 billion in total nonresidential construction and an additional $2.2 billion in residential construction. In 1979, the city of Houston became the first American city to issue over $2 billion in building permits in a single year, a total of $2.14 billion for an increase of more than 33 percent from 1978.

In 1978, the Houston metropolitan area led the nation's urban areas for the fourth year in succession in the number of housing starts, a total of 60,306.

TOTAL CONSTRUCTION- HARRIS COUNTY

1970 - 1979 — Increase: 399%

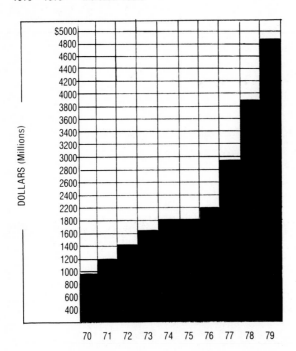

DOLLARS (Millions)

$5000
4800
4600
4400
4200
4000
3800
3600
3400
3200
3000
2800
2600
2400
2200
2000
1800
1600
1400
1200
1000
800
600
400

70   71   72   73   74   75   76   77   78   79

SOURCE: Houston Chamber of Commerce

MEDICAL SCIENCES

The Texas Medical Center in Houston is internationally renowned for its research facilities and educational contributions. The Medical Center has grown into a large complex, housing four general hospitals, five specialized hospitals, two medical schools, a school of public health, a dental school, a graduate school of biomedical sciences, two nursing

The proficient Life Flight helicopter service, a feature of Houston's Hermann Hospital. The three-helicopter service flies outlying patients to inner city medical care.

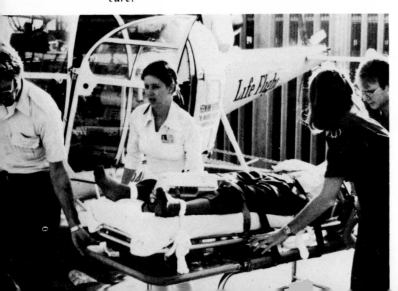

schools, a library, an institute of religion, several research organizations, computer facilities, several specialized training facilities, a cancer center and a heart center. Hundreds of patients come from around the country to avail themselves of the services offered by the Texas Medical Center.

MARINE SCIENCES

Over 300 Houston firms in all are involved in offshore activities world-wide. These firms are engaged in the design and manufacture of instrumentation, corrosion control, underwater pipelines, offshore production platforms, oil spill recovery and control equipment, oceangoing vessels, research of tides and currents, medical aspects of deep sea activity and marine biology. Marine research activity is conducted by Rice University and the University of Houston, both part of the Gulf Universities Research Consortium, and Texas A & M University.

SHOPPING

Shopping in Houston is pleasant, convenient, dazzling and occasionally surprising. There is something to satisfy every taste, and something to accommodate every pocketbook. From the small corner novelty shop to the large multi-tiered shopping mall, eager shoppers can find items ranging from a 12-carat emerald to a Queen Anne chair; from a Paris original to an antique automobile; even a 50¢ scarf. His and her's submarines may be bought or ordered. Just name it and chances are it can be found somewhere in Houston's consumer wonderland.

The variety of stores and merchandise results partly from Houston's position as the third largest seaport in the United States. Enterprising shop owners can readily import items from around the world. Extraordinary shopping opportunities include the area's wealth of handmade items. Prosperity has brought many fine collectables to the city throughout the decades. These now show up on the local market, while Houston dealers canvass the nation for antiques and unusual merchandise.

Although large shopping centers have mushroomed in all major suburban areas of Houston, most major stores have a location in the central business district. The largest of the stores are Foley's, Sakowitz and Palais Royal.

Three types of shopping centers are found in Houston: regional, community and neighborhood. The regional centers are large complexes such as enclosed air-conditioned malls and include two or more major department stores, along with a variety of smaller specialty shops. Community shopping centers, on the other hand, are smaller and have one or more department stores and a supermarket. Neighborhood centers, by contrast, feature a supermarket, drug store, or both, in addition to several smaller shops. These centers usually spring up as soon as a new housing development comes into being.

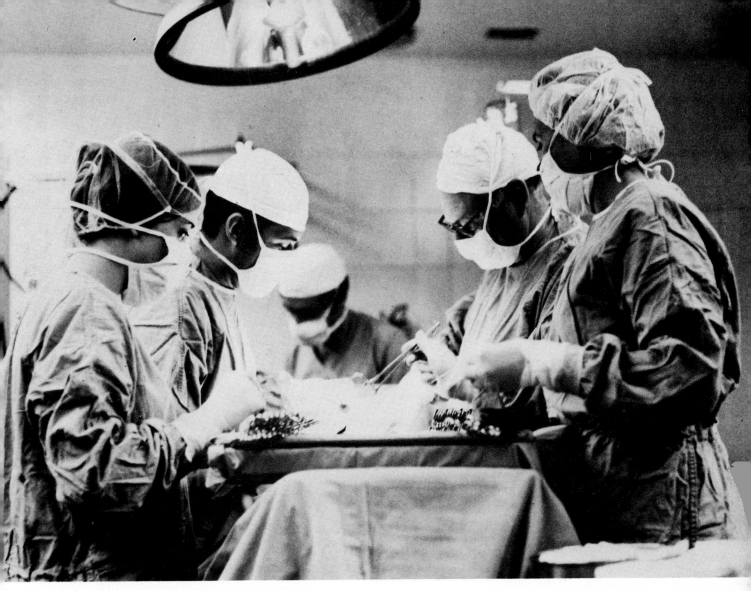

Perhaps the most impressive and popular of Houston's shopping malls is the Galleria. This spectacular enterprise has received both international and national acclaim. Located on Westheimer, west of South Post Oak Road and Loop 610, the multipurpose, multi-level complex embraces 200 shops and restaurants, hotels, movie theaters, offices, a tennis club, parking for thousands of cars and an ice skating rink. Nearby there are also four fashionable department stores, Joske's, Neiman-Marcus, Lord and Taylor, and Marshall Field, as well as other stores, offices and restaurants. A creation of famed developer Gerald Hines, its inspiration came from Milan's Galleria Vittorio Emmanuele and New York's Rockefeller Center. Like the Galleria in Milan, Houston's Galleria brings shops and walkways together under one clear, barrel-vaulted roof, and like Rockefeller Center, it sports an ice skating rink.

The largest shopping mall in Houston is Sharpstown Mall on the Southwest Freeway, where convenience and variety are offered in a beautiful and relaxed atmosphere. The newest is Greenspoint Mall at the north part of town. Town and Country Village, at Katy Freeway and West Belt, serves as a tourist attraction as well as a shopper's heaven. The

An inside view of the Texas Medical Center Cardiovascular Operating Room, one of Houston's renowned medical specialties.

complex includes ten movie houses and dinner theaters, a hotel, restaurants, boutiques, department and grocery stores, banks and office buildings. Within half a mile on Katy Freeway is the Memorial City Shopping Mall with several major department stores and numerous small shops.

Westwood, at U.S. Highway 59 and Bissonnet, houses two major department stores and a total of over 90 shops and is one of the most popular malls. A profusion of skylights enhances the mall's flowers, trees and waterfalls, and hundreds of tiny lights and a glass elevator grace its central courtyard.

In addition to the many malls around Houston, there are several specialty centers with an assortment of unusual boutiques and gift shops. Westbury Square, for example, located between Chimney Rock and Bellfort, is an old world style market. Outdoor art shows are weekend features. Carillion West and Woodlake Square, two recent shopping developments, are other specialty centers with colorful Old World atmosphere, housing fashionable restaurants and stores.

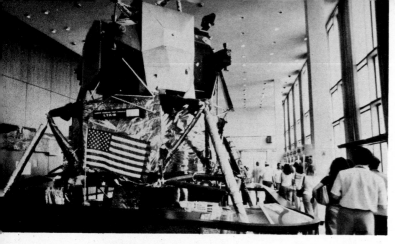

NASA's Visitor Center: a lunar module test article LTS-8, a display representative of equipment used in the manned space program.

Texas has a four percent sales tax on purchases of 10¢ or more. The City of Houston adds to this a one percent sales tax and a one percent Metropolitan Transit Authority (MTA) tax. Sales taxes are not levied on certain items, such as prescription drugs, food for out-of-store preparation and fertilizers.

Texas "blue laws" prohibit the purchase of particular items on Sundays except where the stores choose to close on another day of the week instead. Twenty-six generic items which cannot be sold include clothing, household goods, cars and jewelry. Houston stores which stay open seven days a week rope off these departments on Sundays.

CHALLENGES FOR THE FUTURE

Houston's phenomenal growth will continue in the future, but Houston will face numerous challenges as it prospers, expands and moves into the twenty-first century.

The maintenance of the quality of life in Houston is important to its economy. Air pollution from industrial emissions and vehicle exhaust is a problem which faces most modern American urban areas. Houston has taken strong steps to solve these problems. The ship channel was cleared and marine life has reappeared in it. Currently the city is working to substantially reduce ozone pollution, although most parts of town show relatively small amounts of pollutants.

Houston's transportation needs are in a constantly changing state. Houston airport facilities are being expanded to meet the rapidly growing number of air passengers.

Because of its heavy reliance on the automobile, Houston is now attempting to develop transportation alternatives. The Metropolitan Transit Authority has been established to provide effective solutions.

Local government has been restructured to increase participation among various groups. A new formula has been put into effect for at-large and district representation in the Houston City Council.

OUTLOOK

It is estimated that Houston's metropolitan population will grow by 32 percent in the decade of the 1980s to a total of 3.9 million. This implies that over the same period there will be a 43 percent increase in the number of households, a 47 percent increase in the number of employed persons and a 46 percent increase in the number of passenger cars.

Houston will also continue to grow as the petroleum capital of the nation. Much of the research and development for new energy forms will come, most likely, from Houston's scientists. The city will experience continued economic advancement as a center of international finance.

The average Houstonian pays only 4.7 percent of his income to state and local governments in the form of taxes while, in comparison, in New York City the figure is 19.1 percent. Houston's taxes are lower than any other major urban area in the United States. This will continue to stimulate the city's economic development as it has done in the past.

Heavy industry is growing faster in Houston than in the nation as a whole, and the average plant capacity utilization rate in 1979 was 84.4 percent, compared to an expected national average of 81 percent nationally, or three percent greater efficiency in Houston.

Among Houston's other advantages are a low cost of living compared to other major United States urban centers, a favorable business climate providing an incentive for corporate relocation, and an appealing spot in the center of the Sun Belt. Thus, the young and dynamic city looks forward as it enters the decade of the 1980s to an even greater era of economic growth and development.

Houston-Galveston Area Economic Projections

ECONOMIC INDICATOR	1973	1974	1975	1976	1978	1980**	1982*	1983*
Non-Agricultural Empl.(Thous.)	959	1,032	1,095	1,161	1,262	1,388	1,494	1,551
Industrial Production** (1967-100)	159	164	169	181	217	242	280	300
Retail Sales ($ Millions)	6,306	7,737	8,933	10,665	15,925	16,100	19,200	20,900
Personal Income ($ Millions)	12,450	14,400	16,740	19,190	23,867	29,000	34,600	37,800

*Estimated by Texas Commerce Bancshares Economics Division.
**Industrial production calculated for Houston Area Only.

PART IV

THE CITY looks at the city government, how it works, its institutions, programs and public services, its rules, regulations and customs, then follows the city's fanlike growth pattern and the intricate transportation system which serves it on land, in the air and on the sea. Finally, it explores some of the numerous neighborhoods which compose the metropolitan area of Houston. These few were selected either as representative of the part of the city in which they lie or because they possess a particular feature which should be noted. Thus, each neighborhood is described, with its special character, its history, its residents and its facilities, what it wants and what it offers, in order to create together the colorful and diversified town called Houston.

GOVERNMENT

Houston city government has a long standing tradition of governing with day-to-day participation of the city's residents. Citizens from all walks of life participate in city council sessions and actively influence their elected representative's actions and decisions. Much of the city's growth can be attributed to the local government's attitude of cooperation with the business community. Houston is the major American city with the least amount of regulations and restrictions. The wish to help the city's growth and prosperity along and not to restrict it has been the city government's policy throughout the decade, and thus it can take pride in its record of achievement, as well as in the close and intimate relationship it maintains with its citizens, their needs and their aspirations.

Houston Mayor Jim McConn presides over a council meeting in city hall.

The City of Houston has a strong mayor form of government; the mayor exercises administrative powers while the council is the legislative arm of city government. Nine council members are elected by citizens in their districts and five are elected at-large by city-wide vote, all for two-year terms. Elections are held in odd-numbered years. The only other elected city official is the controller. Department heads are appointed by the mayor, subject to council confirmation. The usual voter qualification rules apply if one wants to vote in Houston.

James J. "Jim" McConn, the present mayor, a homebuilder by profession, has held that office since 1977 (he was reelected in 1979). From 1971 to 1977 he had been a member of the city council. He presides over all meetings of the city council, with voting privileges, but does not have the power of veto. McConn's other functions as mayor include

administering oaths and signing ordinances, motions and resolutions of the city council; seeing that all laws and ordinances are enforced; making recommendations to the council for the welfare of the city; submitting to the council an annual budget; advising the council as to the city's financial condition and needs.

The mayor's staff includes one senior executive assistant and seven executive assistants. The senior executive assistant is the mayor's liaison with the city council and deals in personnel matters and powers of appointment. The seven executive assistants serve as liaison between the mayor and the city departments of public safety, local intergovernmental administrative and support departments, federal urban development programs, community services, and citizens assistance employment and training. In addition to the mayor's immediate staff, the office embraces nine divisions: Affirmative Action Division; Citizens Assistance Division; the Community Development Division; the Comprehensive Employment and Training Act Division (CETA); the Policy Planning Coordination Division; the Area Agency on Aging; the Communications Division; the Economic Development Division; the Fair Housing Division. Most divisions are located at City Hall, 901 Bagby.

All council members are elected for two-year terms by the qualified voters of the entire city for specific places on the council. The City of Houston, however, is divided into nine districts (Districts A, B, C, D, E, F, G, H and I). To represent the council, a candidate for council member must be a resident of the district to be represented. One council member is elected to represent each district, and five are elected to specific at-large positions.

The council has the power to enact and enforce all ordinances necessary to protect life, health and property within the city; to preserve and promote good government order; and to provide for the general welfare of the city and its inhabitants. Among the council's specific functions are confirming the appointment of all department heads and civil service commissioners proposed by the mayor; establishing any office it considers necessary for conducting the city's business or government; determining public utility rates; leasing or disposing of city-owned real estate; levying assessments against property; serving on the city's Board of Appraisement; hearing appeals from decisions of various appointed officials of the city; and administering oaths in matters pertaining to municipal affairs.

Council members are Jim Westmoreland, an attorney; Eleanor Tinsley, a civic leader and former Houston school board member; Johnny Goyen, a real estate broker; Homer L. Ford, an architect; and Judson Robinson, Jr., a mortgage banker and the

The Honorable James McConn, former homebuilding executive, is now serving a second term as Houston's mayor.

Controller Kathryn J. Whitmire is currently serving her second term.

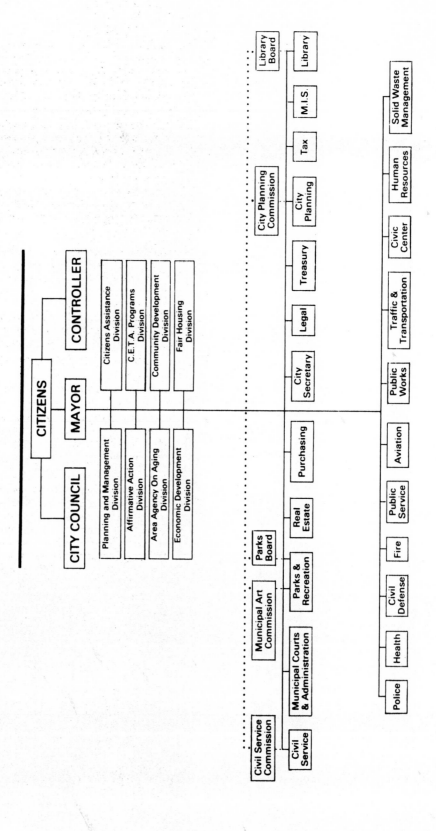

CITY OF HOUSTON ORGANIZATION CHART

CITIZENS

CITY COUNCIL — MAYOR — CONTROLLER

Planning and Management Division
Affirmative Action Division
Area Agency On Aging Division
Economic Development Division

Citizens Assistance Division
C.E.T.A. Programs Division
Community Development Division
Fair Housing Division

Civil Service Commission — Civil Service

Municipal Art Commission

Municipal Courts & Administration

Parks Board — Parks & Recreation

Real Estate

Purchasing

City Secretary

Legal

Treasury

City Planning Commission

Police

Health

Civil Defense

Fire

Public Service

Aviation

Public Works

Traffic & Transportation

Civic Center

Human Resources

Solid Waste Management

City Planning

Tax

M.I.S.

Library Board — Library

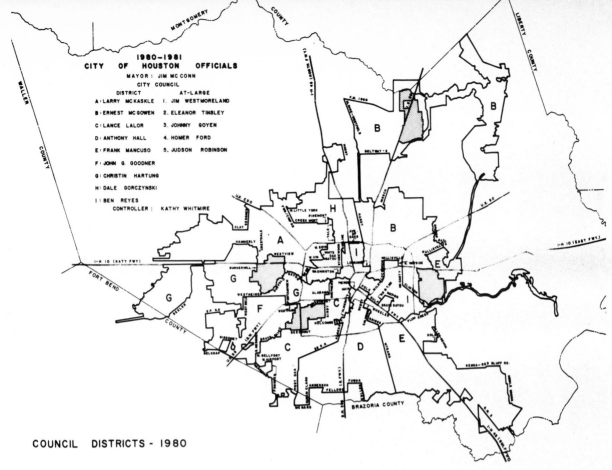

1980-1981
CITY OF HOUSTON OFFICIALS
MAYOR : JIM MC CONN
CITY COUNCIL
DISTRICT   AT-LARGE
A : LARRY McKASKLE   1. JIM WESTMORELAND
B : ERNEST McGOWEN   2. ELEANOR TINSLEY
C : LANCE LALOR   3. JOHNNY GOYEN
D : ANTHONY HALL   4. HOMER FORD
E : FRANK MANCUSO   5. JUDSON ROBINSON
F : JOHN G. GOODNER
G : CHRISTIN HARTUNG
H : DALE GORCZYNSKI
I : BEN REYES
        CONTROLLER : KATHY WHITMIRE

COUNCIL DISTRICTS - 1980

first black elected to the council; Larry McKaskle, a rental property owner; Ernest McGowen, Sr., a former letter carrier and former Houston school board member; Lance Lalor, a former state representative and former administrative assistant to the mayor and Anthony W. Hall, Jr., director of a health-testing program and former state representative.

Councilman Larry McKaskle is the representative for District A.

The map shows the Houston council districts. There are nine district council members and five council members-at-large. The mayor presides at all meetings of the city council.

Councilman Ernest McGowen, Sr. is the representative of District B, one of the newest redistricted minority wards.

Councilman Lance Lalor represents District C. He is a former state representative.

Former state representative Anthony Hall serves on the city council from District D.

Councilman Frank O. Mancuso is the representative for District E.

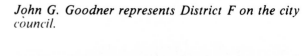

John G. Goodner represents District F on the city council.

ABOVE: *Houston buildings tower gracefully over diversely landscaped sections of the city, including ultramodern Greenway Plaza.* BELOW: *Downtown near City Hall.*

ABOVE: *Popular exertrails are found at Hermann Park.* BELOW: *Memorial Park, where the jogging craze is alive and well in Houston.*

District G councilwoman Christin Hartung is the first woman to serve on the council as a district representative.

Councilman Dale M. Gorczynski is the representative for District H.

Former State Representative Ben T. Reyes is a councilman from District I, one of the newly redistricted minority wards.

Councilman at-large Jim Westmoreland.

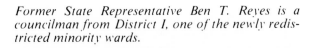

Councilwoman at-large Eleanor Tinsley, one of the first women to serve on the council.

Councilman at-large Johnny Goyen.

Councilman at-large Homer L. Ford.

Councilman at-large Judson Robinson, Jr., the first black to serve on the city council.

Other councilmen are: Frank O. Mancuso, a sales representative and one-time professional baseball player; John G. Goodner, a land management and real estate man; Christin Hartung, a former executive assistant to the County Judge; Dale M. Gorczynski, former director of the Harris County Youth Program; and Ben T. Reyes, a former state representative, former treasurer of the Texas Democratic Party and, in 1979, the first Mexican-American elected to council office. In 1979, Tinsley and Hartung became the first women elected to the Houston City Council.

COUNTY

Harris County, in which most of Houston is located, is governed by the County Commissioners' Court, which is composed of the county judge, elected from the county-at-large, and four commissioners, each elected from a separate precinct. They all serve four-year terms. The County Commissioners' Court is not a court in a usual sense. It is an administrative body primarily responsible for county courthouses and jails, appointment and employment of county personnel, setting county tax rates, administering budgets, approving county contracts, building and maintaining county roads and bridges and establishing county libraries and parks. Moreover, the court acts as the governing body for the Harris County Flood Control District.

The present commissioners are Tom Bass, a political science professor; James (Jim) Fonteno,

formerly a commissioner for the Port of Houston Authority and former Baytown municipal court judge; Bob Eckels, former trustee and president of the Houston Independent School District; and E. A. "Squatty" Lyons, a former businessman and past president of both the County Judges and Commissioners Association of Texas and the County Judges and Commissioners Association of South Texas. Jon Lindsay was elected county judge in 1974, the first Republican in over a century to serve as the chief executive officer of Harris County. He was reelected in 1978 to a second four-year term. He presides over the five-member County Commissioners' Court and serves as the chief administrative officer of county government. He is the only member of the court elected by the entire county and so must represent all county residents in matters before the court. Originally a civil engineer, Judge Lindsay has internally increased the duties of his office by becoming involved in the technical planning of road and bridge improvements, flood control projects, county construction plans and parks. Judge Lindsay is active in many organizations. He is chairman of the Harris County Juvenile Board and chairman of the Policy Advisory Committee of the Multimodel Transportation Planning for the State Planning of the Gulf Coast Region. He is also vice-chairman of the Conference of Urban Counties.

The sheriff, one of the elected county officials, serves a four-year term. Jack Heard, the present sheriff, is a former assistant director of the Texas

County Judge Jon Lindsay presides over Harris County's Commissioners' Court.

Jack Heard, former Houston police chief, is now sheriff of Houston's Harris County.

Harris County Commissioner Tom Bass, a professor of political science, represents Precinct 1.

James Fonteno, Harris County Commissioner for Precinct 2.

Harris County Commissioner for Precinct 3, Bob Eckels.

Harris County Commissioner E. A. "Squatty" Lyons represents Precinct 4.

Department of Corrections and a one-time Houston chief of police. The principal law enforcement officer in the county, his major duties include serving as conservator of the peace; acting as an executive officer of the county and district courts; and maintaining custody of prisoners who have been committed to jail.

Other elected county officials serving four-year terms are the tax assessor-collector, county clerk, district attorney, county attorney, county treasurer and district clerk.

Nonlegislative governmental bodies in the county are water districts. The water district boards are elected by homeowners within the district and are regulated by state law.

Water districts are responsible for water and sewage treatment. They set the rates for the service, sell bonds to maintain and expand the facilities and levy property taxes. Water districts are organized by the developer of a subdivision. In and around the Houston city limits are small, incorporated towns and villages, such as Pasadena, Bellaire, West University Place, Pearland, Tomball, Galena Park and LaPorte. Most are governed by a mayor and city council and are responsible for property taxes, deed restrictions, zoning, and police and fire protection within their boundaries.

Annexation, under Texas law, has enabled Houston to expand its tax base by assuming bonded indebtedness through the use of municipal water districts. Annexation of an area adjacent to the city may be initiated by petition to city council by a majority of the area's voters and property owners. However, city council may annex territory lying adjacent to the city by ordinance with or without consent of the inhabitants annexed. State law permits cities with populations in excess of 100,000 to annex up to five miles of the areas outside their corporate limits. This clearly includes Houston. Annexation

China's Vice Premier Deng Xiao Ping visited Houston when he came to the United States. Pictured from left to right are Senator John Glenn, Mayor McConn, Madame and Vice Premier Deng and Mrs. McConn.

increases the property tax base which supports Houston by bringing more area which can be taxed into the city. State laws permit deannexation but bond funds for capital improvements must be reimbursed to the city.

STATE

The Houston area is represented in the state capital in Austin by 6 senators and 14 representatives. Among the many branches of Texas government, departments and agencies located in Houston are the Department of Public Safety, the Railroad Commission, the Texas Employment Commission, the Texas Research Institute and the Welfare Department.

The Houston-Galveston Area Council represents more than 15 cities and 13 counties. The council is headed by Charles Doyle as president. Benjamin Bobavec serves as vice president, and Mickey Deisin is the secretary of the council. The council deals with grant applications and local governmental matters, including community planning, economic development, aging, alcoholism, land usage and transportation. It is a multipurpose agency with optional membership.

FEDERAL

The Houston area is represented in Washington by five Congressmen, Bill Archer (R), Jack Brooks (D), Robert Eckhardt (D), G. T. Leland (D) and Ronald Paul (R) as well as the two Texas Senators Lloyd Bentsen (D) and John Tower (R). Among the important and sizeable branches of federal departments and agencies in the Houston area are the National Aeronautics and Space Administration (NASA), the Immigration and Naturalization Service and the Veterans Administration.

TRANSPORTATION

MOTOR VEHICLES

During 1979, Harris County motor vehicle registrations increased by 33,841 (2 percent) over 1978 figures: passenger cars, 12,365 (1 percent); trucks, 11,966 (3.4 percent); all others, 9,510 (3.4 percent). Motor vehicle registrations in Harris County (as of December 31, 1979) were:

Passenger cars 1,295,361

Trucks 359,712

All other vehicles 292,618

Total registrations 1,947,691

Houston is working on several alternatives to reduce traffic congestion and to increase urban mobility. The annual average daily traffic (AADT) on urban freeways, suburban/rural and recreational freeway locations rises an average of 7.5 percent a year, a 20.6 percent increase from 1968 to 1978. The total yearly volume, from which the AADT is derived, of course, rises, too. The Metropolitan Transit Authority (MTA) which began operation in January, 1979 is the first step taken by the city in dealing with the mass transit problem. Future plans include a number of elevated transit ways over the freeways and automated trains.

FREEWAYS

The freeway system in Harris County spans 411.2 miles of roadways, 207.2 of which are complete and 204 miles of which are at various stages of development. Interstate Highways 10 and 45 intersect and Highway 59 intersects with both 10 and 45. The total planned system of freeways will involve 11 freeways radiating from the center of the central business district in three concentric loops. The first loop is an elevated system circling the central business district. The second is Interstate Loop 610 at a six-mile radius from the center of the central business district. The third loop is the proposed Beltway 8. A planned 88-mile facility which will circle the city at a 12-mile radius and will be six to nine miles outside Loop 610, Beltway 8 is presently open to traffic between Interstate 45 and US 59 and serves Houston Intercontinental Airport. Houston has a good network of primary and secondary highways.

AIR SERVICE

Houston is an international air transporation hub for the Southwest. The air service system,

Map showing the main thoroughfares in Houston as well as several points of interest.

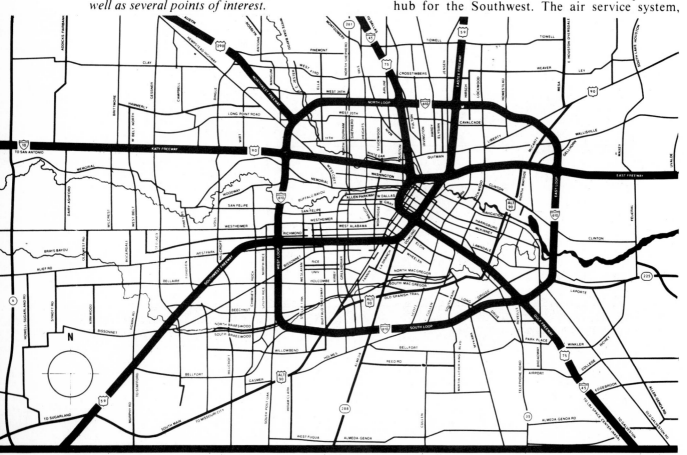

1. Aline McAshan Arboretum and Botanical Gardens
2. Astrodome/Astrohall Complex
3. Astroworld
4. Bayou Bend Museum
5. Bear Creek Park
6. Contemporary Arts Museum
7. Downtown
8. Farmers Market
9. Galleria
10. Greenway Plaza
11. Hermann Park (includes Burke Baker Planetarium, Miller Theatre, Museum of Natural Science, Zoological Gardens)
12. Hobby Airport
13. Houston Baptist University
14. To Intercontinental Airport
15. Memorial Park
16. Museum of Fine Arts
17. Port of Houston
18. Rice University
19. Sam Houston Inspection Boat
20. Summit Sports Arena
21. Turning Basin
22. Texas Medical Center
23. Texas Southern University
24. University of Houston
25. University of St. Thomas

conceived of years ago in Houston, is however, approaching the saturation point much sooner than planners projected.

In 1979, 1,006,286 international passengers arrived in, and departed from, Houston. The same year, Houston air facilities served some 9.9 million domestic passengers. In 1979, 222,663 air carrier operations and 348,417 general aviation operations took place in Houston. Air cargo, during 1979, totaled 86,593 short tons.

Airlines providing direct international flights to 31 foreign cities from Houston include Alia Airways, American Airlines, Aero Mexico, Air Canada, Air France, Braniff International Airways, KLM Royal Dutch Airlines, Pan American World Airways, Texas International Airlines, Cayman Airways and VIASA (Venezuelan International Airways). Twenty-one air carriers maintain offices for flights leaving from Houston and 46 others maintain "offline" sales offices, that is, for carriers not presently operating in Houston. Domestic interstate passenger service from Houston Intercontinental Airport is provided by US Air, American Airlines, British Caledonian Airways, Delta Airlines, National Airlines, Continental Airlines, Eastern Airlines, North Central Airlines, TWA, and Texas International Airlines. Tejas, Hammond Flying Service, Commutair, Chaparral Airlines, Houston Metro Airlines, Rio Airways and Royale Airlines offer commuter service from Houston.

The Federal Aviation Administration has designated Houston one of 22 large United States air transportation hubs, which means Houston serves one percent of the total travelling population in the nation. Other transportation hubs include the Chicago, Miami, Los Angeles and San Francisco Airports. Air passenger volume increased 16 percent in 1979 to 13.5 million. Houston Intercontinental Airport became operational in June, 1969. The $110 million Houston Intercontinental Airport, which opened in June, 1969, covers approximately 8,000 acres between Interstate Highway 45 and US 59, about 16 air miles north of downtown Houston. The $52 million Terminal C development underway at Houston Intercontinental Airport, scheduled to be functional in 1981, will have a linear configuration in contrast to the satellite layouts of terminals A and B. To be located immediately east of the Host Hotel, Terminal C has been designed to accommodate the needs of Continental Airlines, Texas International Airlines and Metro Airlines until 1990. A fourth terminal, Terminal D, which is scheduled to open in 1983, will serve an additional 6.6 million people a year and will also have a linear configuration. The planning of Terminals E and F will probably also come in the 1980s. A $15 million to $16 million interterminal train will run between terminals A, B and C and the Host Hotel and will open simultaneously with Terminal C.

Currently, Trailways provides ground bus transportation service from Intercontinental terminals to downtown, business center and suburban terminals. A special limousine service leaves from the Galleria's Houston Oaks Hotel. Trailways leaves from five different locations including the Hyatt Regency, Post Oak and Greenway Plaza. In addition, taxi service to and from Intercontinental is available and there are automobiles for hire.

William P. Hobby Airport, 10 miles southeast of the central business district, provides facilities for private and corporate aviation as well as for commercial airlines. Approximately $4 million is being spent for a new parking facility for Hobby Airport. Phases one through three of this will be completed by 1982. Hughes Airwest, Ozark Airlines and Southwest Airlines provide interstate passenger service from Hobby. The 1,300-acre airport and its 80-acre terminal complex are being readied for a multimillion-dollar capital expansion program designed to upgrade and update existing facilities. Hobby Airport's re-emergence as a commercial air transport facility is underscored by the 39 percent increase in passenger traffic, a total of 2.6 million passengers during 1979. Plans are being formulated to open the middle and west fingers of the terminal to commercial airline use. This would increase the number of gates from eight to twenty available to aircraft. Hughes Airwest has pledged $30 million for the construction of a new grand rotunda at Hobby. The city of Houston has also recently reopened Airport Boulevard as a four-lane traffic artery. Monroe Road is being improved to provide easy entry and exit from Hobby.

METROPOLITAN TRANSIT AUTHORITY

The Houston Metropolitan Transit Authority (MTA), or "Metro" for short, has a fleet of 631 air-conditioned buses, which feature Easy Rider monthly passes for passengers, and serves an area of 1,312.5 square miles. The Metro currently operates the longest contraflow bus lane in the United States. The nine-mile-long lane connects the downtown business district with the northern portions of the city on Interstate 45. It is used daily by buses and van pools. The current fleet of 631 buses will be expanded to 1,500 to serve the growing needs of the region. While the MTA contemplates acquiring some 326 more air-conditioned buses to crisscross the city and suburbs (at a basic fare of 40¢ with 10¢ for each additional zone up to 60¢; express fares are higher), it also plans to retire at least 50 of the existing fleet. Among major cities, Houston is unique in not having a rapid transit system. In 1978, estimated revenue passengers totaled 44.5 million. Meanwhile nine park-and-ride routes provide express bus service to the central business district for commuters from Westwood Shopping Center, the Gulf Freeway, the Southwest Freeway at Bellaire, the West Loop at Beechnut, FM-1960's Church of Christ, the inter-

sections of Interstate 45 and Kuykendall road, Kingwood's Church of Christ and the Alief Independent School District's football stadium. MTA's 14 Metrolift vehicles provide door-to-door service for handicapped and elderly passengers who cannot use regular buses. A 24-hour notice is required for service. In the MTA Carshare program, computer matching creates carpools. While at present there are only 8,041 Carshare participants, a 10 percent annual expansion is anticipated through 1983.

The MTA has also begun advanced studies of a proposed one billion dollar 13.5-mile-long transit rail line through southwest Houston, the first segment of a regional system of approximately 90 miles. The Southwest Freeway-Westpark Corridor which might fulfill this function has been mentioned as a possible transit rail route. It could be a travel section extending from downtown Houston to Beltway 8 in western Harris County. Several options exist for the final form of the project. It may become a busway (a buses-only roadway), or a conventional commuter rail line. The downtown section of the project would be able to incorporate a mile-long subway under such streets as Main or Fannin. These would serve to complement the first segment of the projected regional rail line.

TAXICAB SERVICE

In comparison to a city such as New York, Houston's taxicab service is limited. The Yellow Cab

A Metro bus on its park-and-ride route provides express bus service to the central business district for commuters.

Company, whose fleet numbers over 900, is by far the largest of the approximately 20 taxi service companies in Houston.

INTERCITY BUS SERVICE

Express motor coach service for passengers and small packages is available from Houston to numerous short and intermediate distance points on Trailways, Greyhound, Kerrville Bus Company, and Texas bus lines.

RAIL SERVICE

Six major rail systems operate 14 lines of mainline track radiating from the city, and two switching lines serve the industrial area plus the Port: Burlington Northern, Katy, Missouri Pacific, Rock Island, Santa Fe, and Southern Pacific and trunkline railroads. Some 30 other railroads maintain "offline" offices here. Amtrak passenger service is available on two routes: daily each way Houston-Chicago to Temple-Laredo-Chicago and three times a week New Orleans-Houston-Los Angeles.

MOTOR FREIGHT SERVICE

Some 32 common carrier truck lines operate daily schedules serving Houston as the southwestern distribution center and provide direct routes to the

East, the Midwest and the Pacific coast. In addition to these general commodity regular route carriers are Houston's regulated truck services. These include an exceptionally large number of specialized operators such as commodity and irregular carriers, oilfield equipment haulers, 14 tank truck lines and household carriers and scores of other specialized carriers. More than 200 local delivery trucking firms operate in the expanding commercial delivery zone.

OIL AND GAS TRANSMISSION

One of the nation's most important oil and gas transmission centers, Houston is the location of 25 percent of the major natural gas pipeline companies in the United States; 10 are headquartered here while four maintain operating divisions in Houston. These 14 companies operate more than 122,878 miles of natural gas pipelines throughout the nation. The concentration of pipeline operations in the city itself includes 13 crude oil and products pipelines and 21 gas pipelines.

PORT OF HOUSTON

The Port of Houston is an important feature of Houston's transportation system. In 1979, the Port of Houston handled a record high of 122.3 million short tons of cargo, a 9.9 percent increase over the previous year's total. During 1979, a total of 41.9 million short tons of imports and 23 million short tons of exports passed through the Port of Houston.

The Turning Basin of the Houston Ship Channel, a 50-mile inland waterway connecting the city with the sea lanes of the world, is four miles east of the

The tourboat Sam Houston *taking visitors up and down the ship channel.*

central business district. Most of the channel has a minimum width of 400 feet and a depth of 40 feet. In the fiscal year 1979, receipts of the Port of Houston customs collections totaled $261,239,547.

More than 180 steamship lines offer regular service between the Port of Houston and some 250 ports throughout the world. In 1978, 5,527 ships called at the Port of Houston. More than 100 wharves are in operation in the city. Private terminals of the large industrial complex line both sides of the channel. Since 1957, the Port of Houston Authority has spent more than $140 million on improvements and on construction of new facilities.

Container service was initiated in Houston in 1956. In 1970, a new 16-acre container marshaling yard began operations. Phase one of the new container ship/barge facility at Barbours Cut was completed in 1972 when the first LASH (containers Lighter Aboard Ship—than land, that is) wharf became operational. A second phase added in 1977 includes two container wharves and a roll-on—roll-off platform. A third container wharf is also under construction at Barbours Cut. (See Port.)

INTRACOASTAL WATERWAY

The 1,777 mile intracoastal waterway links Houston with 9,812 miles of commercially navigable waterways in the mid-continental regions of the Mississippi River and with some 2,500 miles of waterway in the Gulf of Mexico to the south. Some 8,410 miles of these waterways provide at least a nine-foot draft. Low cost barge transportation service is offered by nine common carrier lines and many contract and specialized operations along these waterways.

NEIGHBORHOODS

With its population nearly double that of 20 years ago, Houston has experienced fan-like wedges of growth in recent years to its north, south and west.

Until 35 years ago, the city consisted essentially of a densely-settled area of roughly 73-square-miles. Today the difference between country and city—or suburbs and city—has largely lost its meaning; Houston merges into the countryside in such a way that it is difficult to say where the city stops and the suburbs begin. Surrounding the core area of Houston is a continually growing complex of residential subdivisions, shopping centers and industrial-office parks that are reaching farther and farther into what was once open country.

Since most of Houston's growth has occurred during the age of the automobile, the city has developed in a style designed to accommodate the motor vehicle as the principal mode of transportation. The flat terrain of the upper Gulf Coastal plain, with no geographical barriers to development, has permitted the creation of a widespread major thoroughfare and freeway system. Interstate Loop 610, for example, now defines Houston's inner city. The West and North belts circle suburban Houston of the 1960s and the early 1970s. Texas Highway 6 and Farm-to-Market Road (FM) 1960, and their extensions west and south, represent suburbs of the late 1970s and the 1980s. Beyond are the outlying reaches of the unincorporated area of the city where residents seek better prices on land and homes. A house bought in an inner city neighborhood in the 1950s for $15,000 has a market value today of $125,000; hence the movement outward from the inner loop to the ever-expanding outskirts. Houston is an extensive city with an overall gross density of some 2,500 persons per square mile. Houston's corporate boundaries have relentlessly continued to expand with annexations of nearby areas.

Houston's lack of zoning restrictions, too, has contributed to the outward growth of the city. It is a real estate broker's paradise with a minimal level of local governmental controls interfering with its pattern of growth. The relative absence of restrictions on apartment complex development, for example, has resulted in an apartment construction boom, making rents in Houston lower than in other major cities where controls abound.

Furthermore, there are more commercial uses of land in predominantly single-family housing areas. For example, convenience stores and strip shopping centers have proliferated throughout Houston and its vicinity, making shopping and services more available to residents. However, because of lack of zoning, most neighborhoods draw up deed restrictions to preserve the atmosphere of the individual neighborhood. Moreover, it is a peculiar Houston trend that most areas adjoining major thoroughfares—both arterial and collector streets—will be adapted to a variety of commercial and multi-family uses. Numerous pockets of business activity have developed in the past 20 years throughout the city, outside the central business district. Finally, the amount of acreage as yet undeveloped in numerous subdivisions in unincorporated Harris County portends that Houston's urban encroachment will continue well into the 1980s.

More than 30 neighborhoods from among the countless subdivisions in the greater Houston area have been selected for discussion. The selection depicts the diversity, movement and growth of the city into the outer reaches of unincorporated Harris County. Such older incorporated entities as Bellaire and West University Place are represented, as are the more recently incorporated Memorial villages. Such outlying neighborhoods as those in Fort Bend County to the southwest, and extreme eastern (Pasadena), southeastern (Clear Lake), northwestern (FM-1960) and western (Katy) parts of Harris County are included in this representation.

Considered in-town and southwest, **MEYERLAND** is bounded on the north by Beechnut, on the west by Chimney Rock Road, on the east by Interstate 610 and approximately to the south by Braeswood Boulevard.

Meyerland, launched as a suburban subdivision in the 1950s by the First Mortgage Company, was comprised of 1,200 acres, and is made up of 2,700 lots. Twenty independent builders developed houses in the cost range of $18,000 to $40,000. The development was advertised as having "lower prices than River Oaks or Tanglewood, but with an architectural control board which approved all plans." Today, the interiors of many Meyerland homes have been renovated to include modern conveniences while retaining the original exteriors.

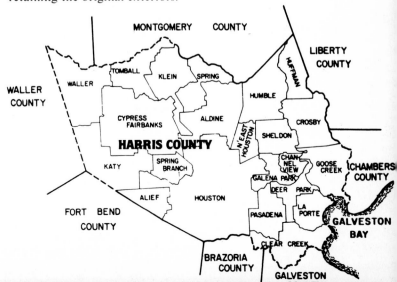

Wooded lot in Bellaire.

Meyerland has the ambience of a classic American suburb and lacks the problems of Houston's older neighborhoods. Its all-American suburban flavor is shared, in some respects, by the neighborhoods of **Spring Branch-Memorial and the Memorial villages.**

Because of the deed restrictions and the lawn ordinance promulgated by the developers, Meyerland homes have well-kept lawns. Most of the homes were designed for the multi-car family with a garage for every home. Some of these garages have since then evolved into garage apartments. The neighborhood has 11 religious institutions, including two modern synagogues. Meyerland Plaza, covering 850,000 square feet and one of the Houston area's major shopping malls, is located at Loop 610 West and Beechnut and boasts 60 stores and restaurants.

Ranch-style home in Meyerland.

Not far from Meyerland and also in the Southwest area is the city of **BELLAIRE,** which had about 200 residents at the time railroadman W. W. Baldwin incorporated it in 1918. Typical of the early real estate developers in Houston, Baldwin arrived in the city around the turn of the century as a vice-president of the Burlington Railroad. He opened a lumber company in West Moreland (now a part of Montrose) before purchasing 9,700 acres of the former William Marsh Rice ranch several miles southwest of town. He began promoting the new addition he named Bellaire—the Burlington Railroad had served Bellaire, Ohio—and gave it the slogan, "City Homes for Country People or Country Homes for City People." Edward Teas planted trees in the bald subdivision in 1908 and, in 1910, Baldwin's electric streetcar opened, replacing mule-drawn carriages.

As a result of post-war industry and the development of the petrochemical industry, more and more families sought homes in Bellaire, which boomed in the late 1940s and into the middle 1950s. Four thousand five hundred homes were built during this period—there are now a total of 6,000. With 19,000 residents and about 600 townhouses situated in an area encompassing 3.7 square miles, Bellaire is the largest incorporated entity in the area surrounded entirely by Houston. The median age is 29, the average price of a home, $65,000. Unlike Houston proper, Bellaire is a zoned city. Its property owners spend time at the Bellaire community center in numerous public hearings on problems ranging from zoning code revisions to the cost of home sewage taxes.

When West Loop 610 was constructed through Bellaire in the late 60s, the property from Bellaire's northern boundaries south to Bellaire Boulevard, previously restricted to residences, was re-zoned for office buildings or "planned development offices." About 85 percent of Bellaire is residential and 15 percent is business. Only 8 percent of the business area has been developed.

The planned development offices included the construction of buildings for Texaco, Inc., Prudential, Sun Oil Company, Sperry-Univac and Northern Natural Gas Company. Wayne-Duddleston, Inc., is planning a $100 million office-hotel complex. Apart from these offices, Bellaire has its own central business district, laid out in 1950. Bellaire is bounded by Bellaire Boulevard and Bissonnet, Chimney Rock and Third Avenue and features various retail businesses. It has two large shopping centers, Triangle and Eagle, and several smaller strip shopping centers.

Five elementary schools serve Bellaire, (there is no junior high school) and Bellaire High School enjoys an excellent reputation. Bellaire West General Hospital serves the Bellaire neighborhood and 18 churches of various religious denominations are located within the city limits.

Next to Bellaire lies the two-square-mile city of **WEST UNIVERSITY PLACE,** with a population of 15,000. Incorporated in 1925, it is situated west of Rice University. West University Place is is predominantly Caucasian. The city is divided into actual blocks, something unusual in the Houston area.

An older house in West University Place.

Residents of West University Place pride themselves on living in a city within a city. As a city, West University Place has its own charter, mayor, city hall, tax and zoning system. Other services not shared with the city of Houston include water and sewage, police and fire departments and ambulance service. Besides a traditional police force, the West University Place police, like some of their European counterparts, patrol the area on bicycles.

West University Place itself has only one school, an elementary school, but is within the Houston Independent School District which offers junior and senior high facilities for its residents.

West University Place has many recreational facilities, including a public swimming pool, tennis courts, parks, handball courts, a weight room, community center and a branch of the Houston Library. There are three areas set aside for commercial establishments. Otherwise the neighborhood is strictly zoned for dwellings.

There are few lots left in West University Place, and homes which sold for $7,000 in 1925 now go for $30,000 to $50,000. West University Place is a folksy, sought-after middle class neighborhood whose property values have risen steadily with the years. The area which began as a poor farm built on a bog,is now composed mostly of single-family dwellings, with few townhouses or apartment complexes.

Trees have flourished in West University Place, nourished by its moist terrain. Pecan, ash, oak, cottonwood, and magnolia trees are abundant in the neighborhood, and are peculiar to it. In addition, West University Place backyards are full of plants including ivy, aspidistra, passion-flower and thickly blooming honeysuckle.

SOUTH SIDE PLACE, bounded on three sides by West University Place, is a well-established older neighborhood. Like West University Place, it has many trees that thrive in the once swampy terrain.

The population of 1,450 is mostly Caucasian, although South Side Place has a sizeable Hispanic population. Inhabited mainly by lawyers and doctors, South Side Place is a white collar, upper middle class neighborhood. There are no schools within its boundaries; children first attend the West University Place Elementary school and, later, Houston Independent School District schools. There is a civic club for men, a civic club for women and a garden club.

Other South Side Place facilities include a park run by a paid director, a clubhouse, a swimming pool, and various outdoor activities.

Originally an area of flat land consisting of small farms, **EAST FORT BEND COUNTY** has become highly populated in recent years and is demonstrative of Houston's outward southwesterly growth. More westerly than Meyerland, Bellaire, West University Place and South Side Place, this growing area comprises four incorporated entities or cities: Missouri City, Stafford, Sugar Creek and Sugarland. All are located within 30 minutes of downtown Houston. They straddle US 59 and State Highway 6. Two major subdivisions in the area are developed around golf courses. The lavish landscaping compensates for the sparsely-wooded area.

Located due south of US 59, the East Fort Bend County communities enjoy many amenities. The Fort Bend Independent School District includes two high schools, three junior high schools and 11 elementary schools. There are several parks in the area, one of which covers more than twelve and one-half acres. Other facilities include baseball diamonds, playgrounds and an olympic-sized swimming pool. Golf is a major pastime and there are four country clubs. Stables are available year-round to provide boarding services, rentals and horseback instruction for riding enthusiasts. Hull Field is the local base for private commuter planes.

Incorporated in 1956, **MISSOURI CITY,** adjacent to Houston proper, has over 20,000 inhabitants, half of whom commute to Houston. A good percentage of home owners are corporation executives and professionals. Homes range in price between $50,000 and $300,000. There is little commerce here. The larger companies here are the ACF Industries, Savage Laboratories and the E-I-M Company.

SUGARLAND,13 miles southwest of Houston, is the location of one of the world's largest sugar refineries. The community started as a company town when W. T. Eldridge, Sr. organized the Imperial Sugar Company in 1907. A new town was laid out, and a public school, church and hospital were provided. A 75 percent glass, eight-story refinery building, opened in 1926, dominates the countryside. For years, Sugarland was famous for its prison farm which supplied labor for the sugar cane fields.

Most home owners in Sugarland are industrial workers. Besides the sugar industry, oil industry equipment is manufactured for worldwide marketing. Nearly half of the 10,000 residents are between the ages of 18 and 49. Homes range in price from $50,000 to over $125,000. The city, which has grown at a rapid rate, has seen later development in its Venetian Estates, a tract with individual boat landings formed off Oyster Creek. Sugarland has a mayor and council form of government.

STAFFORD is located 10 miles southwest of Houston. There is some open land, but no heavily wooded area and there are no lakes. The major industries in the city include Texas Instruments and the Houston Fabricating Company. Stafford's nearly 6,000 inhabitants are mostly college-educated and the median age of its residents is 27. The city has a mayor-council form of government.

A southwest suburb of Houston, **SUGAR CREEK** is the story of the creation of a multi-million dollar city community from over 1,000 acres of undeveloped farm land. A group of Houston real estate investors and developers acquired a cattle ranch and turned it into Sugar Creek in 1968, a 200-million-dollar community of elegant homes, lakes and a championship 27-hole golf course. Now Sugar Creek also has its own commercial center, including Sugar Creek National Bank, a full-service shopping center and office park as well as required public utilities.

Some 1,000 families live in the Sugar Creek community, with a distinctive blend of architecture. The price of homes ranges from $175,000 to $500,000. The gracefully winding streets also accommodate elegant townhomes and garden homes starting at $100,000. The Sugar Creek Country Clubhouse, a stately 33,050-square-foot Georgian structure, includes elegantly appointed rooms for entertaining and dining, meeting rooms, locker rooms, kitchens, and executive offices. A separate building complex houses the golf shop and the office of the resident golf professional and staff, the poolside kitchen, dining room, and activity room. In addition, there is an olympic-sized pool with a unique in-the-water gazebo. Sugar Creek boasts a tennis center with eight lighted courts and a tennis shop.

The Fort Bend Independent School District, on the eastern boundary of Sugar Creek, is a system recognized throughout the state for its pace setting educational programs and facilites. The Sugar Creek community was selected by the *Ladies Home Journal* as one of the twenty best planned suburbs in the United States.

Two major arteries, Houston's South Main and the Southwest Freeway, connect Sugar Creek to downtown Houston, providing proximity to Houston's outstanding cultural, entertainment and medical facilities. Sugar Creek is, in essence, a home in the country, yet an inseparable part of Houston.

ALIEF, a neighborhood partially annexed to Houston in 1977 and 1978, lies southwest of the central business district and southwest of the communities of Bellaire and West University Place. State Highway 6 runs through this area southwest of Houston. The story of Alief exemplifies Houston's growth through annexation and also Houston's subdivisional mixture of country and city. The city of Alief proper, however, has not been annexed by its larger, ravenous megalopolis.

Jacamiah Seaman Dougherty, school teacher from the Midwest, initiated rice farming in southwest Harris County, in the area which would become Alief, in 1894. Named Alief, in honor of the community's postmistress, the town was established

Subdivision living in Alief features uncrowded spaces.

in 1897. The first cotton gin was built in 1905. The first Harris County Flood Control District, No. 1, was organized in Alief in 1909. A storm in 1915 blew the roof off the three-story school, built in 1911. Electricity came to the area in 1935.

Cotton and dairy farming eventually replaced rice farming, and today ranching and industry (primarily Brown and Root Engineering offices) have largely supplanted farming, although much open country and old pasture land still covers the neighborhood. Now, with a population of 75,000, the Alief average age is 35; its median income is $18,000; the median value of its houses, $50,000 and the mean level of education, college. Alief is a middle to upper middle class suburb, with homes ranging from $40,000 to $100,000. Brick veneer housing dots the neighborhood.

The support residents lend its school system distinguishes Alief. Newcomers have been attracted not only by the moderate and contemporary housing, but also by the good educational facilities afforded by the Alief Independent School District (AISD). Alief has ten elementary schools, three junior highs, and two high schools. A fantastic growth rate has been the story of the Alief Independent School District for the past seven years. An increase in enrollment of 1,100 students per year since 1970 will result in a student enrollment of 18,000 by 1984. There are several private day care centers.

In November of 1979, Alief approved a $43 million bond issue which will be used, among other things, for the construction of two elementary, one junior high and one high school. Thanks to the school ad valorem tax on residential and industrial property, which brings in additional funds to the schools, Alief's independent school district is definitely solvent.

Alief is still a good property location for the middle class family to purchase, but the value of single-family houses, raw land prices and construction costs have indeed rocketed since 1972. Ultramodern apartment complexes, with an average monthly rental of $225, are cropping up in Alief's open fields.

The area has established its own sense of community with the advent of banks, savings and loan companies, diversified businesses, a regional shopping center, hospital, office parks and office buildings.

In addition, Alief is a research center with seven major firms doing total or partial research in their field. Shell Oil, Gulf Oil, Superior Oil, Dresser, Inc., Texas Instruments, Uncle Ben's Rice, Inc., and Western Geophysical are all represented.

Alief has many shopping centers, including Bellwood at Brays Forest; Beltway Center at Bellaire; Kelly's Plaza on Boone Road; Kirkwood Plaza on Kirkwood; and Westwood Fashion Place on Bissonnet at the Southwest Freeway. Offices are scattered throughout these shopping centers and there is an office park behind the Beltway Center.

The neighborhood's health needs are met by Alief General Hospital, the Kirkwood Medical and Dental Center and the Imperial Point Medical Center.

TANGLEWOOD, to the north of Alief and close to town, is a predominantly white and upper class neighborhood between San Felipe Road and Buffalo Bayou, Voss and Sage roads. There are approximately 2,000 homes, ranging in price from $230,000 to $1,000,000 dollars, and a population of some 7,000.

Tanglewood was founded 30 years ago by a well-known developer, William G. Farrington. Once on the outskirts of Houston, Tanglewood is now considered a part of the inner city suburbs. Deed restrictions have kept apartment complexes from mushrooming amid the tree-shaded neighborhood. Townhouses and highrise condominiums flourish immediately beyond Tanglewood's borders. The value of homes has risen significantly because of the construction of the nearby Galleria I in 1969 and of Galleria II in 1977. There are no churches, shopping centers, hospitals, or businesses within the boundaries of Tanglewood.

Tanglewood is within the Houston Independent School District. However, there are no elementary schools in the immediate neighborhood although the Rogers Jr. High and Lee High Schools are located nearby. There are no day care centers. The Tanglewood Homes Association is the local civic group and its members are Tanglewood lot owners. This association provides garbage pick-up and security patrol service.

Tanglewood is distinctive as a classic American suburb. The ranch style home, as elsewhere in the sprawling city of Houston, is the rule. The well-manicured lawn and backyard, often with pool and carport, typify the Tanglewood landscape.

The **SPRING BRANCH-MEMORIAL** neighborhood is bordered on the south by Interstate highway 10 (Katy Freeway), on the north by Hempstead Road, on the east by the South Post Oak Road and on the west by Addicks Dam off Clay Road. It is to the northwest of Bellaire and West University Place.

SPRING BRANCH, within the city limits of Houston, is also bordered by the Memorial villages on the south and the city of Spring Valley on the west. It is a predominantly Caucasian middle-class neighborhood with smaller percentages of blacks, Hispanics and Asians.

Apartments in the Spring Branch area.

Spring Branch Independent School District serves the Memorial villages of Bunker Hill, Piney Point, Hedwig, Hilshire and Hunter's Creek and the city of **SPRING VALLEY.** It has 23 elementary, eight junior and six senior high schools. The population of the Spring Branch-Memorial area, which the school district encompasses, is about 200,000.

Bear Creek Park is the major park in the area. There are three day care centers and a range of civic clubs which include private country clubs, a Dad's Club and the YWCA. The Spring Branch-Memorial Sports Association and the Spring Branch-Memorial Chamber of Commerce serve the area.

Organized sports activities include jogging, little league football, soccer, ice hockey, and baseball. Also available are girls' basketball, soccer, volleyball and softball facilities and golf links, racquetball and tennis courts.

Single family dwellings available in many different styles range in price from $40,000 to 150,000. A one bedroom apartment rents for an average of $220 to $320 a month. Townhouses sell for $60,000 and up.

Spring Branch, one of the earlier suburban areas to develop in Houston, is today considered "close-in," although some distance from the central business district.

Over 60 churches, serve the many different denominations of Spring Branch residents. Three branches of the Houston Library operate in the Spring Branch area. It has two major regional shopping centers and many specialty shops. There are two hospitals with emergency room services, Spring Branch Memorial and Sam Houston Memorial. Among the businesses and industries with branches in Spring Branch are Brown Oil, the Igloo Corporation, Texas Corrugated Box Company, Cameron Iron Works and Louisville Title Company.

To the east of Spring Branch between Buffalo Bayou and the Katy Freeway, amidst the trees along West Memorial Drive, are the independent municipalities of **HUNTER'S CREEK VILLAGE, BUNKER HILL, PINEY POINT, HILSHIRE** and **HEDWIG VILLAGE;** collectively known as the **MEMORIAL VILLAGES.** The City of Houston surrounds them. For the last 20 years, the Memorial villages have embraced a tightly zoned and affluent pocket of suburbia with comfortable, often elegant homes. They are like River Oaks in their affluence and similar to Bellaire as independently incorporated cities. They lie in the country to the north of Westheimer Road, to the south of Katy Freeway and to the east of Tanglewood, the Houston Country Club and beautiful Memorial Park.

The estimated population of these villages ranges from 3,300 to 5,000. The strictly residential Memorial villages are zoned, and since the city of Houston is not, the city may not annex them. Each village incorporated separately in 1954 and 1955 and their independence from the city of Houston gives them decided tax advantages. As of 1979, the city tax on a $150,000 home in Hedwig Village, for example, was $231 while the tax on the same home in Houston would be $1,216.

The villages however, do not enjoy certain municipal services. There are no community centers, and no clinics, although Rosewood General Hospital and its adjoining clinics and medical offices at Rosewood Medical Center as well as the Memorial City Hospital are accessible. There is but one park and it's in Hedwig Village. Memorial Park doesn't overlap with the villages, but it is in the area and is easily accessible to village residents.

All five of the villages originally shared the cost of police protection; in 1976 Hedwig Village formed its own police force. Mayors and council members make up part of the volunteer force while the adjacent Spring Valley Fire Department provides all of the villages with fire protection.

Families who moved here partly because of the excellent Spring Branch Independent School District—the boundaries of which include the villages—have remained. Unlike the relatively undeveloped neighborhoods of Woodlands and Alief, the Memorial villages are nearly completely developed.

Houston's growth towards the west between Highway 6 and the city of **KATY** has been amazing. This area of Harris County and the subdivisions along west Interstate 10, represent a rapidly growing metropolitan region and a flourishing segment of suburbia. It is predicted that as much as 23 percent of Houston's housing growth will be in the Katy-west

Plant life at Spring Branch apartments.

Houston area in the next two or three years. The boundaries of the neighborhood are Highway 290 to the north, Katy to the west, Dairy Ashford to the east and Westheimer to the south.

Katy-west Houston has a major advantage which many suburban communities do not enjoy—a tremendous number of employment opportunities available within a radius of a few miles. Shell Oil Company's office facilities will be added on the north side of Interstate 10 at Dairy Ashford, supplementing office buildings between Highway 6 and Gessner and the still expanding Park Ten development. Other key employers moving to the area include Conoco Oil, Hudson Engineering and Exxon.

Gerald Hines Interests, a major Houston area developer, has plans to build two office towers at Eldridge and Highway 6 and Browning Ferris will move west from its current downtown facilities.

While the general area is referred to loosely as Katy, the town of Katy proper lies 30 miles west of Houston's central business district, with a population of 5,000. Incorporated in 1945, Katy began as a farming community.

Most of the work force, whose median income is $24,000 per year, is employed in industrial occupations. The Exxon Company gas plant, for instance, employs a large number of local residents. Most of the industrial plants are on Highway 90, which divides north Katy from south Katy. Ranching continues to be a major business factor. Since many residents of Katy's newer subdivisions do commute to Houston, there is a strong interrelationship between Houston and Katy.

There are a number of civic organizations, such as the Optimist's Club, the Rotary Club, garden and literary clubs and sports organizations.

There are several organized sports activities, including soccer, football and baseball. The Katy Park Department organizes summer activities and Easter egg hunts for children.

There are privately owned leisure retreats, such as the Green Meadows Golf Club, and public facilities such as V.F.W. (Veterans of Foreign Wars) Park, Thomas Park, Woodlands Park and Katy City Park.

Within the city limits, there are two elementary schools, a junior high school and a high school.

Four private day care centers provide care for young children and the Katyville Healthcare Center serves the needs of the aged.

Homes in this predominantly white community range from $40,000 to $140,000. Local, state and national news are covered by a weekly newspaper, *The Times*. Katy has thirteen churches, including Lutheran, Catholic, Mormon, Assembly of God and

The birth of a subdivision in Champions.

Jehovah's Witnesses. Katy operates under an aldermanic form of city government.

HOUSTON NORTHWEST, which takes in FM-1960, Jersey Village, Spring and Cypress-Fairbanks, is a growing area second only to Katy-west Houston in the burgeoning construction of new homes and business growth. Houston Northwest is approximately 20 to 25 miles north-northwest of Houston's central business district. The area encompasses Houston Intercontinental Airport and is about 70 miles from Galveston. Houston Northwest is home to more than 350,000 people with more than 250 square miles of land covering more than 100 residential subdivisions. The area ranges from 100 to 180 feet above mean sea level and is heavily forested. Its semirolling terrain is drained by hundreds of scenic streams, creeks and bayous.

Its history dates back to the Orcoquisac Indians who hunted deer, bear and buffalo in the area. Treks along Spring and Cypress creeks have uncovered several Indian camps. In addition, German, French and Spanish explorers charted the area as early as the 1600s.

During the 1960s, Houston Northwest was a sleepy, hidden woodland intersected by several farm-to-market roads. It was a haven for golfers, farmers and early northside settlers. Today, more than 250 square miles are enclosed within the triangle formed by FM-1960, US 290 and US 59.

Major employers in the Houston Northwest include airlines and agencies in the aviation industry, several major school districts, Goodyear, Tenneco, Chicago Bridge and Iron, Drilco, Plains Machinery, Houston Natural Gas, Southwestern Bell and numerous other light industrial and manufacturing plants. This business activity takes place in an attractive tax economy which features neither personal nor corporate income taxes at the state level.

The majority of Houston Northwest residents live in single family homes located on individual lots in subdivisions. Approximately 625 families are moving into the area every month. Homes range in price from $39,000 to $50,000.

Route **FM-1960** between FM-149 and Interstate 45 has become a center of commercial activity. Numerous office buildings, shopping centers, restaurants and residential subdivisions line both sides

Large waterfront house in Champions.

of the busy thoroughfare. The **CHAMPIONS VILLAGE I** and **CHAMPIONS VILLAGE II** commercial developments total over 150,000 square feet of office space. These are developments of Joe McDermott, Inc., as is Creekridge near FM-1960 and Interstate 45.

Schools have kept pace with the rapid growth by investing more than $200 million in new school construction in the past six years. Cypress-Fairbanks, Klein, Spring and Aldine independent schools are all highly regarded. The current student population in the area and surrounding district totals about 80,000 and some of these local districts are expecting to double.

Houston Northwest offers the recreational opportunities of the famed Champions Golf Club. Champions is one of 16 golf courses in the area, including the Woodlands, now the site of the Houston Open.

Lakes Conroe, Livingston, Toledo Bend and other smaller lakes and creeks offer fishing and boating facilities. The county's Bear Creek Park, Spring Creek Park, Mercer Arboretum, Cypress Creek Parkway and Klein Park are either in the heart of or within minutes driving time from Houston Northwest.

The Houston Northwest Medical Center recently opened a six-story facility. Parkway Hospital also provides full medical services. In extreme emergencies, Life Flight transport is available to the Texas Medical Center in nearby Houston. Life Flight helicopters fly from Hermann Hospital while the military staffs a nearby MAST unit at Hooks Airport.

Only ten years ago FM-1960 was a farm-to-market road that wound quietly through the edge of the East Texas woods. FM-1960, in 1980, is a major road serving one of the faster growing sections in the United States. What were once leisurely country drives are now busy streets nearly comparable to Houston's principal thoroughfares.

The **CYPRESS CREEK-1960** area is some 20 to 25 miles north to northwest of Houston's central business

Natural beauty maintained in modern neighborhood.

district. It falls in a green belt of beautiful pines, both loblolly and shortleaf. Most of the growth is between Interstate 45 and FM-149, but the community is rapidly growing to the north and south of FM-1960, east of Interstate highway 45 and west toward the US 290-Addicks Dam area. Much of this area is outside the Houston city limits. It is another example of Houston's growth into unincorporated Harris County. FM-1960 is definitely not an inner city suburb.

The origin of FM-1960 can be traced to the early 1960s. At that time a group of golf enthusiasts built the Champions Golf Club on Cypress Creek. The first residents were principally families with grown children. Real estate developers soon saw the value in the territory and created residential subdivisions such as Champions, Greenwood Forest, and Huntwick.

The homes in FM-1960 fluctuate in price from **$50,000 to $350,000. The average home owner is** young. Many of the couples currently moving into the neighborhood are professionals in search of a pastoral elegance. Some two hundred home builders are striving to meet the couples' needs in eighty or so subdivisions between Interstate 45 and US 290. Nearly 200,000 currently live in the FM-1960 area and another 50,000 are expected to move there in 1980 alone.

FM-1960 growth may be attributed to the residential benefits of the neighborhood. Most structures are single family homes, with few apartment complexes.

Many businesses and shopping centers serve the subdivisions in typical Houston style, mixing the commercial and residential areas as in the Tanglewood-Galleria area. There are more than 350 shops and supermarkets located in nine shopping centers and 18 strip centers. Four more shopping centers are under construction and six more are on the drawing boards.

The residents in FM-1960 with school-age children are served by three independent school districts, Cypress-Fairbanks, Klein and Spring. Nineteen new schools were built in the FM-1960 area during the past two years and several more are under construction.

In addition, the Cypress Creek Parks Project is now underway to provide children with plenty of safe open spaces to play in. The project will purchase 4,000 acres along the 43-mile stretch of Cypress Creek. The proposed open space parks will consist of hike and bike trails with an abundance of picnic areas. The Cypress Creek Parks Project should be a distinctive feature of FM-1960. In addition, individual subdivisions have community programs which provide an opportunity for children to participate in team sports such as swimming, tennis and Little League baseball.

FM-1960 has the ambience of a small town. It exists in two worlds, that of metropolitan Houston and the unhurrried style of country living. It has been predicted that the FM-1960 area of Houston northwest will be annexed to Houston in the next several years. The community has already held forums to discuss pros and cons.

The incorporated city of **JERSEY VILLAGE,** northwest of the central business district, is bounded on three sides by Cypress-Fairbanks. Part of the outer northwestern band of Houston's most recently developed neighborhoods, it is in no sense an older, inner city suburb. Rather, it exemplifies Houston's fan-like outgrowth. The ethnic breakdown of the city of Jersey Village is largely Caucasian. It is a residental neighborhood of middle income, white collar workers with over 800 homes and 2,500 to 3,000 residents.

Jersey Village's single family homes run from $60,000 upward. There are deed restrictions against the construction of apartments, but Jersey Village plans call for building townhouses in the near future. Originally a dairy farm community, the city of Jersey Village was incorporated in 1955.

The city of Jersey Village has two schools, Post Elementary and Jersey Village Senior High, part of the Cypress-Fairbanks Independent School District. A community club plans social functions. There is one major park with a pool and playground, several smaller neighborhood parks and one day care center.

The city of Jersey Village organizes a six-week summer recreational program for neighborhood children, featuring pottery, art, twirling lessons, and gymnastics. Various organizations also use the parks for other sports activities. Church denominations serving the area include Methodist, Baptist and the Church of Christ.

There is one major shopping center, with a bank, a supermarket, a western shop, and a savings and loan association. Shopping is also possible at points on Center and Jones streets and along the Northwest Freeway. There are no major businesses in the planned residential community of Jersey Village. The city of Jersey Village has a 10-man police force and a 30-man volunteer fire department.

CYPRESS-FAIRBANKS, another northwestern neighborhood, resulted from the joining together of two communities in the early 1940s: the German agricultural area of Cypress and the Italian waterstop and railroad junction of Fairbanks. It is a 186-square-mile neighborhood with a population of 70,000 in the middle to upper socio-economic level. Cypress-Fairbanks is bounded on the south by Clay Road, on the north by Cypress Creek, Faulky Gully, and Grand Road, to the west by an imaginary midpoint line between the towns of Cypress and Hockey, and to the east by Bingle Road and the Burlington Railroad. In economic terms, it is a neighborhood whose population is half white collar and half blue collar.

The Cypress-Fairbanks Independent School District includes 12 elementary, four junior high, and three high schools. There are many civic clubs in the neighborhood and six day care centers. Bear Creek Park and the county park along Cypress Creek are the available neighborhood parks. Bear Creek Park is open 7:00 A.M. to 10:00 P.M. seven days a week, year round. Heavily wooded with pines and oaks, the park affords facilities for trailers, tent campers and hikers. Picnickers may use roadside drive-ups and concrete tables as well as barbecue grills. There are plans for a new park—Barbers Park—to the south of Interstate 10.

There are about 30 churches representing such faiths as Baptist, Roman Catholic, Lutheran, Assembly of God and additional Protestant denominations. There are no shopping malls, but Willowood Mall is accessible at the Intersection of FM-1960 and FM-149 and Northwest Mall at Hempstead and Highway 290. Two hospitals have applied for a charter and a third is in the planning stage.

Over 1,000 businesses operate in the Cypress-Fairbanks area. Cameron Iron Works, one of the leading iron producers, is headquartered in Cypress-Fairbanks. Other companies in the area include Texas Instruments, Houston Lighting and Power, and various oil tool firms. The neighborhood also features small businesses like dress shops, pharmacies, and hardware stores.

Cypress-Fairbanks is served by the Cypress-Fairbanks and Cypress Creek Volunteer Fire Departments. The encapsulated city of Jersey Village and the city of Houston offer police protection.

Cypress-Fairbanks has some 24,000 single family dwellings which range in price from $50,000 to $250,000. One bedroom apartments rent for a monthly average of $255 a month. Three or four areas in the neighborhood have townhouses, selling for between $50,000 and $90,000.

SPRING, also part of Houston northwest, is 25 miles northwest of downtown Houston along Interstate 45, sandwiched between the incorporated cities of Tomball and Humble, west of Lake Houston, and south of Conroe. The total Spring area, which covers part of Highway FM-1960, had a 1978 population of over 200,000. The ethnic distribution in Spring is approximately 80 percent white and 20 percent black.

Spring's crime rate is low. Mostly a white collar neighborhood, Spring has its own private garbage pick-up service.

Spring, which grew up around what was once a railroad turnaround, has experienced increasingly rapid growth in the last few years. Contemporary style homes range in price from $50,000 to $100,000. In addition to single family dwellings, there are numerous apartments available with rents in the $200 to $400 a month range. Townhouses are priced from $40,000 to $70,000.

The Spring Independent School System serves parts of Aldine, Klein, and Conroe in a triangular configuration. There are eight elementary schools, three middle schools, and two high schools. There are five parks in the Spring area and about 100 civic clubs, with at least one to each subdivision.

The Spring area's leaders have organized numerous sports and children's projects, including Boy Scouts and Girl Scouts and church-affiliated activities. There are 15 day care centers.

The neighborhood of Spring has about 50 different churches, mostly Protestant and Catholic in denomination. The Greenspoint Shopping Mall is accessible to Spring residents and so are various shopping strips along FM-1960. There are three hospitals, but very few business enterprises. Spring has its own volunteer fire department, but relies on the Harris County police for protection.

Modernistic townhouses in Montrose.

Located 31 miles northwest of Houston's central business district, the town of **TOMBALL** is situated on Highway 290, between Interstate 45 and Highway 149.

Until 1850, Tomball was a farming community. With the movement of the Rock Island Railroad through the town, people in other pursuits began settling in Tomball. When oil was discovered in the area in 1933, it attracted more people. In 1937, Tomball became an incorporated town.

Tomball's population is 42,090 and recreational facilities include a swimming pool, cinema and country club. Spring Creek County Park is a lovely wooded area in the town. The Tomball Community Hospital provides medical care for the area. The Tomball volunteer fire department has 30 members, 13 of whom are certified by the state.

The **WOODLANDS** in south Montgomery County is 23,000 square acres of heavily wooded terrain 14 miles north of Houston Intercontinental Airport. Woodlands, a community designed to be a hometown in itself, is located 30 miles north of downtown Houston and eight miles south of Conroe, along Interstate highway 45. Bounded on the east by Interstate 45 and the Montgomery and Harris county line to the south, the city of Shenandoah is on the north. Woodlands is a mostly white community with a population of 8,200. A majority of the residents are administrative, managerial and technical professionals. Woodlands, like Cypress-Fairbanks, FM-

Brand new Atascocita neighborhood.

1960 and Humble, is an outgrowth neighborhood of Houston with much room left for future development.

The Woodlands has five schools within its boundaries: W. E. Wilkerson Intermediate School, Knox Junior High, Hailey Elementary, Lamar Elementary and McCullough High School. An as yet unnamed elementary school is under construction. Civic clubs include A.A.R.P., The American Association of University Women, The Ladies Community Golf League of the Woodlands, The Rotary Club and the Christian Women's Club. The Woodlands area is in the unincorporated portion of Montgomery County, It is administered by the Montgomery County Commissioners' Court. The four commissioners are elected from four precincts throughout the county. A county judge also sits on the commissioners' court and is elected by the county at large.

Houses range in price from $40,000 to $400,000 and apartments run from $146 to $360 a month. There are 144 townhouse units. Currently, 20,000 of the 23,000 square acres remain undeveloped.

The Woodlands encompasses an industrial park, a trade center, a retail commercial area and a wharf shopping mall. The gigantic Mitchell Energy & Development Corp. and the Schlegel Manufacturing Company are in the process of moving into the area.

A vast array of shopping facilities are available locally. There are many retail outlets along Interstate 45 and its major intersections in the Woodlands Wharf shopping center and along other thoroughfares. Other shopping facilities are available to the north in Conroe and to the south in Houston proper.

Woodlands and southern Montgomery County health facilities include Doctor's Hospital in Conroe, Woodlands Health Center, Houston Northwest Medical Center and Medical Center Hospital.

HUMBLE is located at the intersection of US Highway 59 and FM-1960 in the northeast corner of Harris County, east of FM-1960 and south of Kingwood, and is approximately five miles from Houston Intercontinental Airport. The city of Humble was incorporated in 1932 and operates under a council-manager type of government. Its strategic location on US Highway 59 and FM-1960 affords quick connection with points in Houston, the Gulf Coast and East Texas. Covering an area of approximately ten square miles, Humble sits atop a heavily wooded knoll, close to lakes and recreational facilities. It is also a prime center for fishing and hunting enthusiasts.

The first people who settled in Humble were lumbermen and cattlemen. Humble Oil began operating an early oil field from which the town took its name. The population of Humble, a predominantly white neighborhood, is 10,000. There is today an even blend of blue and white collar workers and, with the proximity to Intercontinental Airport, many of the residents work at the airport.

Humble has its own independent school district, with two elementary schools, one junior high school and one senior high school. North Harris County Junior College is located within its environs.

The residents are served by three newspapers, the *Humble Echo,* the *Humble News Messenger* and the *Lake Houston News.* McKay Clinic and Northeast Medical Center provide health care for the area and the city is 18 miles from the Texas Medical Center. Township and Kingwood centers serve the shopping needs of the city's residents.

For golfers, there are Kingwood, Forest Cove, Atascocita, El Dorado and Tejas golf clubs. Swimming is available at the city swimming pool and at various residential club pools. Cezeaux Memorial Park organizes summer activities for children and has Little League football and baseball teams.

The 2,500 homes in Humble range in price from $35,000 to $150,000. There are 39 churches, representing ten different religious denominations. Several civic organizations and clubs are present, including the Rotary and Lions clubs and the four subdivisions also have their own civic organizations. Humble has a low crime rate. It operates its own police and fire departments.

KINGWOOD, a self-contained community, is a well planned development northeast of Houston, beyond Humble. It is near Houston Intercontinental Airport, near FM-1960, and close to Lake Houston. Advertised as a "livable forest" and boasting an

House in Kingwood subdivision.

abundance of trees, the distance from Houston to Kingwood is 22 miles via the Eastex Freeway.

Unincorporated and divided into nine villages (with at least five more planned), Kingwood is currently home to some 15,000 people. It is estimated that Kingwood will ultimately be home to between 70,000 and 75,000 persons.

The King Ranch, Inc. acquired the property in 1967 and the original developers were the Friendswood Development Company, a subsidiary of Exxon. A popular suburb largely inhabited by oil company employees, most residents commute to Houston to work.

Kingwood is an affordable place to live for people in most every income bracket. Sherwood Trails homes range from between $40,000 and $50,000; Elm Grove and Hunters Ridge feature those from $50,000 to $100,000; and Trailwood and Bear Branch homes run from $90,000 to $140,000. Kings Forest homes run from $150,000 upward.

Residents pay for their own police and fire protection, garbage collection, mosquito fogging and the maintenance of pools, streets and green areas. Unannexed and unincorporated, the Kingwood Community Action Committee actively serves to promote the best interests of the community. An active suburb with many businesses relocating there, Kingwood enjoys a high quality of life. Kingwood's excellent recreational facilities include a country club, pools in each subdivision, bike paths, Lake Houston, stables, and Little League sports.

THE HEIGHTS lies across the Buffalo Bayou, northwest of the central business district. It is bounded by Interstate 610 to the north, Interstate 45 to the east, White Oak Drive and 11th Street to the South and Durham to the west. The Heights is an older neighborhood undergoing restoration. Residential development of its 4.7 square miles began in the late nineteenth century. An early example of Houston's growth through annexation, the Heights was once an exclusive upper-income neighborhood

An elegant wooden home in the Heights.

annexed by Houston in 1918. Even in its early days, much of the Heights had paved streets, street lights, telephone service, fire protection, a street car line, city water, gas and electricity. Despite the absence of deed restrictions lot sizes were originally rigidly governed (50' x 100') to insure low population density. Today, with 16 persons per residential acre, the Heights has one of the lowest levels of local population densities in Houston.

Around 1970, Houstonians in search of affordable homes rediscovered the Heights. Real estate transactions, according to a local bank, doubled from 1972 to 1973. Homes which sold for $20,000 in the 1970s sell today for at least $40,000. Those who wish to restore can buy homes for between $30,000 and $40,000. Victorian and California-type homes and mature pecan and oak trees dot the neighborhood, so that it resembles, at its best, a picturesque small town. Residential structures tend to be of wood frame construction and more than 60 percent were constructed prior to World War II. Its present population of 37,000 is 80 percent Caucasian, about 16 percent Mexican-American, and approximately two percent black. Unusual for Houston, nearly 17 percent of the Heights' area residents do not own automobiles.

The Heights has 11 public schools, two private elementary schools (one Catholic and one Lutheran) and one religious institute, Gulf Coast Bible College.

Characteristic houses in the Montrose area.

There are eight public elementaries, two junior highs, and one senior high school; Heights' schools are part of the Houston Independent School District.

Health facilities include Heights Hospital and the West End Health Center. There is one day care facility, Fulbright Child Care Center, and there are six parks.

Community programs include the Senior Citizens Program, the Neighborhood Program, Heights Day Care and Training Center, Maebridge Community Living Center of Houston and Rotary's Variety Boys Club. Architect Janet Wagner is trying to have a 39-square-block area in the Heights added to the National Register for Historic Places. Should this come about, the Heights will receive federal funds to aid in improving streets, drainage and lighting, and receive a five-year moratorium on taxes.

MONTROSE is a diverse area of 24,572, which includes numerous artists and one of the largest gay populations in the United States. Montrose, which began about 1912 as an elegant residential suburb, is one of Houston's oldest neighborhoods. Architects are now restoring old homes and defining precise boundaries, which run by Buffalo Bayou to the north, Richmond and Westheimer to the south, Dunlavy Street to the west and Main to the east. The strip along Westheimer has emerged as Houston's Greenwich Village. Montrose has a low percentage of children under five (6.4 percent) and a high percentage of senior citizens, with 23.5 percent of the population 55 years or older. This large concentration of senior citizens necessitates special services in terms of public transportation and various social services. The black population comprises 3.5 percent while 18.5 percent is Mexican-American and 78 percent is white.

Originally a residential neighborhood, much of Montrose has now been converted to other uses. Currently, commercial land use is concentrated along the thoroughfares of West Dallas, Gray, Shepherd, and Main streets with stores, restaurants, family businesses and many convenience stores.

Approximately half of the houses in Montrose were built in the 1920s and the remaining structures date from the 1930s. The housing is generally a mixture of brick and wood structures, with both slab and pier and beam foundations. There are several business establishments of historical significance in Montrose, notably the building that houses Matt Garner's Bar-b-que, which has been at the same location for 40 years.

Montrose has three public elementary schools within its boundaries, including Wilson Elementary, part of the Houston Independent School District. Medical facilities include the Cerebral Palsy Treatment Center, Jefferson Davis Hospital, and the City of Houston Department of Public Health.

One of the newer homes in River Oaks.

Service centers abound in the Montrose area. Among these are the Chicano Training Center, the Child Care Council of Greater Houston, Inc., the Family Service Center of Houston and Harris County, the Harris County Juvenile Department, the Harris County Center for the Retarded, Inc., Houston Metropolitan Ministries, the Houston School for Deaf Children, the Inlet Drug Crisis Center, the Lighthouse for the Blind, the Texas Institute for Rehabilitation and Research, the Texas Department of Public Welfare, the Texas Youth Council, Turning Point, The Hope Center for Youth and the Montrose Neighborhood Service Center.

RIVER OAKS is a prestigious, elegant residential neighborhood, west of the central business district, bounded by Buffalo Bayou, Westheimer Road and South Shepherd Drive. An inner city suburb, it is one of the best planned and maintained upper class neighborhoods in the United States.

River Oaks' founding stemmed from the desire of a group of Houstonians to organize a country club in 1923. Charter members of the Country Club soon realized that the land surrounding the club grounds

would be ideal for home sites, and so they took options for areas in an adjacent 1,500-acre tract. Will Hogg, a member of the famous Hogg family, purchased most of the tract and then formed the River Oaks Corporation to develop it into a community known as the River Oaks Country Club Estates, a planned community complete with a shopping center. Hogg also formulated a plan for a Civic Center, to be rendered in Spanish Renaissance Revival style. The corporation required that any buyer would have to pay an annual maintenance fee based on the size of the buyer's property. Many of the residents employed garden experts and outstanding landscape architects to beautify the River Oaks residential lots.

The community's development was nearly complete by the middle 1950s, with over 1,400 homes. Hugh Potter, who created the River Oaks Property Owners Association in the 1950s, was instrumental in enforcing the strict building and maintenance requirements of the River Oaks Estates. River Oaks' deed restrictions specifically ban business structures, duplexes, apartment houses and residential outbuildings. Hospitals may not be built in River Oaks and hedges or fences over four feet require the written consent of the Property Owners Association. Thus, the community is essentially composed of expensive single family residences. The few empty lots in River Oaks are owned by River Oaks residents. "For Sale" signs on homes and garage sales are not permitted.

River Oaks most exclusive section is Homewoods, an area including Bayou Bend, the former residence of Will Hogg's sister, the late Miss Ima Hogg, who donated Bayou Bend to the Museum of Fine Arts.

A large River Oaks dwelling is valued up to $2 million. Some smaller homes are valued as low as $100,000 and family homes usually range in price from $150,000 to $1 million. There are no shopping centers, except for the small River Oaks shopping center on Westheimer which is one of the oldest in Houston. St. John's School, Lamar High School, River Oaks Elementary School and St. John's Church are nearby.

To the south of River Oaks, is the **SOUTH MAIN** area. There are 55,000 people employed in the South Main area, making it the second largest employment core in Houston. About 35,000 residents live in this downtown easterly area which encompasses some of **Houston's oldest and most historic deed-restricted** neighborhoods, such as Shadyside, Broadacres, Shadowlawn and Southampton Place. The area also includes the renowned Texas Medical Center, the Astrodomain, Hermann Park, Rice University and the city's major art museums. It is the cultural, institutional and recreational hub of the city. The South Main area also contains large tracts of undeveloped inner city land.

Some of the major accomplishments of the South Main citizens in the 1970s have been the 127 trees planted on Main Street, the designation of the south freeway as a scenic drive prohibiting billboards, the establishment of "brown bag" musical concerts in the Texas Medical Center, the retention of the High School for Performing and Visual Arts in the arts corridor and the installation of a $250,000 fountain.

Residence in Southampton Place.

SOUTHAMPTON PLACE is bounded on the north by Bissonnet, on the south by Rice Boulevard, on the east by Ashby and on the west by Greenbriar. The 161-acre Southampton Place is less suburban in ambience than other Houston neighborhoods. An older and deed-restricted neighborhood west of Hermann Park and east of West University Place, Southampton Place grew up next to Rice University, 10 years after the university began classes. In 1922, Southampton principally consisted of one street, Sunset Boulevard. As the years went by, it developed into a hospitable, small, friendly neighborhood.

Members of the Southampton Civic Club have joined to preserve the residential, single-family community ordained by 50-year old deed restrictions. The restrictions stipulated, among other things, the prohibition of apartment houses in Southampton Place. The Civic Club renewed these restrictions in 1973 for another 50 years. Southampton, thus, continues as a neighborhood of homeowners. Houses in Southampton range from $100,000 to $200,000, while these same houses went for $22,000 to $35,000 ten years ago.

Moving clockwise through East Houston, the **FIFTH WARD** is bounded on the west by Eastex Freeway, on the south by Buffalo Bayou, on the east by Lockwood Street and on the north by a series of residential streets, including Brewster, Gregg and Lucille. The density of population is 30 persons per residential acre, the average housing density is 9.1 and the median income is $5,030. As of the last census in 1970, the population stood at some 24,000 and is predominantly black.

At the turn of the century, the blacks were a decided minority among Houston's residents. After World War II, however, migrations of blacks from Louisiana, rural Texas, and rapidly growing neighborhoods to the north and west of the central business district introduced the black predominance to the Fifth Ward's ethnic makeup.

The Fifth Ward has five elementary schools, one junior high, and one high school. There are seven day care centers. One shopping center serves the area. Finnigan Park and several smaller parks are nearby.

The community's Baptist church is the pillar of faith as well as the cultural and social center for the ward.

Public health clinics within commuting distance of or within the Fifth Ward include Casa de Amigos Health Clinic, Lyons Avenue Health Clinic and the Mobile Dental Unit.

Most houses in the neighborhood are of wood frame construction and are the single family detached type. Single-family dwellings account for 62 percent of all the houses.

Local agencies operating in the Fifth Ward are the Julia C. Hester House, Wesley House Community Center, the Ethnic Arts Center-Hope Development, and the South Coast Community Services Association and its various subdivisional stations.

Another lower-income predominantly black neighborhood, the **FOURTH WARD** has been mobilizing to preserve its heritage. By the 1880s, blacks owned most of the property south of Congress and west of Main. By 1900, it was flourishing. Now, it is mostly a lower-income neighborhood, bounded by Allen Parkway, Interstate 45, Bagby, Taft and Tuam, and apartment renters constitute 85 percent of the neighborhood.

Currently, Fourth Ward landlords, realtors and developers are seeking to sell Allen Parkway Village, a 1,200-unit low-income federal housing project which they would like to tear down in order to construct housing for renters. Two million dollars has been set aside for the widening of West Dallas, the area's main thoroughfare, connecting downtown and the Montrose and River Oaks area. This was approved by voters in an April, 1979 bond election.

The Fourth Ward has an estimated population of over 25,000, with 15.9 people per acre. It has a larger than average number of school age children, as well as large numbers of elderly people. It has a disproportionately small number of people in the labor force. It is 72 percent black, 9 percent Mexican and the remainder is white. It has one elementary school and one junior-senior high school which is part of Houston Independent School District. Medical services are available to residents at the Cerebral Palsy Treatment Center, Jefferson Davis Hospital and the City of Houston Department of Public

Health. Two Houston fire stations serve the neighborhood. Two day care centers are accessible to Fourth Ward residents.

Also in East Houston is **DENVER HARBOR,** which is considered a "barrio," or Spanish speaking neighborhood. North of the Houston Ship Channel, Denver Harbor is located 3.5 miles east of Houston's central business district. The area is bounded on the north by Wallisville Road, on the east by Lockwood Drive, on the south by the Ship Channel, and on the west from Wallisville to Market by Wayside Drive, and from Market to Old Clinton Road by McCarty. The total land area is 5.9 square miles and the total population is 20,029, giving a population density of 5.3 people per acre. The ethnic breakdown is 55.8 percent Mexican-American, 32.6 percent white and 11.6 percent black. The housing in Denver Harbor is mostly wood frame structures with pile and beam and block foundations. The remaining quarter of the homes have a slab-type foundation. The average value of housing in Denver Harbor is below that of Houston as a whole, with the 1970 average value of Denver Harbor homes being $8,723. The average apartment rents for $64 a month.

Denver Harbor has a large number of non-residential structures. Most of the commercial ship development along Houston, Market and Lyons was built prior to the construction of the Interstate 10 freeway. Some of the industrial structures along the ship channel are older, but most of the construction has been completed within the last 20 years.

There are four schools within the boundaries of Denver Harbor. These are all part of the Houston

Independent School District. The schools are Mc-Reynolds Junior High, Pugh, Eliot, and Scroggins Elementary Schools. There are also several vocational schools within the area.

There are no public day care centers in Denver Harbor. There is a Harris County Mental Health and Mental Retardation Center.

MAGNOLIA is a neighborhood on the southeast side of Houston. The 7.8 square mile neighborhood lies due south of the Houston Ship Channel. Magnolia has a population of 45,201 and is also a barrio. It has the second highest percentage of Hispanics (48 percent) in Houston and one of the lowest black populations (4 percent). The number of Caucasians (48 percent) equals that of the Mexican-Americans.

The blue collar community of Magnolia evolved with the Houston transportation system. Harrisburg, due south of Magnolia, extended itself over Brays Bayou in 1826, and Houston rose up to its north, on Buffalo Bayou in 1836. The Harrisburg Road came to serve both cities and yielded, in the late 1800s, to railroad tracks laid down by Mexican laborers. Mexican and black workers dredged and widened Buffalo Bayou by 1914, making way for the entry of the first ocean-going vessel along the new ship channel. Jobs were created for Magnolia residents, loading and unloading southern cotton on railroad cars and ships. Mexican women worked in jute mills, making gunnysack material for binding compressed cotton bales. The construction of Harrisburg Freeway, an addition to the 69th Street Bridge and Navigation Boulevard, will boost industry and commerce in the 1980s.

The Catholic church, in particular the Immaculate Heart of Mary Catholic Church on 76th Street and Avenue K, ministers to the spiritual needs of the inhabitants of this barrio.

The housing structures in Magnolia are fairly old. The most valuable housing is found south of the FHH railroad and is predominantly wood frame structures with pier and beam and block foundations. There are also some brick structures with slab foundations.

The eight schools within Magnolia are Southway, J. R. Harris, Briscoe, De Zavala and Franklin elementaries, Deady and Edison junior highs and Milby senior high.

The City of Houston Department of Health runs a clinic in Magnolia, open from 8:00 A.M. to 4:00 P.M., whose services include mental health and preventive health care.

The city of **LA PORTE,** 30 miles southeast of Houston, wedged between two ports, slightly north of Galveston Bay and south of the dense industrial area of Houston, is renowned for its proximity to San Jacinto Monument and its recreational area, the Sylvan Beach Park on Galveston Bay. The population of the city is 18,000, with a median age of 32. Industry is the primary source of employment, providing a median income of $15,000.

Residents in search of recreational pursuits have access to the Fairmont Park City Pool, city tennis courts, Baywood Country Club and San Jacinto College golf course. The Port Theater adds a cultural dimension to the city's activities, and local youth can find activities at the La Porte Community Center and the North Side Center.

The major health-care facility serving the area is the Harris County Health Center. The city government functions under a mayor and four councilmen. Shopping facilities are available at Sylvan Plaza, Oak Center and Bay Plaza. Information on world and local events is published in the weekly newspaper, *The Bayshore Sun.*

Deer Park, Pasadena, Gulfgate and Friendswood are all part of Houston's North Channel neighborhood, so named after the Houston Ship Channel. Deer Park, for example, named for a private park for deer which had occupied the site, began with the opening of a railroad station in 1892. By 1940, Deer Park had four businesses and a population of 100. The 1980 population is estimated to be 27,973.

DEER PARK is located in the southeastern quadrant of Harris County. It is bounded on the north by the Houston Ship Channel, on the west by the city of Pasadena, on the south by Houston and Pasadena, and on the east by the township of Lomax. Located in the industrial section of Harris County, Deer Park covers 14 square miles and it is 20 miles southeast of downtown Houston. Incorporated in 1948, it is actually not a part of Houston (like Humble and Tomball), but it is considered part of the greater Houston metropolitan area.

Deer Park borders the site of one of the Houston area's major tourist attractions: the San Jacinto Monument, the site where General Sam Houston and 650 soldiers defeated General Santa Anna and his 1,350 force army, making Texas an independent nation. The San Jacinto Monument was built between 1936 and 1939. Another Deer Park tourist attraction is the Battleship *Texas.*

The Deer Park median family income is estimated to be $20,800 and the median age is 25. There were 406 businesses on the city tax roll at the beginning of 1980. There are about 6,562 single family housing units and 1,292 apartments in Deer Park. Since incorporation in 1948, Deer Park elects a board of five aldermen, a mayor and a city marshal. The office of city marshal was abolished by ordinance in 1956 and a regular police department with an appointed chief was substituted.

RIGHT: *Miles upon miles of highways provide access for residents of Houston neighborhoods to any point in the city.*

The Deer Park Independent School District, currently commemorating its 50th year, has eleven schools, including one 4-A high school, three junior highs and seven elementary schools, serving about 8,400 students.

Covering 54.5 square miles to the southeast of Houston lies **PASADENA,** one of the larger incorporated cities within the Houston metropolitan area. Pasadena, with a population of over 130,000, is bounded to the south by Clear Lake, to the west by South Houston, to the east by Deer Park and to the north by the ship channel. An agricultural community when it was founded in 1895, Pasadena has retained its original community flavor while participating in the explosive growth around it.

Once inhabited by the peaceful hunting and farming Coushatta Indians, Galveston businessman Colonel J. H. Burnett incorporated the city in 1928, then one square mile. Pasadena was known as the strawberry capital of the world until the petrochemical industry began local operations. The Houston Ship Channel along Pasadena's east boundary, was dredged between 1910 and 1920. This brought in ship channel industries along with their personnel.

Pasadena is a thriving blue collar community with a monthly influx of 350 to 400 families and a median income of $18,639, second highest for a city in Texas after the Dallas suburb of Richardson. The median value of its homes is approximately $30,000. Thirty-six thousand students attend four high schools, nine junior highs, and 27 elementary schools there.

Pasadena is home to the nationally known country-western club, Gilley's. Sports and dancing are popular pastimes in the city and several large dance pavilions ring with music there. Some 85 churches, representing 20 denominations, serve the community. The city has 23 parks and playgrounds. Pasadena also has undeveloped land without immediate plans for its development.

The entrance to Olde Oaks subdivision, one of the many subdivisions in the Houston area.

There are four hospitals, three nursing homes, three home nurse services and several chiropractic clinics in the city. There are about 13 major shopping centers. Pasadena's tax rate is 60 percent of the assessed basic market value or $1.10 per every $100 evaluated.

Another neighborhood in the southeast quadrant of the city, nearly seven miles from the central business district, **GULFGATE,** covers nearly eight square miles. It is bounded on the north by Griggs and Telephone Road and Winkler Drive, on the east by Plum Creek and Sims Bayou, on the south by Bellfort Road and on the west by the Atchison, Topeka and Santa Fe Railroad tracks. Its population of nearly 36,000 is predominantly white with a sizable portion of it Spanish surnamed. A quarter of the residents are under 18 while 17 percent are 55 and over, with the majority between 18 and 55 years of age.

Single family residential development is the favored type of land use while commercial development constitutes the second largest use. Small businesses and services such as restaurants and entertainment establishments, convenience stores and new and used automobile dealerships proliferate throughout the neighborhood. The housing occupancy rate in the neighborhood is high, although between 20 percent and 25 percent of the total acreage remains undeveloped.

Recreation and open space uses are found in greater concentration in the eastern extremity of the neighborhood and along Sims Bayou. There are seven pools.

The Gulfgate area is served by seven elementaries, two junior highs and one senior high school, all in the Houston Independent School District. Four non-profit day care centers are located in the Gulfgate area. Gulfgate Shopping City is a major shopping center located at the intersection of Interstate 45 South and the South Loop.

Again to Houston's southeast, **FRIENDSWOOD** is found in Galveston County, near the boundaries of Harris and Brazoria counties. Lying on the border of the greater metropolitan Houston area, Friendswood is within driving distance of major industrial and commercial areas as well as recreational sites in the Houston-Gulf Coast area. Friendswood was founded in 1895 by Quaker pioneers seeking a peaceful place to farm and raise families. Today, heavily wooded subdivisions dot the banks of Clear Creek.

Approximately 8,500 people live in Friendswood. Friendswood's schools, medical facilities and proximity to large shopping malls and recreational facilities make the neighborhood attractive for families with children. Home buyers may find an abundance of developed and undeveloped properties, heavily wooded tracts and land for raising horses in close-knit suburban communities and in beautiful rural areas.

Galveston Bay water sports, such as boating, skiing and fishing are only a fifteen-minute drive from Friendswood. Nearby bodies of water include Trinity Bay, Clear Lake and the Gulf of Mexico at Galveston. Four city parks and a nearby county park provide Little League ball fields, picnicking, tennis and a party pavilion.

Friendswood is governed by a mayor and city council; their administration is supervised by a city manager and a planning and zoning commission. A local police department, fire department and emergency medical corps serve those who live in the Friendswood vicinity.

BAYTOWN is considered a suburb of Houston. In the coastal plains sector of Harris County, something of a company town, Baytown is 30 miles east of Houston, 50 miles west of Beaumont and 40 miles north of Galveston. With an estimated population of 58,000, Baytown is approximately 27 square miles of primarily wooded land.

The city of Baytown has a city manager form of government with a council composed of six members and a mayor. There are approximately 139 doctors and three hospitals. The three hospitals are Gulf Coast, Baytown and San Jacinto Methodist. Goose Creek Consolidated Independent School District, accredited since 1921, has eleven elementary schools, four junior highs, two high schools, one parochial school and three special education schools. Lee Junior College is located in Baytown.

Baytown features two railroads, one passenger bus line and one private airport. All major truck lines serving Houston also serve Baytown.

Baytown has five banks and three savings and loan associations conveniently located within the city. Baytown's major source of employment includes

refining rubber, chemicals, carbon black and steel plants. Major companies are Baytown Olefins, Carter Oil, Exxon Chemical, J. M. Huber Corporation, National Gas Odorizing, Texas Eastern Transmission, United States Steel Corporation and the Mobay Chemical Company.

Historically, the earliest known settlers in Baytown were Indians. Some have been traced back as far as 600 or 1,000 years. The last known tribe to inhabit the area was the Karankawas, who left shortly after Texas Independence was won in 1836.

The first residents of Baytown played a major role in one of the world's most important military battles, the Battle of San Jacinto. Shortly after this battle, General Sam Houston, first provisional president of the Republic of Texas, took up residence in Baytown. After the Civil War, the trading post of Baytown officially sprang up at the site which is now Baytown Country Club.

Governor R. S. Sterling, after whom Baytown's newest library and high school is named, founded the Dayton-Goose Creek Railroad and helped Baytown become what it is today. Other than building the railroad and organizing the Humble Company, he laid out the townsite for what is now Baytown.

By 1915, successful tests gave proof that the Baytown area would make a profitable oil field. Humble Oil and Refining Company located its largest plant in Baytown in 1918 and subsequently gave Baytown the industrial shot in the arm it needed. As early as 1937, Humble started installation of new refining equipment which formed the backbone of production of toluene to be used in TNT during World War II. Nearly all of the TNT used by the Allies came from Baytown.

In January of 1948, Goose Creek and Baytown consolidated to form the present city of Baytown.

Residential construction of Charterwood homes.

Contemporary home in Clear Lake.

The Baytown-La Porte Tunnel of Texas highway 146 was opened in 1953. This structure under the Houston Ship Channel replaced a ferry and has facilitated travel between the north and south sides of the channel. It cost in excess of 10 million dollars and is the most expensive foot-by-foot construction in the state highway system. Highway 73 (Interstate 10) is a short-time super highway between Houston and Port Arthur. This facility is another east-west artery serving Baytown.

Southeast of Houston, midway between the city limits of Houston and Galveston, the **CLEAR LAKE** area encompasses 125 square miles located in Harris and Galveston counties. Annexed to Houston in December 1978, Clear Lake is another example of Houston's growth through annexation. Clear Lake is a composite community of nearly 100,000 people, embracing eight incorporated cities, major unincorporated areas and related industrial, commerical, government and suburban areas. Municipalities in the area include Webster, Nassau Bay, El Lago, Taylor Lake Village, Seabrook, Kemah, Clear Lake Shores and League City. Unincorporated communities or developments within the area include Clear Lake City, a planned community with shopping centers, an industrial park, office buildings and a country club; the Bayport Industrial Development, extending from Clear Lake to Galveston Bay south of Shore Acres near the Houston Yacht Club; and the Lyndon B. Johnson Manned Space Center. Located south of the Houston Ship Channel, Clear Lake is an outlying area like many other neighborhoods. Seventeen neighboring towns surround Clear Lake, with area populations exceeding 300,000. Homes in the Clear Lake area range in price from $45,000 to $350,000. The occupations are varied and the percentage of skilled professionals is sizeable.

Access to Galveston Bay and the Gulf of Mexico invites participation in fishing and a variety of water sports. Kemah and Seabrook are popular for boaters and water-skiers. Nature lovers and outdoor types will enjoy Armand Bayou Park, located in the heart of Clear Lake. The 2,000-acre park is a convergence of three ecosystems—Southern mixed hardwood forest, the Gulf Coast tall grass prairie, and an estuarine marsh—which support a rich and diverse plant and animal community. Striped skunks, red wolves, bobcats, great blue herons and over 180 species of birds live and breed there.

New home construction is on the rise in Clear Lake City. The 5,000th home was built in 1977 in one of its eight subdivisions. Building continues in the upper class subdivision of Brook Forest, with two new subdivisions underway, Oakbrook West and Meadowgreen. In El Lago, a $30 million subdivision is on its way on Taylor Lake, known as Taylorcrest. Several hundred waterfront homes will be built there. Also, Seabrook continues to grow, offering new homes near Galveston Bay. Meanwhile, in League City, a number of developers are beginning various residential projects, totalling more than 2,500 homes.

A large number of Clear Lake residents work near home; there are now more than 925,000 square feet of office space in the area. Among the newest is the NASA One office complex situated along Carlton Bayou in Nassau Bay, representing a $9 million investment. New office developments planned for the area will add some 300,000 square feet in office space in the next several years, binding the area from Clear Lake City to League City.

PART V

THE CULTURE tells about the exciting diversified cultural opportunities Houston can offer: museums and galleries, ballet, symphony, opera, theaters and libraries. The press, radio and television media and their service to the growing city and its residents are related. A delineation of education in Houston follows, including public and private institutions, colleges and universities, continuing and vocational education, as well as special courses. Subsequent sections describe health, education and research, and the medical center for which Houston has achieved international recognition.

ARTS

As the 1980s open, culture is abloom in Houston. Much of the dynamism invigorating the city's cultural life is stimulated by the increasingly international orientation of the city's business and professional communities, with an accompanying broadly based financial support of the arts. Memorable purchases by or for the city of outstanding pieces of sculpture provide significant art experiences for Houstonians. Music, ballet and experimental theater presentations all find enthusiastic response from Houston viewers.

THE CULTURAL CLIMATE

To coordinate cultural programs the city of Houston established the Municipal Arts Commission in 1964. Through the activities of the commission, funding for cultural programs has now improved significantly. Under the auspices of the Houston Chamber of Commerce, corporations and firms in the city are able to make a one-time financial contribution for cultural programs by donating money to the Combined Arts Corporate Campaign. This concept of support for the arts is modeled after an approach adopted by the National Commission

The impressive Jesse H. Jones Hall for the Performing Arts.

for the Arts. Another source of funding has been the use of a percentage of hotel occupancy taxes to support the arts. In 1978, the city was able to raise over $1.2 million through this source.

Support for the arts on both individual and corporate levels mirrors the city's financial health, indicated by the fact that fund raising campaigns meet and often exceed their goals. When the Ford Foundation gave the Alley Theatre a $1 million construction grant requiring matching local funds, the matching million was raised in almost 60,000 individual gifts, with Houston Endowment contributing the civic center site on which the Alley Theatre now stands. Other institutions have benefited from similar public spiritedness, such as that of Miss Nina J. Cullinan, who contributed $400,000 for the construction of Cullinan Hall, a glass and steel exhibition hall added to the Museum of Fine Arts in 1954. The Brown Foundation's donation of $4 million for the construction of Brown Pavilion, the most recent addition to the museum and the $2 million Cullen Foundation contribution for acquisitions in memory of Agnes Cullen Arnold, for the Museum of Fine Arts, have also helped the arts to flourish in Houston.

A new element in Houston's cultural life is the international perspective as evidenced by subtle programming changes in the city's museums and concert halls. Houstonians have been able to view such exhibits as *Peru's Golden Treasures, Imperial China: Photographs 1850-1912, Costumes from the Arab World* and *MA: Space and Time in Japan,* through the cooperation and efforts of foreign consulates, the Institute of International Education (I.I.E.) and other local institutions.

Excellent cultural facilities exist in the city. The Oscar Holcombe Civic Center is the cultural nexus of the city. The civic center complex includes Jesse H. Jones Hall for the Performing Arts, the Coliseum, the Music Hall and the Albert Thomas Convention and Exhibit Center.

Jones Hall, with a seating capacity of up to 3,001, houses the Houston Symphony, Houston Grand

The Sam Houston Coliseum seats 11,500 and includes the Music Hall with an additional 3,036 seats.

Opera and Houston Ballet. Opened in 1966, the hall is a frequently used prizewinning building, with elegant teakwood interior panelling.

Built in the 1930s, the 3,036-seat Music Hall offers a pleasant and practical setting for concerts, stage revues, recitals, lectures and convention meetings.

The well-equipped Sam Houston Coliseum, a 11,500-seat arena plus a 50,000-square-foot exhibit space, lends itself equally well to conventions, trade shows, meetings, sporting events, concerts, ice shows and circuses.

Albert Thomas Convention and Exhibit Center is the fourth and newest of the civic center buildings.

Houston Symphony Orchestra performs at Jones Hall, which also houses the Houston Grand Opera and Houston Ballet.

The Albert Thomas Convention and Exhibit Center, the fourth and newest of the civic center buildings, has 300,000 square feet of space and the ability to serve a banquet of over 3,000. Apart from hosting national conventions, the Albert Thomas Convention Center provides facilities for antique shows and auctions, flower shows and automobile and boat exhibits. Thirty-five hundred vehicles can be accommodated in two underground parking garages.

All of the major art forms—music, opera, theater, ballet, modern dance and visual arts—thrive in Houston. All are affected by the stimulus of the vision of unlimited horizons which pervades the business, scientific and educational communities.

MUSIC

Miss Ima Hogg was instrumental in founding the Houston Symphony Society in 1913. The group was reorganized in 1931 with a full-time conductor. Beginning in the 1950s, and later under the direction of General Maurice Hirsch in 1960, the Houston Symphony emerged as a national institution. It attracted such international conductors as Efrem Kurtz, Ferenc Fricsay, Leopold Stokowski, Sir John Barbirolli, Andre Previn, Andre Kastalonetz, Sir Thomas Deasham, Sir Malcolm Sargeant and Lawrence Foster. The Symphony Society has evolved into a nationally acclaimed orchestra of 94 musicians.

It performs numerous concerts for children, and thousands of children attend each year. Many concerts are played in Texas points, while tours by the orchestra have been conducted in cities throughout the United States, Canada and Mexico. In cooperation with the Houston Parks and Recreation Department, the Symphony Society provides free open-air concerts during the summer at Hermann Park's Miller Outdoor Theatre and at other places in the city. The symphony musicians also provide accompaniment for opera, dance and other special presentations and are active locally in music education and chamber music. These musicians provide a substantial number of teachers of music in the area schools and colleges.

Various other symphony ensembles have sprouted in Houston, some of which also perform at Jones Hall. Among these are the Houston Pops Orchestra, Houston Youth Symphony, Symphony North, Houston All-City (school) Orchestra and the orchestras of the Houston Baptist University, Texas Southern University and the University of Houston. Houston's claim to the title of Space City of the world was recently confirmed and enhanced musically when the famous composer Karl Heinz Stockhausen directed the first presentation outside of Germany of his opera *Sirius* at the University of Houston in Clear Lake. Other major musical groups in Houston include the Contemporary Chamber Ensemble, Houston Chamber Orchestra, Lyric Art String Quartet, Shepherd Quintet, Virtuoso Quartet, Woodwinds of Houston, Bay Area Chorus, Community Chorus of Houston Parks and Recreation, Concert Choral Society of Houston and the Gilbert and

Sullivan Society of Houston. The Houston Symphony Chorale, the Society for the Preservation and Encouragement of Barber Shop Quartet Singing in America, Sweet Adelines, Tuesday Musical Club, American Guild of Organists, Houston Classic Guitar Society, Houston Harpsichord Society and the Music Guild represent still other musical ensembles.

On the lighter side of the music scene, concerts and solo performances by recording stars and artists can be enjoyed in sports arenas and concert halls. Clubs and restaurants offer jazz, rock and rhythm-and-blues. Country and western music, on the air, in outdoor concerts and in restaurants, perpetuates Houston's frontier heritage. Gilley's, a country and western club in nearby Pasadena, (the largest of its kind in the nation) was recently chosen as the setting of a movie, *Urban Cowboy*, starring John Travolta.

OPERA AND DANCE

Formed in 1956 as a professional company, the Houston Grand Opera has become one of the leading performing arts companies in the nation. It presents a full season of varied productions at Jones Hall, including both foreign language and English versions, as well as an annual free Spring Opera Festival in the Miller Outdoor Theatre. It has enjoyed high acclaim for presentations in New York, Washington and other cities. Plans are in process for the erection of a magnificent Opera House designed specifically for the performance of opera.

The highly acclaimed Houston Ballet, founded in 1955, and formed into a professional company in 1969, offers a complete season of performances as well as performances on tour. Like the symphony, the Houston Ballet conducts classes for both children and adults. Various other dance groups provide performances and instructions throughout the city. Among these are the Houston Jazz Ballet, Houston Contemporary Dance Theatre, Dance Center, Discovery Dance Group, Houston Allegro Ballet, Metropolitan Concert Ballet Group, Royal Academy Ballet Theatre and the Space Dance Theater.

Traveling dance groups that have recently toured Houston include the Royal Ballet, Alvin Ailey Dance Company, Joffrey Ballet, Les Ballets Trocadero de Monte Carlo, Hungarian Folk Ballet, Lucnica Czechoslovakian Folk Ballet and Yatran Ukrainian Dance Company.

A scene from Der Rosenkavalier, *one of many operas performed at Jones Hall.*

The Nina Vance Alley Theatre seats approximately 1,200 people.

THEATER

Theater lovers in Houston may choose from a wide selection of productions performed by professional, amateur and dinner theater groups. In 1946, a high school drama teacher, the late Nina Vance, armed with penny postcards, launched a campaign to establish a community theater, and the Alley Theater, now renamed Nina Vance Alley

Mexican dances, one of the many attractions held at the Miller Outdoor Theatre in Hermann Park.

Theatre, was born. Housed in one of the most sophisticated theater buildings in the world, the widely acclaimed Nina Vance Alley Theatre stages major dramatic works, such as Mikhail Roschin's *Echelon,* a contemporary Russian play directed by its original Russian director, Galina Volchek.

Theatre Under The Stars (TUTS) is another popular theatrical organization. It has expanded its annual free summer productions of lavish musicals to include similar presentations in a season of professional productions. It offers four productions at the Music Hall. TUTS also operates the Humphreys School of Musical Theatre.

Other notable professional and amateur theatrical organizations in the Houston area include the Country Playhouse, Alief Community Theater, Baytown Little Theatre and Channing Players. Clear Creek Community Theater, Dean Goss Dinner Theatre, Hamster Theater, Chocolate Bayou Theater, Houston Shakespeare Society, After Dinner Players, Main Street Theatre, Equinox Theatre, Comedy Workshop, Theatre Suburbia, Theatre Showcase, Windmill Dinner Theatre and area university players groups represent additional theatrical organizations.

MUSEUMS

Houston takes pride in its museums, and in contrast to most other major American cities, admission to all of these museums is free. The Museum of Fine Arts houses an expanding and significant collection of art in its main location and provides a continuing series of major loan exhibitions featuring fine and applied arts. At another location is Bayou Bend, the former home of the Hogg family, donated by Miss Ima Hogg to the museum. Bayou Bend features one of the foremost collections of American furniture and decorative arts of the period from the seventeenth to the mid-nineteenth centuries. Aside from the Bayou Bend collection of decorative arts, the museum exhibits the Samuel H. Kress collection of 26 paintings of the Spanish and Italian Renaissance, the Hogg collection of paintings by

Frederic Remington, and part of the Percy S. Straus collection of old masters and French impressionists. The museum also conducts a professional art school with junior and adult classes, called the Alfred Glassell School of Art. The school occupies a splendid separate building, erected especially to house the classes and exhibits dedicated to teaching the visual arts.

The Contemporary Arts Museum offers exhibitions of modern works, not limited to paintings and sculpture. Unlike traditional museums, it exhibits the work of artists in different fields and media (such as woodwork, music, dance and film), emphasizes regional art, and distributes Texas art exhibits throughout the state. The Contemporary Arts Museum was started as an amateur effort in 1949. Patrons John and Dominique de Menil agreed to underwrite the salary of the museum's director and the museum is now a major cultural force in the city.

Set on four acres of land at Hermann Park stands a three-level museum which includes the Houston Museum of Natural Science, the Museum of Medical Science and the Burke Baker Planetarium. This museum encompasses the Isaac Arnold Hall of

Space, which has an open diorama depicting the amazing Mercury, Gemini and Apollo manned spacecraft missions; the Moody Foundation Hall of Chemistry; the W. W. Fondren Hall of Energy; the J. Brian Eby Hall of Gems and Minerals, which houses one of the largest amethyst specimens as well as a wide variety of sparkling gems and minerals; and the Roy and Lillie Cullen Hall of Communications, highlighted by a collection of antique instruments. The main level features displays ranging from dinosaurs to petroleum science as well as artifacts of North and South Americans. On the third level are halls devoted to Texas historical scenes and wildlife dioramas, murals depicting Africa's magnificent wildlife and geography and a marine display emphasizing Gulf coastal habitats of Texas. The Museum of Medical Science, also on the third level, features a $25,000 transparent female anatomical mannequin. Capable of revolving, it is equipped with a recorded message that describes the different parts of the body

Ima Hogg's Bayou Bend mansion, donated to the Museum of Fine Arts, houses an outstanding collection of furniture and decorative arts.

Brown Pavilion at the Museum of Fine Arts.

as they individually light up. The Burke Baker Planetarium invites spectators to a dazzling show of the bright lights of passing meteors, stars, comets and other wonders of the universe projected onto an overhead dome, 50 feet in diameter, simulating the night sky.

A place of meditation and a gathering place for religious events, concerts and international colloquia, the Rothko Chapel was commissioned by Dominique de Menil and her husband, the late John de Menil. The chapel contains 14 huge abstract canvasses of the late Mark Rothko, illuminated only by a single skylight. The effect is one of utter simplicity. The paintings conjure up a quiet, sombre and meditative atmosphere. The chapel is highly acclaimed as Rothko's masterpiece and it was his final work before his demise. The *Broken Obelisk,* a striking sculpture commemorating the late Dr. Martin Luther King, is an elongated metal cube of cor-ten steel; the creation of sculptor and painter Barnett Newman, it rises like King Arthur's sword, Excalibur, from a rectangular pond in the chapel park.

The San Jacinto Museum of History is housed at the base of the 570-foot San Jacinto Monument on the San Jacinto Battlefield. The museum depicts the cultural development of Texas in chronological order from the American Indian civilizations of.the New World through the time of the Texas Republic to its current status as the Lone Star State. The museum's exhibits include documents, maps, engravings, paintings, pioneer tools, coins, costumes, guns and other weapons.

Rice Museum, on the Rice University campus, and the Sarah Campbell Blaffer Gallery, at the University of Houston, feature exhibits of major international works of art.

ART EXHIBITS AND GALLERIES

Taking advantage of the favorable weather conditions, various outdoor art festivals are held throughout the year in Houston. The Main Street Festival, one of the largest public art festivals in the nation, is held two weekends each spring. The festival showcases work by hundreds of artists and craft people, simultaneously presenting continuous entertainment on several outdoor stages. The Westheimer Colony Art Festival, held in the spring and fall, features the works of local and national artists. The Houston Festival, international in scope, brings together artists and art work from all over the world.

One of the important developments on the Houston arts scene since the early 1950s is the emergence of art galleries for fun and profit. Prior to World War II, art works and antiques were acquired elsewhere. Only a few antique shops, notably Herzog's, The Shabby Shoppe and James Bute's paint store offered art works and antiques for sale.

Art galleries that have sprung up since the 1950s include the Dubose Gallery, opened by Ben Dubose in 1966, and Meredith Long's Houston Galleries, opened in 1957. Each of these galleries has focused attention on local, national and international artists in Houston. Opening with the "Paris School" paintings of Herbert Meers and David Adickes, Dubose later added the monochromatic landscapes of Henri Gadbois. Meredith Long's Houston Galleries made headway in 1959 with an exhibition of the works of Childe Hassam, several of which were sold for $6,000 to $9,000. Today, in short, a good number of Houston galleries exhibit the works of local artists. Dorothy Hood, the abstract painter known for her large canvases of pale, dream-like forms, impressionist William Anzalone, muralist John Biggers, Charles Schorre, Lamar Briggs, abstract master of acrylic technique, and phantasist Kelly Fearing have gained exposure through these galleries.

MEDIA

Newspapers, magazines, television and radio programs influence the culture of people everywhere. In Houston, a city with a growing communications network, the diversity of cultural appeal demonstrated by the media reflects the wide background of today's Houstonians.

DAILY PAPERS

Since the 1830s, when the *Telegraph-Texas Register* relocated in the city, Houston has always had a newspaper. Continuing that tradition in the 1980s are the city's two major newspapers, the Houston *Post* and the Houston *Chronicle*. The *Post* is the older of the two, but the *Chronicle* has the larger circulation.

Although the current *Post* began publication in 1885, it evolved from the firm foundation of an existing tradition, the *Telegraph-Texas Register*. When Rienzi Johnston and Julius Watson purchased their rights and created the *Post*, one of Johnston's proteges was young William P. Hobby who worked his way up the ladder to attain the position of managing editor in 1905. Later, Hobby became governor of Texas, but returned to the *Post* at the end of his tenure as its president. In 1931, he married Oveta Culp, who later became the *Post's* editor-in-chief and chairman of the board, a position she still holds today. The *Post,* with its simple, straightforward format, prides itself on reporting complete stories. Reporter Gene Goltz received a Pulitzer Prize in 1966 for doing just that. The *Post* entered the 1970s with a move to its present Southwest Freeway location and in 1979 it registered the nation's largest annual readership gain. The *Post* has a daily circulation of 327,858.

Original building of the Houston Post *which began publishing a paper in 1885 after acquiring the* Telegraph-Texas Register.

The *Chronicle* began publication in 1901. Today, it ranks third in the United States in advertising; it is first in the Southwest in terms of circulation and amount of classified ads. Much of this success can be attributed to the man who took over the paper in 1926, builder-philanthropist Jesse H. Jones. He moved the *Chronicle* to its current building at Texas and Travis streets, quarters which he continued to expand in later years. The *Chronicle* also publishes the only locally edited weekly rotogravure, *Texas Magazine*. The *Chronicle* has a daily circulation of 348,601.

WEEKLIES

The best known of the local weeklies is the *Houston Business Journal*, covering local business facts and opinions. In February 1980, the Scripps-Howard chain purchased Cordovan Publishing Company, the original publishers of *Houston Business Journal*.

Nine of Houston's neighborhood community newspapers, which were owned individually or by small groups, were purchased in 1979 by News America, Inc., of New York, with the aim of making these papers, with 18 zoned editions, rival the two dailies in local news coverage. Their combined circulation is over 318,000, and they are distributed free on Wednesdays.

An older, established publication is the *Jewish Herald-Voice*, which carries the Jewish community's local, state and national news. Founded in 1908 by Edgar Goldberg, the current editor is Joseph Samuels. Regular issues of the tabloid-size weekly come out on Thursdays, and special magazines appear on the eve of the Jewish New Year and Passover.

Formerly called The *Houston Tribune*, The *Texas Tribune* is the "Voice of Free Enterprise." This conservative weekly, founded in 1964, emphasizes news and commentary with sections devoted to special events. It comes out on Thursdays and has a circulation of 23,000. Houston also has two black-oriented papers, the *Forward Times* and The *Informer*. The latter has been in circulation since 1893 and is published on Thursdays while the former, a Wednesday paper, is a winner of awards for community service. A Spanish language weekly, *El Sol of Houston*, appears on Tuesdays.

MONTHLIES

There are 26 monthly publications in Houston. Foremost among them is *Houston Magazine*, published by the Houston Chamber of Commerce. It focuses on business and civic affairs, dealing primarily with the arts and the economy. Annual features include "100 Top Public Locally Based Companies" (June), a convention guide (November), a report on office development projects (February), and a newcomer's guide (Spring). Its circulation exceeds 16,000.

Recently acquired by Dallas Southwest Media Corporation is *Houston City Magazine*. It began publication in 1977 as *In Houston*. A metropolitan magazine in its scope, *City* has regular departments and is heavily feature-oriented, with a circulation currently exceeding 50,000.

Houston Home/Garden gained a new logo during the 1979 streamlining of the magazine, but its format has not changed. It was and still is a hometown guide to living in Houston. Everything from decorating to landscaping is discussed. Two special gardening issues and an outdoor living publication are printed annually. With an over 92,000 circulation, *Houston Home/Garden* is the most widely distributed publication in Houston, aside from the two daily papers.

NEWS BUREAUS

News bureaus maintaining permanent offices in Houston include: Associated Press, *Chemical and Engineering News*, Fairchild Publications, *Forbes Magazine*, *Fortune Magazine*, Houston News Service, *Los Angeles Times*, McGraw-Hill (*Business Week*, *Chemical Engineering*, *Chemical Week*, World News Bureau), *Metro News*, NBC News, *Newsweek*, *The Journal of Commerce*, *The New York Times*, *The Oil and Gas Journal*, *Oil Daily*, *People Magazine*, Southwest Press Relations Newswire, *Texas Business*, *Time Magazine*, United Press International, *U.S. News and World Report*, *The Wall Street Journal* and *The Washington Post*.

RADIO STATIONS

The oldest radio station in Houston, *KPRC (950)*, started broadcasting in 1925. Until the beginning of World War II only three radio stations—*KPRC, KTRH* and *KXYZ* operated in the Houston area. Today, licensed AM and FM stations abound in the Houston greater metropolitan area. Of these, five stations play primarily rock music. *KULF AM (790)* is the only general AM rock station. On the FM wave bands *KRLY (93.7)* is heavily disco-oriented. *KAUM (96.5)*, Houston's only network locally owned-and-operated station (ABC), combines rock music with news; *KFMK (97.9)*, a recent rock entry, was formerly a religious station; *KILT (100.3)* features the popular "Jay and Jolly" morning show, and *KLOL (101.1)* plays progressive rock.

The formats of *KILT-AM (610)* and *KRBE-FM (104.1)*, both "Top 40" stations, are contemporary. *KCOH-AM, (1430)*, *KYOK-AM (1590)*, and *KMJQ-FM (102.1)* are the rhythm and blues frequencies. Country and western music has a large following in Houston, and several radio stations inluding *KIKK-AM (650)*, *KIKK-FM (95.7)*, *KFDR (105)*, *KENR-AM (1070)* and *KNUZ-AM (1230)* devote their entire programming to it. *KYND-FM (92.5)* and *KODA-*

FM (99.1) present beautiful music. The only middle-of-the-road and golden oldies station in Houston, *KQUE-FM (102.9),* is also one of the city's original FM stations. Paul Berlin, a local radio personality for the past 30 years, is heard on this station. Two AM stations, *KTRH (740)* and *KPRC (950),* offer news-talk-sports programming. *KTRH* is a CBS affiliate and the flagship station for the Houston Oilers. *KPRC,* affiliated with NBC, has been the flagship station for the Houston Astros games for almost 20 years. *KYOK-AM (1590)* is part of the National Black Network.

AM stations with various other formats include *KEYH (850), KLAT (1010)* and *KLVL (1480),* which broadcast in Spanish. Additionally, Houston AM radio includes *KRBZ (1460), KBUK (1360),*

The Houston Chronicle *ranks third in the nation in advertising and first in the Southwest in circulation.*

KFRD (980) and *KGBC (1540), KIKR (900), KILE (1400)* and *KXYZ (1320). KXYZ* is a religious contemporary station while *KHCB-FM (105.7)* also features religious programming. On the FM side, there is *KUHF (88.7),* National Public Radio station, noncommercial, playing jazz. *KPFT (90.1),* also noncommercial, has a controversial free-form style. *KLEF (94.5)* is Houston's only classical music station along with regular hourly news. It boasts the daily (8:30 A.M.) commentary by Houston's foremost commentator, award-winning Fred Nahas. *KGOL (107.3)* plays top 40 music and *KMCV (106.9)* is religious.

TELEVISION

There are three network affiliates, two independents, an educational channel and five cable TV companies. NBC, CBS and ABC are represented in Houston respectively through *KPRC* (Channel 2), *KHOU* (Channel 11) and *KTRK* (Channel 13).

KPRC was the first of the three to air in 1950. It soon became renowned for its excellent live remote broadcasts of news and sports events. In 1954, KPRC presented the first color program in the area and in 1965, it was the first local station to broadcast entirely in color. Today, it has Houston's largest local news department and originates some national network broadcasts. Its president, Jack Harris, is a well-known figure in the broadcasting industry. Anchorman Ron Stone has been called "the Walter Cronkite of Houston" and is highly regarded among his viewers, whom he greets with his familiar "welcome, neighbors" salutation.

Originally based in Galveston, *KHOU* moved to Houston in 1953 under the auspices of its current owners, the Corinthian Broadcast Corporation. It still maintains a permanent Galveston bureau. Over the years, *KHOU* set many local precedents. It was

Public television Channel 8, KUHT, the educational channel in process of filming PTV Potpourri.

the first station to begin daily editorials, engage an anchorwoman, hire a black anchorman and expand the 5:00 P.M. newscast to one hour. *News Center 11* is still the only hour-long news show in Houston. *KHOU* has advanced its programming outside of the news, most notably with "The Bum Phillips Show" and Houston's "PM Magazine." News remains its strong suit, however, and *KHOU* has had its share of great moments and newscasters. For instance, the 1961 coverage of Hurricane Carla brought national acclaim for *KHOU* reporter Dan Rather. Eventually Rather moved to the national news sector and gained acclaim on CBS's "60 Minutes" program and has since been named "CBS Evening News" anchorman, due to succeed fellow Houstonian Walter Cronkite in 1981. Current *KHOU* anchorman Steve Smith is by far a special favorite in Houston's living rooms, where his magnetic smile and easygoing bearing lend both charm and confidence to his professional and clear delivery of the area's daily news.

The ABC affiliate *KTRK*, Channel 13, began operating in Houston in 1954 as a full color station. Anchorman Dave Ward, unmatched with his unique, personal touch, lends its "Eyewitness News" a sincere air of expert reporting and creative interviewing style which Houstonians love and respect. Ward has led his station to first place in the ratings since 1977, and

Channel 2, KPRC, Houston's NBC affiliate, located on Southwest Freeway, energizes the airwaves with its broadcasting and news coverage.

is instrumental in building its special Houstonian image and its strong involvement in community affairs. The news program is also the stage for top rated, through controversial, consumer advocate Marvin Zindler, who has earned national fame with his highly successful campaign in defense of consumers and underdogs. *KTRK* lays claim to the biggest "first" in Houston: first area coverage of a local story via satellite, a story, appropriately, about the space shuttle. Local programs include "Good Morning, Houston," "Live at 5," and "Turn On," dealing with teenage problems. *KTRK* sponsors the Jefferson Awards, a national contest whose participants are locally chosen for noteworthy public service.

KRIV, Channel 26 is a local station acquired by the Metromedia network, which is also available on 35 CATV's with 180,000 subscribers. *KRIV's* ratings have since risen remarkably since it was taken over by Metromedia, which provides most of its programming and is noted for its production facilities and live-and-tape ability. The most popular of *KRIV's* offerings are telecasts of Houston Astros road games.

The top independent station in the city, *KHTV*, Channel 39, is also the most powerful station on the Gulf Coast, with a five-million-watt signal reaching over 260,000 CATV homes on 54 cable systems. Owned by Gaylord Broadcasting Company, *KHTV* is a programming innovator. Originator of the five minute hourly news capsule, "News Before the Hour," Channel 39 is a founding station of Operation Prime Time mini series. *KHTV* is also a top ranking producer of commercials and programs. It has complete videotape and modern studio facilities, including a news transmitter and plans for satellite service in the Southwest.

The format of *KUHT*, Channel 8, the educational channel, sets it apart from all of the local stations. As the first Public TV station to go on the air in the United States, *KUHT* broadcasts PBS programming almost exclusively. Public affairs oriented, Channel 8 presents many service subjects in its specials and on its seven regular shows. One program, "Sports Unlimited," is now nationally distributed. Funding for *KUHT* comes partially from program sponsorships and private contributions which are mostly through "Act for 8," a voluntary community support group. They hold four annual drives, the most familiar of which is the *KUHT* Auction, the on-air marathon of selling donated items for the support of Channel 8. The station has a monthly program guide, *The Public Times,* available by subscription.

Channel 11, KHOU-TV, with, from left, Alexis South, weather; Steve Smith, news; Amanda Arnold, news; Dan Patrick, sports.

Cable TV companies, still in their developmental stages, are Houston's newest TV family members. Each company has its own section of town within which to operate. Gulf Coast Cable TV, in the southwest and west, competes for most advanced network status with Warner Amex, which purchased Houston Cable TV in the Northwest. Gulf Coast aims for 25 active channels, a two-way system and a local origination facility for producing commercials. Warner Amex counters with plans to deliver 35 service channels. Storer, a network with an originating studio, owns the former Houston Community Cablevision territory in the northeast and the MECA in the southeast offers 25 channels. The smallest cable system, Westland Cable, is located in the southwest and plans a sitcom satellite service.

EDUCATION

Houston's formal educational institutions reflect its residents' increased cultural awareness, especially over the past 20 years when Houstonians and their institutions of learning have demonstrated a sharpened alertness to the state of the arts and a heightened willingness to contribute and be sensitive to their city's artistic climate.

Concern for education in Houston goes back to the 1830s when early attempts were made to structure the school system. Beginning with Mrs. E. A. Andrews' school in 1837, through Zerviah Noble's in 1851, most of these schools were run in the homes of the teachers providing a rudimentary form of education. Houstonians had to go elsewhere for college preparatory level studies. The year 1844 heralded the earliest effort to provide college preparatory studies, when H. F. Gillet opened the Houston Academy. The Academy was a forerunner of the city high school system. The private approach to education gave way in 1876 to the municipal controlled system.

From these modest beginnings Houston has become a leading educational center, attracting scholars, researchers and students from the nation and the world. Educational institutions, ranging from preschool through postgraduate levels, flourish in Houston and its greater metropolitan area. Nearly a dozen senior colleges and three junior colleges are within the city, and more than half a dozen other senior and junior colleges lie within commuting distance. Numerous commercial, trade and business schools open their doors to those seeking such instruction.

ELEMENTARY AND HIGH SCHOOL EDUCATION

Public education in Houston started in 1876, when Houstonians approved a city controlled system of free education for children up to age 14. Later, in 1923, direct city control over administrative and fiscal matters was eliminated when the Houston Independent School District (HISD) was created. Today, the Houston Public School System is the fifth largest in the nation, with over 193,000 pupils in attendance at all grade levels. As the fifth largest school district in the United States, the Houston Independent School District is able to offer its

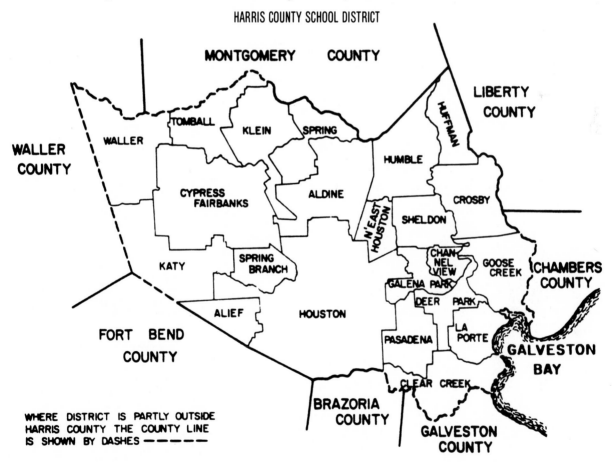

HARRIS COUNTY SCHOOL DISTRICT

WHERE DISTRICT IS PARTLY OUTSIDE HARRIS COUNTY THE COUNTY LINE IS SHOWN BY DASHES - - - - -

students the finest academic and vocational education in the Southwest. There are twenty-two school districts in Harris County. The HISD, due to its size and proximity to local businesses and community agencies, is available to offer more services to students than any other school district in the county.

Included among the district's programs is the HISD Magnet School Program. Under the magnet school concept, students residing anywhere in HISD may apply for admission to one of these special schools. The district offers fifty-six magnet programs. Each program emphasizes, in addition to the basic skills, studies in the fine arts, sciences, languages, math, engineering, literature, health and medical professions, vocational careers, performing and visual arts and classes for the academically gifted. Magnet programs are offered for all grade levels, from kindergarten through grade twelve. These schools include the Aerodynamics Academy; the College Prep High School; the Community High School, which promotes students' interest in their community at large; the Contemporary Learning Center, which meets the needs of those students not responding to traditional methods of education; the Foreign Language Academy; the Fundamental High School, which serves those students who need more help in vocational and technical training schools; the High School for the Performing and Visual Arts; the

The Statue of William Marsh Rice sits in the center of the quadrangle at Rice University, facing Lovett Hall.

Petro-Chemical Careers Institute; the School of Communications; and the Vanguard High School, designed for students gifted with general intellectual ability.

The student population of 193,000 is also eligible for other services, including academic counseling, limited health services, career counseling and other services not usually available in smaller districts. Also available are programs and services for students with special needs: those who are physically or mentally handicapped, deaf, blind, orthopedically handicapped or pregnant.

Academic excellence is one of the district's most important priorities. A basic skills program was instituted in 1974. Since that time, HISD student test scores on national basic skills tests on the elementary level have shown an increase in achievement. In fact, students in grades one through six have, for the most part, tested at or above the national levels for the last year. The most recent test score information comparing students from similar socio-economic backgrounds in HISD with those from the surrounding district showed HISD students outscoring their counterparts in other school districts and nationally by as much as seven months.

Community support for the district is seen by the overwhelming approval of voters in 1976 of a $297 million school bond program. This program, the School Facility Improvement Program, is a multi-year new school construction and renovation program

aimed at providing new schools where needed and upgrading the district's older schools. The bond issue was passed by more than a two to one margin by Houston voters and was made possible without a tax increase to taxpayers. The program is now into phase three, and most of the projects are well ahead of schedule.

As a result of Houston's annexation of outlying areas, several independent school districts are now within the corporate boundaries of the city of Houston, but operate independently of HISD. These school districts serve Houston's "bedroom communities" and are considered to be very successful. Among the highly rated districts are Spring Branch, Aldine, Alief, Cypress-Fairbanks and Klein, districts which enjoy a good reputation and attract parents seeking quality schools for their children. Other school districts in the area, are Channelview, Clear Creek, Crosby, Deer Park, Galena Park, Goose Creek, Huffman, Humble, Kirby, La Porte, North Forest, Pasadena, Sheldon, Spring and Tomball.

Parents who prefer private school education have many schools from which to choose. There are at least 19 parochial and private schools in the area which offer grades 1 through 12, while many others offer fewer grades. Among the highly rated private schools in Houston are St. John's School, Kinkaid, Duchesne Academy of the Sacred Heart, The Awty School, The Jewish Community Center and the Bryman School. These schools graduate many National Merit finalists and semifinalists and their students perform very well on the Scholastic Aptitude Test. Tuition in these schools ranges from under $1,500 a year for preschoolers to nearly $3,000 a year for students of high school age.

HIGHER EDUCATION

Until 1912, when the William Marsh Rice Institute for Literature, Science and Art opened, Houston had no institution of learning above the high school level. Today, Rice University is internationally acclaimed as a top ranking graduate and postgraduate school. It has rightly earned a reputation as the "Harvard of the South." A co-educational nonsectarian institution, the school started through a bequest left by William Marsh Rice, who at the time of his death in 1900 was considered one of the two wealthiest men in Texas. Princeton University's Dr. Edgar Odell Lovett, Rice's first president appointed in 1907, spent a year on a world tour recruiting faculty members. Scholars of world renown and statesmen such as Julian Huxley, Bernard Shaw, H.G. Wells, Woodrow Wilson and General John J. Pershing came to teach or lecture at the school. During Rice University's 1962 golden anniversary celebration, President John F. Kennedy accepted Rice's gift of a 1,000-acre site to the federal government for the space center and made his famous prediction that the United States would place a man on the moon before 1970.

Rice, which is internationally renowned for its outstanding science and engineering programs, also offers study in other major academic areas. Its million-volume library system, is one of the largest libraries in the Southwest. Rice maintains a low faculty-student ratio and has a limited enrollment of approximately 4,000 students.

The University of Houston grew out of the public school system. In 1927, the Houston Independent School District formed a Junior College division that offered courses at several high school campuses. Seven years later, it became a four year college with the authority to grant degrees. The University of Houston has Hugh Roy Cullen, Sam Taub, the M. D. Anderson Foundation and other individual donors to thank for its early growth and rapid development. Now a part of the state university system, the University of Houston is the largest university in the city. In its four campuses—Central Campus, Downtown College, Clear Lake and Victoria, it offers course work in most major areas of study to over 40,000 students in undergraduate through post-doctoral levels.

Texas Southern University also began in 1926 and was absorbed into the Houston Independent School District Junior College System in 1927. There it became known as Houston College for Negroes. It was later acquired by the state and it operated as the Texas State University for Negroes, adopting its present name in 1951, when it accepted students irrespective of color. The university offers course work in many major fields of study, granting degrees through the doctoral level. Texas Southern University has had several outstanding educators and alumni. Among its former presidents, Dr. Samuel Nabrit was the first black to serve on the prestigious Atomic Energy Commission and Dr. R. O. Lanier served as Ambassador to Liberia. Barbara Jordan, now a Professor of Government at the Lyndon B. Johnson School of Government at the University of Texas, served as Congresswoman and was a member of the committee to impeach President Richard M. Nixon during the Watergate break-in proceedings in Washington. Texas Southern University now has a student body of nearly 10,000.

Houston Baptist College was founded in 1960, but, awaiting construction of its facilities, did not open until 1963. In 1973, its name was changed to Houston Baptist University. The school was the first Baptist college in Texas to be located in a major metropolitan area. It provides a Christian liberal arts education for a limited number of qualified students. The university offers courses in most major academic areas, grants bachelor and master degrees and serves some 2,000 students.

The University of St. Thomas, founded by the Basilian Fathers in 1947, offers undergraduate work in most areas of the arts and sciences and grants

The modernistic Crooker Student Center at the University of St. Thomas.

master degrees in education and theology. It has approximately 2,000 students.

The Alfred C. Glassell, Jr., School of Art is a non-accredited art institution affiliated with the Museum of Fine Arts, offering art courses to 700 adults and 400 juniors of high school age and younger. Founded 50 years ago, it functions much like an art department of other universities. It now occupies a new and modern building erected to give it the needed facilities for its purposes.

Houston Community College, with over 30,000 students, is the largest community college system in the area. Like the University of Houston before it, the present community college program is an out-growth of the Houston Independent School District. Other local community colleges include the North Harris County Community College, with an enroll-ment of 5,000, and San Jacinto College, with an enrollment of 10,000.

There are several junior and senior colleges within commuting distance of Houston. Among these are two state universities, Huntsville's Sam Houston State University and the Prairie View

A & M University. Also within commuting distance are six junior colleges, the Alvin Community College, Brenham's Blinn College, Texas City's College of the Mainland, Baytown's Lee College and Galveston and Moody Colleges, both in Galveston.

Undergraduate and graduate medical education are strongly supported by the many institutions in Houston's internationally acclaimed Texas Medical Center, situated just southwest of the central business district. The M.D. Anderson Foundation was the motivating force behind the development of Houston as a great center of health, education, study and practice. In 1943, the city sold the Foundation 134 acres adjacent to Hermann Park. At that time, the only medical facility in the area was Hermann Hospital, built in 1925. The Texas Medical Center Corporation was formed in 1945 to oversee the development of the property. Since that time, the Texas Medical Center has grown incredibly fast, and now occupies over 320 acres. Today, as a result of the work of famed heart surgeons, Drs. Michael DeBakey and Denton Cooley, it is recognized worldwide as a center for heart surgery. The researchers and technicians of the M.D. Anderson Hospital and Tumor Institute have gained international recognition for their achievements in cancer research and therapy. Many other individuals and institutions within the Texas Medical Center have contributed to its success as a world leader in medical education and research.

One of the center's oldest institutions is the Baylor College of Medicine. The only private medical school in Texas, Baylor was founded in Dallas in 1900, moved to Houston in 1943, and, in 1969, separated from its parent institution, Baylor University, a Baptist school in Waco.

The medical center's largest institution is the multi-unit University of Texas Health Science Center, the inclusive name applied to the many University of Texas institutions located in the Texas Medical Center. Among these institutions are: the Cancer Center (M.D. Anderson Hospital and Tumor Institute), the new U.T. Medical School, the Graduate School of Biomedical Sciences, the Dental Branch and the Dental Science Institute, the School of Public Health, the School of Allied Health Sciences, the School of Nursing, the Speech and Hearing Institute, and the Division of Continuing Education.

The TSU cheerleaders and their mascot, a pink bunny, raise the spirits of the spectators at a football game.

Other Texas Medical Center institutions include Texas Woman's University-Houston Center, the Texas Institute for Rehabilitation and Research, the Texas Research Institute of Mental Sciences, the University of Houston College of Pharmacy and the Institute of Religion and Human Development.

Additional Texas Medical Center institutions include, Ben Taub General Hospital, the City of Houston Department of Public Health, the Harris County Medical Society, Hermann Hospital, the Methodist Hospital, St. Luke's Episcopal Hospital, the Shriners' Hospital for Crippled Children, Texas Children's Hospital, Texas Heart Institute, and the Houston Academy of Medicine-Texas Medical Center Library. Another associated institution, the College of Nursing of Prairie View A & M University, is located away from the complex, in the southwestern part of Houston, and yet another is the University of Texas Medical Branch at Galveston.

Legal education is offered at three major law schools: the Bates College of Law of the University of Houston, the Thurgood Marshall School of Law of Texas Southern University, and South Texas College of Law.

There are three religious educational institutions in Houston: Gulf Coast Bible College, Southern Bible College and Texas Bible College, with an aggregate enrollment of 20,300 students. Houston Baptist University, the University of St. Thomas and the Institute of Religion also offer courses in the field of religion.

PART VI

THE LEISURE LIFE deals with another side of life in Houston: that of fun and games, food and wine, shows and plays, parks and resorts. Considered an ideal convention city because of the number and variety of its hotels, restaurants, and clubs, Houston provides visitors and residents alike with an unusual mixture of sophisticated cuisine, music and art. It is a haven for fun loving explorers of night-life and devotees of sports, be they participants or spectators. All these exist side by side with the regional specialties of the American west, such as Texan and Mexican cookery, bronco busting and rodeo, hunting and fishing, swimming and boating, hiking and biking, riding and walking, camping and outdoor barbecues. And thus we round out the success story of the city of destiny, while the next chapter is being written . . .

OUTDOORS

Houstonians have neither forgotten nature nor neglected the need for recreation. The city offers its residents numerous parks, resorts and indoor and outdoor activities for adults and children. At present, Houston has 276 parks encompassing 6,133 acres of land and 12,236 acres of water. These parks include five 18-hole golf courses, three tennis centers, 52 community recreation centers, 85 neighborhood tennis courts, 38 swimming pools and 287 softball, baseball, football, soccer and rugby fields. Many of these recreational facilities, available to the public, are utilized by the Houston Parks & Recreation Department (HPRD) for classes in everything from arts, crafts, dance and drama to sports for children and adults.

Park visitors may pursue independently such outdoor activities as jogging, camping and biking, during the winter and summer. Many parks offer riding trails, playgrounds, water sports, picnicking and nature study. Residents may enjoy gymnastics, square dancing and round dancing. Children six years and up may learn judo, karate and self-defense in Houston parks and therapeutic recreation for the blind, deaf, developmentally disabled and occupationally handicapped is also available.

Houston is particularly proud of its exer-trails. The Memorial Trail, a $100,000 three-mile, rotted pine bark loop beginning west of the Memorial Tennis Courts, drew 879,000 exercisers in 1979. Recently completed, the Braeswood Exer-Trail runs from Hermann Park to Bissonnet at the Southwest Tennis Center, and an additional ten miles to Mason Park will be ready in 1980-1981. Unusually enough, Houston will feature an exer-trail for the handicapped, opening in Hermann Park in July, 1980.

The Houston Parks Department is now implementing a three year, $40 million appropriation to establish more "passive recreation space" parks. These park spaces are especially designed for children

Children participating in a project sponsored by the arboretum at Memorial Park.

and the elderly. In addition, a group known as the Park People, has come together within the past year to promote park land acquisition, parks legislation

Tourists at the Aline McAshan Botanical Hall in Houston's Arboretum and Botanical Gardens, Memorial Park.

and donation of park space. The most significant donation to date has been the Brown Foundation's gift of Herman Brown Park in Northeast Houston, an 850-acre plot valued at $10 million.

Most Houston parks devote themselves to nature and recreation. Neighborhood parks abound, but for a variety of activities there are two large parks, Hermann and Memorial. Perhaps the most versatile of the two is Hermann Park. South of the central business district and bordering the Texas Medical Center complex, Hermann Park encompasses 410 acres of well kept area. It features the most elaborate playground in the city, along with picnic areas, a recreation center, a golf course, minitrain rides, fishing ponds, horse and jogging trails, ball fields and "places to visit." The last include the Hermann Park Garden Center, a meeting place for botanical groups, a site for flower shows and the home of three beautiful gardens (rose, camellia and fragrant), through which visitors may wander. From here visitors can reach the Houston Zoological Gardens by foot. The Zoological Gardens contain both a main zoo and a children's zoo. A large variety of animals reside in both gardens and cages, making for a day of fun and communing with nature. Nearby centers of interest include the Museum of Natural Science, the Planetarium and Miller Theatre, the outdoor haven for many free spring and summertime cultural events.

Houston's largest park, Memorial Park, extends for miles in every direction. On a sunny Sunday some 20,000 people will flock to Memorial Park where Houstonians can partake in jogging, golfing, swimming, baseball, tennis, soccer, polo, archery and rugby. However, no camping is allowed. The large Houston Park and Recreation Department greenhouse, which supplies greenery to the city, is also in Memorial Park.

Houston is the hub of a veritable resort area which surrounds the city. The white sandy beaches and warm waters of the Gulf of Mexico are fifty miles to the south of the city and the Texas Hill Country with its piney woods, ranches, lakes and streams is within driving distance from the city to the northwest.

Houston's highway and freeway systems afford easy access to Galveston Island, fifty miles to the south. Often referred to as Houston's playground, Galveston is a popular beach retreat for swimming, sunbathing and deep-sea fishing.

Another popular recreation area south of Houston is the Sylvan Beach and Pavilion, a Harris County facility for outdoor recreation located at the La Porte section of Galveston Bay. Open throughout the year for fishing, it offers picnic areas, playgrounds, boat launches and an air-conditioned banquet and dance pavilion for private parties.

North of Houston are three lakes offering a recreational haven. Lake Houston is located in the northeast quadrant of Harris County, just east of Humble. Lake Houston is a man-made lake on the San Jacinto River, created in 1954. It is used largely as an arena for water skiers and small-boat sailors and is also a fisherman's haven. The lake teems with channel catfish, blue catfish, black bass, perch, crappie and yellow catfish. Lake Houston is bordered on its south shore by Alexander Deussen Park, which offers such public facilities as picnicking areas, concessions, camping, pavilion and free boat launching. Atascocita Country Club, a private membership organization, is located on the west end of the lake.

Lake Livingston is both the largest and the deepest of the three lakes. It has a shoreline of 650 miles and lies almost midway between Interstate 45, at the northern end near Huntsville, and US highway 59, at the southern end at Livingston. Of the three lakes, Livingston offers the widest range of accommodations, with everything from public camping sites to private

Children's activities in the arboretum.

developments and a large-scale resort, including two restaurants and elegant overnight facilities.

Lake Conroe is the area's newest artificial lake and one of the best black bass havens in Montgomery County. This clear water, 20,985-acre reservoir began

Bicycles in the park, waiting for someone to take them places.

filling in 1973. It is located about 50 miles from downtown Houston, 25 miles north of the burgeoning FM-1960 area, and about four miles west of Interstate 45 at Conroe. Created on the San Jacinto River, it is 19 miles long and five miles wide.

Major resort and residential developments have sprouted up around Lake Conroe. Two popular ones are Walden and Corinthian Point. Walden features a marina, clubhouse, golf course, tennis courts and swimming pool. Corinthian Point is less than a mile away from the Sam Houston National Forest. Its Yacht and Racquet Club provides tennis courts, a swimming pool, boat docks and boat storage.

Located about 25 minutes from downtown Houston is Woodlands. Covering 2,500 acres, this resort includes residences, a racquet club, two swimming pools, bike trails and an equestrian center. It has two championship golf courses, one of which is the site of the famous Houston Open.

Working ranches also appeal to many Houstonians. One of them, the Nine Bar Ranch in Hempstead, stretching over 4,000 acres, raises registered Santa Gertrudis cattle. Individual group tours are available to the Nine Bar Ranch.

Young Houstonians have a choice of a variety of available activities. Summertime, in particular, offers children many fun activities, including day camps, library programs, zoological gardens, museum programs and amusement areas. In over 50 neighborhood centers, the summer is the time for a veritable explosion of activities. Supervised classes in arts and crafts, drama, dancing, swimming, piano, sewing, music and karate are available to children at little or no cost.

The Boy Scouts, Camp Fire Girls, Girl Scouts, Texas Agricultural Extension Service (4-H Clubs) and the salesmanship Club Camp for children represent a wide range of group and camping activities for young people, which also includes scout troop participation for the handicapped child. Scout activities are part of many community agencies and organizational programs. The YMCA on Allen Parkway has all-day and half-day summer camps. Activities include swimming, gymnastics, nature studies, arts and crafts and cooking. Weekly field trips are available for kindergarten through eighth-grade children.

Some children's activities continue throughout the year. For example, Houston and Harris County libraries serve as centers for youngsters year-round. The main library, in addition to operating a bookmobile, offers a year-round weekly schedule of ASPCA-sponsored pet care classes, craft sessions, puppet and magic shows, films and story hours.

The Children's Zoo, occupying about two acres at the south end of the Houston Zoological Gardens in Hermann Park, attracts many youthful Houstonians. At the entrance to the Children's Zoo is the Aquatunnel, an amazing two-unit display which allows underwater viewing of fish and mammals. This part of the zoo is a complex which permits children to pet, feed, and observe young domestic and gentle wild animals. Elementary and junior high school children can paint animals during June and July.

The artistically inclined youngster can find self-expression in creative workshops at the Contemporary Arts Museum. Classes in painting, drawing, drama, dance and film-making are available for ages four through twelve. The Museum of Fine Arts also has educational programs and exhibits for children.

Children who are interested in science will be fascinated by the Museum of Natural Science, the Medical Museum, and the Burke Baker Planetarium.

The most popular amusement park for the youngster remains, undoubtedly, the 65-acre Astroworld, boasting 11 "adventure worlds" and over 100 rides, shows and other attractions. For the very young, there is the Magical World of Marvel McFey with rides and a play area. Peppermint Park, in addition, is an all weather kiddie park, complete with rides and

Magic and music show performed by the Enchanted Animals at Astroworld's Children's World.

facilities for birthday parties, located in the northwest part of town.

For preschool-age children there is a wide variety of day care centers. These are operated by national chains and franchises, private individuals, churches, community agencies and educational organizations. Cost varies with the nature of the center. The University of Houston, Texas Southern University and the University of St. Thomas have child development centers and preschool programs. The University of Houston and the medical center have day care programs for the children of students and employees. All reputable day care operations are state-licensed.

Many areas in and around Houston afford outdoor activities for both young and older Houston residents. The Arboretum and Botanical Garden, on Woodway at Loop 610, have much to offer the curious and energetic youngster. With five miles of trails and over 100 species of trees and plants, the arboretum is ideal for hiking. Untouched nature and various wildlife reflect the area as it was before the city of Houston came into existence. Guided tours are provided on Sundays, but visitors are free to explore on their own. The Botanical Hall is the locale of special children's and adults' nature courses, exhibits and features. Classes on birds, insects, mammals and weather are held in the Botanical Hall for seven to twelve-year-olds. Membership in the Houston Arboretum and Botanical Society entitles a family or individual to participate in these courses and events.

The Armand Bayou Park is an excellent example of ecological preservation. Found just off Bay Area Boulevard in the Pasadena-Clear Lake area southeast of Houston, Armand is a unique estuarine bayou, flowing through three ecological zones; piney woods, Gulf coast prairie and salt marsh. These provide visitors with a panorama of vegetation and wildlife. Boat rides are offered Wednesdays through Sundays, at 10:00 A.M. and 2:00 P.M. A nature center for birdwatchers opens at dawn on the first and third Saturdays of each month. Guided hikes are conducted at 2:00 P.M. each Saturday by reservation. Armand Bayou Park is open 9:00 A.M. to 5:00 P.M. daily except Monday.

Camping facilities, in addition, are available at several area parks for those who want to "rough it." Bear Creek Park, on Clay Road off FM-1960, is one of the largest. There is a seven-day limit to campers, but much to do during your stay. Water, showers, restrooms and electricity are available as well as picnic tables, shelters, barbecue pits and sheds. It offers hiking and biking trails, fishing in a creek, three complete golf courses (useable for a small fee) with a pro shop and motorcycle race trails. Gates close nightly, so campers need to arrive before 10:00 P.M.

Harris County's Alexander Deussen Park, on Highway 90 by Lake Houston, allows up to two weeks camping. Facilities include boating and fishing on the lake, private concession stands and a mini-

Young lady enjoying quiet and peaceful play in the park.

carnival. Parties may be arranged. Trailers are welcome and there are hookups to lease.

The Dwight Eisenhower Park, also located on Lake Houston, near US 59 North, provides a natural forest environment for camping. Other excellent camping parks are located at Melrose Park, on Canino Road at Carley, featuring tennis, baseball, golf, soccer areas and a meeting hall, and Spring Creek Park, on Brown Road in Tomball.

Three showcase parks are undergoing development. Tranquillity Park, opened in 1979, is a beautiful blend of modern landscaping and architecture in the heart of downtown Houston. It commemorates the Eagle's landing on the moon, guided from Houston and with Houstonian Neal Armstrong at its helm. Nearby at Main and Commerce, an expansion of Allen's Landing Park is underway. The broadest of the three, however, is the transformation of Buffalo Bayou into a linear park for outdoor activities. Covering miles of land and waterscape, the Buffalo Bayou project is one of the most far reaching park development plans in the city's history.

Another long term project is the Cypress Creek Park project in North Houston. When this park opens in 1981, it will transform 4,000 acres of undeveloped land into a natural and recreational retreat. Divided into seven sections, each with its own name, Cypress Creek Park will be a Harris County park. Facilities there will include nature and biking trails, picnic areas, canoe ramps and overlooks, all following the path of Cypress Creek and Spring Creek. There will also be a separate children's playground and a boardwalk around a cypress swamp.

Besides outdoor park activities, other recreational facilities are too numerous to list. There are 33 private country clubs in the area, five golf courses in the park system and five major bikeways throughout Houston. The Mountain, Houston's manmade ski slope, is the only ski facility within the city, located at the intersection of US 59 South and 610 Loop east.

Since routes are not always for bicycles alone, watchfulness is necessary on Houston's numerous bikeways. The Parks Department has maps that distinguish exclusive bike trails, road-edge bike lanes, and bike routes shared with main traffic roadways.

The southernmost and longest bikeway is the Brays Bayou Trail, which begins as a bike route from US 59 south to Rice University, crossing Main Street into Hermann Park. There the bike trail begins, routing the biker through Hermann Park out to a parallel course with Brays Bayou. This scenic route takes the rider past the University of Houston, in and through MacGregor Park, east and north to Gus Wortham and Mason Park, where a picnic and rest area is provided before starting back. For a shorter ride, the T.C. Jester Park trail borders the length of

the west side of the park and leaves the rider plenty of energy for the other sports activities the park offers.

Downtown, there are designated routes for bikers which allow access to the central business district, City Hall and Buffalo Bayou. These roads eventually lead to Sam Houston Park, to the west of which are the Buffalo Bayou and the Allen Parkway Trails. Linked by a trail on Sabine Road, the Bayou and Parkway trails (north and south of Buffalo Bayou, respectively) travel west from the central business district as far as Shepherd Drive. Public parking is available at the start of the trail. Along the way, the trail crosses Waugh Drive, but one may also turn left at this point. This is the beginning of a bike route through the Montrose area which continues south to Hermann Park and the Brays Bayou Trail. The **Bayou and Parkway trails feature large grassy** slopes and flower beds, and are considered the best maintained of the trails. Lighting enables them to remain open 24 hours a day, all week long.

The final and most familiar of Houston's bike trails is located in and around Memorial Park. The Memorial Trail is comprised of several smaller trails. One semi-circles the arboretum. Another runs north from San Felipe, through the southwest tip of the Park to North Post Oak Road. At North Post Oak, a north bound bike route takes the rider to a third trail: a bike lane on Memorial Drive going west to the Villages' residential suburbs. Normal bicycle safety rules need to be followed on all five bikeways to

A young ballet group performs in the open (in downtown Houston) at the annually held Houston Arts Festival.

insure safety, but basically one is free to ride and enjoy some of Houston's most beautiful areas at one's own pace.

In the more populous areas of Houston, especially in the sections just west of the 610 Loop, known as the "Magic Circle," outdoor activities often move indoors. Major shopping malls offer a variety of **sports. At the Galleria, a private club offers a** swimming pool, a jogging track, and ten covered tennis courts. In the middle of Galleria I is a public ice-scating rink. Near Sharpstown Center is the Sharpstown Ice Center, the city's newest and largest ice-skating rink. Tennis courts, racquetball clubs, recreation centers and other such facilities spring up inside buildings throughout this and other such prospering business areas throughout the Houston and greater Houston metropolitan area.

Hand in hand with the arboretums, nature trails, gardens and waterways of Houston are the natural science clubs which take an active interest in the affairs of the parklands. They include the Houston Aquarium Society, Houston Conchology Society, the Houston Gem and Mineral Society and the Outdoor Nature Club. Any of these organizations will gladly answer questions about Houston's natural parks and will welcome your membership.

DINING AND ENTERTAINMENT

For visitor and resident alike, there are numerous spots in Houston in which to enjoy an evening dining out. Houston's 15,000 restaurants include dining establishments whose menus vary from the distinctively Texan to almost any particular international cuisine a diner may desire.

Barbecue and other Texas specialties are served at *Otto's*, ten minutes from the central business district. *The Cellar Door*, with a Victorian and Western setting, serves smoked meats and char-broiled steaks. Portraits of Andrew Jackson and Robert E. Lee adorn the crystal-chandeliered *Confederate House*, where an extensive menu includes broiled lamb chops, fried shrimp and broiled Gulf fish. *Nanny's* decor includes old signs, posters and memorabilia, and the chicken-fried steak and beef stew can be eaten beneath a life-sized portrait of Nanny. An early 1900s railroad station and nine actual railroad cars provide the authentic atmosphere of *Railhead*, offering steaks, prime ribs, seafood and specialty foods, with music every evening in its club. Progressive country music singers entertain in a Texas Hill Country atmosphere at the *Texas Steak Ranch*. More railroad cars, converted into dining rooms, make *Victoria Station*, specializing in prime rib, a unique dining experience. *Cattle Rustlers* in the Sharpstown Mall off US 59 is one of Houston's restaurants featuring an "all you can eat" menu of steaks, baked potatoes and salad bar.

Another part of the native cuisine is seafood. *Don's Seafood Restaurant and Steak House,* close to Houston Intercontinental Airport, has crawfish etouffee, crawfish pie and jambalaya. Fresh lobster flown in from Maine, fresh chowder, Pacific red snapper and crab can be had at *The Hungry Tiger*, a restaurant designed to look like a bustling World War II air freight terminal. *Boston Sea Party* is another "all you can eat" for a flat fee local establishment with a sumptuous variety of sea food. The Kemah docks near *Jimmy Walker's Edgewater Restaurant & Supper Club* provide a special setting in which fresh Gulf seafoods can be devoured in glass-walled dining rooms offering a panoramic view of Clear Lake with its many sailing and motorized

Secretaries and executives enjoy their lunch hour in this downtown outdoor cafe.

pleasure craft. Nationally acclaimed *Kaphan's* restaurant near the Astrodome has a glass-enclosed garden room where Crab Imperial, fillet of trout almandine and prime sirloin strip can be enjoyed. A large variety of oyster dishes are prepared by Kaphan's chefs.

San Jacinto Inn is located near the San Jacinto Battlefield and serves all the seafood, hot biscuits and fried chicken one can eat. Founded in 1917, the inn specializes in seasonal crabs, shrimp and oysters.

Mexican food rounds out Houston's native fare. *Ninfa's Tacos Al Carbon* offerings include *queso a la parrilla* (Mexican fondu) and *sopaipillas* (pastry covered with powdered sugar and honey). *Prima's Mexican Restaurant and Outdoor Cantina* is known for *carne guisada* (well-seasoned stew), *huevos rancheros* (Mexican-styled eggs) and Mexican beer spiced with lime juice and salt. *Molina's Mexico City Restaurant* serves *enchiladas verdes* and frozen margaritas and also features a curio shop with Mexican goods. *El Chico International* has a chain of local restaurants famous for *cabrito* (goat) as well as for its standard Mexican foods, including tortillas, pralines, tamales, tacos and enchiladas.

Austrian food is available at *Restaurant Bismarck,* and the decor is old Vienna. Varieties of schnitzel, Viennese breast chicken and other German foods are featured at *Hofbraugarten* restaurant.

There are several Chinese restaurants in Houston. Szechuan (spicy) and Peking (mild) cuisine are featured at *Shanghai East* in the Galleria amid exquisite old Oriental tapestries, rattan furniture and hanging lanterns. *Hunan's* specializes in the spicy, but not oily or starchy foods of China's Hunan province. Cantonese food is found at several Houston establishments, including the *Ming Palace Restaurant*, which also features seafood and steak on the menu. Some of the best cooked Chinese dishes can be found, with a warm, personal service and reasonable price, at the charming, family-dining atmosphere of the *Lamp of China* on Katy Freeway at Antoine.

English fare is served at the *Red Lion Restaurant & Churchill Pub*, where prime beef and other typically British foods can be enjoyed in an Olde London atmosphere.

Houston has a wide variety of French restaurants. *Foulard's* serves a pale green, subtly seasoned puree called oyster bisque as well as trout Deguerre, a fresh sea trout with white sauce trimmed with minced parsley and fresh chopped tomatoes. Gourmet foods fill the menu at *Maxim's Restaurant Francais.* Capon with wild rice and black cherries, Chateau-

RIGHT: *Tony and Chef Frank proudly display one of the many sumptuous offerings at* Tony's Restaurant.

briand with sauce Bearnaise and red snapper saute are served at *Maxim's,* one of the few cordon bleu restaurants in the United States. *Tony's Restaurant,* featuring a wine cellar with over 120,000 vintage wines, has been described as the "Rolls Royce of Texas restaurants." Located in the heart of River Oaks, Virginia at Westhiemer, the prestigious Brownstone Restaurant, Club and Antique Gallery is a blend of a unique restaurant and club set in the splendor of museum-quality antiques ... all for sale.

Bouzouki music, Greek dances and Greek food are to be found at the *Athens Bar and Grill* near the ship channel. The menu features *spanakopita,* made of spinach and feta cheese, and *tiropitakia,* triangles of filo filled with feta.

Hot or mild curries, including chicken curry, are among the Indian cuisine items at the *Maharaja.* The largely vegetarian fare characteristic of India is also featured at *Tandoor's,* including *dal maharani* (a dish with creamed lentils, spices and onions), *channa masala* (chick peas cooked in spices) and *samosa* (crisp spiced patties of potatoes and peas).

South Pacific foods are a gourmet discovery at *Trader Vic's,* including Indonesian rack of lamb, *bongo bongo* soup and Hawaiian-style Chinese pake dinners.

Houston has an assortment of Italian restaurants. *Arno's* entrees include northern Italian dishes and *Renata's* specializes in veal, fettucini a la Alfredo, ossobuco and cannelloni.

The Window Box Restaurant looks out upon the eye-catching interior of the Hyatt Regency Hotel.

RIGHT: *The multi-level Galleria Shopping complex includes a full-sized ice skating rink open to the public.*

Japanese food, enjoyed in an Oriental surrounding with *samisen* music, is cooked on the spot at *Benihana of Tokyo.*

Kosher-style Jewish food is the feature attraction at *Alfred's of Houston* as well as at the *New York Deli,* in the Galleria area.

Matching the diversity in food, Houstonians and visitors in Houston have a diversity of entertainment available to them throughout the year, particularly at special annual events.

At the end of the first week in January each year, Houston is the site of the International Boat, Sport

The annual Fat Stock Parade through downtown Houston precedes the Houston Livestock Show and Rodeo.

and Travel Show, at the Astrohall, where boating, camping, fishing and hunting manufacturers present displays of their latest equipment.

The Houston Livestock Show and Rodeo brings out the Texan in Houstonians each February. This extravaganza kicks off with a parade featuring at least 6,000 horses and numerous marching bands as trailriders assemble in the center of town on the first day of the rodeo. The rodeo, together with the Houston Livestock Show in the Livestock Show Exposition Building adjacent to the Astrodome, is held during the last week of February and the first week of March in the Astrodome. Various entertainers perform in the rodeo, but the main attraction is the calf roping, bull dogging, bareback riding and saddle bronc riding for which the rodeo is renowned. The world's finest livestock collection can be viewed in

LEFT: *Supremely confident in his Houston zoological kingdom, Ye-Ye the ape contemplates his harmonious surroundings.* ABOVE: *Children are entertained by Astroworld's animal caricatures.* BELOW: *The audience participates in the singing of the national anthem prior to a symphony performance at Hermann Park's Miller Theatre.*

*An artist's concept of downtown Houston
by Houstonian artist Norman Baxter.*

ABOVE: *and* BELOW: Tony's *is a gourmet's paradise, where exquisite food and drink is available in a refined setting.*
RIGHT: *The Houston Ballet presents an outstanding variety of performances, including the* Prodigal Son *(top left).*
The Sleeping Beauty *(top right and bottom),* The Lady and the Fool *(middle left) and* The Nutcracker *(middle right).*

the 22-acre exposition building, where many kinds of livestock are shown and eventually judged and sold. The show draws international attendance.

Each March, a huge assortment of arts and crafts is displayed downtown during the Houston Festival, sponsored by the Chamber of Commerce. Three days in mid-March are devoted to the Science and Engineering Fair, usually held in the Shamrock Hilton, in which junior and senior high school students demonstrate their scientific approaches to the problems of our time. In an accompanying festivity, Houston celebrates St. Patrick's Day with a parade on March 17th. Also, an important military parade is held on Armed Forces Day.

The River Oaks American Tournament, heretofore sponsored by the American General companies and currently by the Houston National Bank, is an exclusive week-long event, held on the first week in April, drawing professional tennis' greatest names. Each April 21st, San Jacinto Day commemorates Texas' independence, and ceremonies are held on the San Jacinto Battleground. Two Houston Open Tournaments are held in May, for golf afficionados on the first week of the month and for tennis fanciers in the middle of the month.

Texas Cyclone, considered the largest roller coaster in the world is located at Astroworld Amusement Park.

Texas Children's Hospital is the beneficiary of the Pin Oak Charity Horse Show and equine grand championships, both held in June at the Astroarena. On June 19th, the Annual Juneteenth Blues Festival is presented in the Miller Outdoor Theatre, celebrating the freeing of Texan slaves. Ringling Brothers and Barnum and Bailey Circus customarily bring their three rings to Houston during the first week in July. Large Independence Day celebrations are held on July 4th at Sam Houston Park and Sharpstown Shopping Center. A Gilbert and Sullivan Festival occupies two nights during the third week in July. During mid-July the Houston Aquarium Society presents a Tropical Fish Show at the Sharpstown Center Mall. Throughout August the Miller Outdoor Theatre is the site of the free Shakespeare Festival presented by University of Houston students. Each September the Miller Outdoor Theatre sponsors a free-admission dance performance.

The Greek Festival in the second week of October, features three days of feasting on Greek cuisine including *pita* (cheese pie), *souzoukakia* (meatballs), *pastitsio* (macaroni and meat casserole) and other Greek dishes. Diners watch the Greek dances accompanied by lively bouzouki music. Every

LEFT: *Gleaming in the bright sunshine, the Astrodome (the world's first domed stadium) symbolizes Houston's progressive attitude.*

People mill and mingle down the street, viewing and buying the various arts and crafts of the Westheimer Art Festival.

weekend in the month of October, the Oktoberfest offers German specialties such as potato pancakes, wurst, strudel and other German delights, as well as dancing to the accompaniment of live oompah bands.

A road and custom car show is held for four days in November at the Albert Thomas Convention Center. Also in November the Sam Houston Coliseum Annex is the site of the South Texas Obedience Club Dog Show. Foley's Department Store holds an annual Thanksgiving Day Parade.

In December, the annual Bluebonnet Bowl football game is held at the Astrodome featuring two top-ranked college teams. The Christmas holiday performance of the Nutcracker Suite and comparably appropriate presentations take place at Jones Hall.

Year-round entertainment is plentiful in Houston and nightclubs and supper clubs abound. Some of

the more famous are the Shamrock Cabaret Theater in the Shamrock Hilton Hotel, the Club at the Marriott Hotel-Astrodome, and the Windmill Dinner Theatre, which presents high caliber Broadway productions.

Gilley's Club in Pasadena is a cavernous country-music lover's retreat where celebrities appear weekly and on weekends. Humorous improvisations can be viewed at the Comedy Workshop on Monday and Tuesday each week while the Workshop's professional company appears during the remainder of the week. Cowboy and Rodeo are appropriately-named country-and-western music dance halls. A pianist performs nightly at the Spindletop, a rotating cocktail lounge that presents a 360-degree panorama of downtown Houston from atop the Hyatt Regency Hotel. National jazz artists appear at La Provence restaurant and at St. Michel. Elan is a charming semiprivate disco on multi-levels complete with backgammon tables. There is music seven nights a week at T.G.I. (Thank God It's) Friday's, and Houlahan's No. 2 features live music as well as excellent food.

HOTELS

For visitors Houston provides an impressive choice of well managed guest facilities. While classic landmarks such as the Shamrock Hilton, the Plaza, and the Warwick remain successful today, Houston's vitality in the 80s is further reflected in its newer and more modern hotels and motels.

Houston has over 26,000 hotel and motel rooms, with more currently under construction. Many cluster in the downtown area. These include the Hyatt Regency, Meridien, Whitehall, Sheraton, Holiday Inn Downtown and Lamar. Others are located in Southwest Houston's Magic Circle, one of the city's fashion and shopping centers, including the Galleria Plaza, Houston Oaks, Guest Quarters, Stouffer's and Marriott on the West Loop. Many hotels and motels are located along the highway 610 Loop or along Interstate Highways 10, 45, or US 59.

The Houston hotel with the most rooms, totalling 958, and currently one of the city's more glamorous buildings, is the $45 million Hyatt Regency. Shaped like a trapezoid and topped by a doughnut-shaped lounge and restaurant, the Spindletop slowly revolves to give its panoramic view of the city. The Hyatt received Carte Blanche's Epicurean Award, and the hotel is itself one of the city's major tourist attractions. Visitors can ride one of the three exterior glass elevators which travel up the facade of the hotel, with spectacular views of the city, and down with a

The Warwick Hotel is an oasis of old-world beauty, brimming with antiques and European artwork.

MECOM FOUNTAIN

The formidable Hyatt Regency Hotel is crowned by the revolving Spindletop Restaurant.

dizzying drop to the lobby through an open atrium. A wall sculpture by Charles Pebworth, "Garden of the Mind," hangs alongside the lobby escalators. The Hyatt is perpetually exciting; it hosts American presidents, visiting foreign dignitaries and local business conventioneers.

The Astro Village Complex, adjacent to the Astrodome and Astroworld amusement park, offers more than 900 rooms in its Astro Village Hotel, Holiday Inn, and Lodge. The Astro Village Hotel boasts the most expensive hotel suite in the world, the Celestial Suite, and has vast convention facilities.

The 398-room Houston Oaks and 498-room Galleria Plaza Hotels are modern and elegant and share the distinction of being part of the Galleria complex. Just across the street is Guest Quarters with

its 211 suites, each of which encloses more than 1,000 square feet of space.

The 786-room Shamrock Hilton remains a Texas institution offering the world's largest hotel swimming pool, four tennis courts, theaters, restaurants, a disco and convention facilities. Legendary millionaire Glenn McCarthy opened the Shamrock on St. Patrick's Day, 1949, with a celebrity-studded gala that resulted in a near-riot when 50,000 Houstonians swarmed the grounds to mix with well-known visitors.

The 394-room Stouffer's Greenway Plaza offers the largest hotel rooms in the city; they average 420 square feet. Like the Galleria Plaza and Houston Oaks, Stouffer's is connected to a shopping-sports-office complex, and, like them, has a rooftop bar with a view of Houston. Next door is the Summit, home of Houston's professional basketball and soccer teams and the site of concerts, circuses, and other sporting events and spectacles.

Houston's older hostelries, the Plaza and the Warwick, rise elegantly at the center of the city's cultural area.

The Plaza has the flavor and ambience of old Europe. Located within the Plaza is Che, widely recognized as one of the finest supper clubs in Texas. The Meridien is the first hotel in the United States built and operated for a prestigious French hotel chain. For those who enjoy a more informal atmosphere, there is Chaucer's, with its bar and restaurant where artists and writers of the Montrose area gather.

The 304-room Warwick radiates a warm and stately elegance. Some of the 60 multi-bedroom apartments offer such luxuries as saunas, oversized beds, custom made furnishings in the style of Louis XV and XVI, marble topped dressing tables, a chandelier of Baccarat crystal, a wood burning fireplace, and antique grand pianos. The north lobby's atmosphere is that of a gracious French salon. Antique paneling was commissioned and hand-carved for the chateau of a prominent French family in the eighteenth century, and came directly from the Paris palace of the Princess Murat. A priceless Aubusson tapestry dominates the foyer, hand-woven area rugs grace the Rose Aurora, with Portuguese marble floors and custom-made furnishings throughout the hotel. Making capital of Houston's year-round subtropical climate, the Warwick Pool Terrace provides guests with a setting for enjoyment of the out of doors. The decor recaptures the romantic nobility of French New Orleans with white and blue sidewalk umbrellas around an elliptical swimming pool. The Fontaine Ballroom, meanwhile, after the bank of twelve glittering fountains which line its arc-shaped perimeter, has entry doors and pilasters with gold leafing from an eighteenth century French chateau.

RIGHT: *The sunken Park Bar commands a view of the glassfront elevators, modern art and architecture of the interior of the Hyatt Regency.*

SPORTS

Sports activities provide Houstonians with a great source of civic pride and national recognition. Not only do the professional and collegiate teams of Houston excel in league competition, but the city has attracted talented sportsmen from all over the world, including football's Earl Campbell, soccer's Kyle Rote, Jr., baseball's J. R. Richard, Nolan Ryan and Joe Morgan, basketball's Rick Barry and Moses Malone, auto racing's A. J. Foyt and hockey's Gordie Howe. In tournament sports, Houston's magnificent facilities and sports patrons have made the city a key stop on many professional circuits, including tennis, golf, rodeo, wrestling and boxing.

PROFESSIONAL TEAM SPORTS

Houston began the decade of the 1960s without a single major league professional sports team. By the 1970s, the city had acquired franchises in baseball, football, men's and women's basketball, outdoor and indoor soccer and ice hockey.

BASEBALL

Houston got its first recognized big league sports team in 1961 when it acquired a franchise in baseball's newly expanded National League. This was a reward for the efforts of civic minded Houstonians, notably County Judge Roy Hofheinz, who had fought for

Second baseman Art Howe forces out Montreal Expos runner.

admission into the league and had gone so far as to lay the foundation for a rival Continental League. Prior to the creation of the new team, Harris County citizens voted a $22 million bond issue for the construction of the world's first domed and air conditioned stadium, an arena in which baseball and other sports teams would subsequently play.

The Houston Colt .45's, the new major league baseball team, had a colorful history beginning with its 162-game inaugural season in 1962 in a temporary park called Colt Stadium, located near the present Astrodome. The Colt .45's beat the Chicago Cubs 11-2 in their opening game and managed to win a respectable 40 percent of their games during the inaugural season, despite the fact that their roster was filled by expendable players acquired in an expansion draft from the league's existing teams. The Colt .45's finished in eighth place in 1962, ahead of the Chicago Cubs and the New York Mets, the other expansion team.

During the three years that the Houston club played at Colt Stadium, players and fans alike had to contend with both humidity and overzealous mosquitoes. The team's management partially solved the weather problem by scheduling a great majority of games at night, including Sunday night games, but it would take an enclosed stadium to vanquish the mosquitoes.

Fine pitching performances highlighted the Colt .45's next two seasons in Colt Stadium. In 1963, Don Nottebart pitched Houston's first no-hitter, a 4-1 victory over the Philadelphia Phillies in which the Phillies remarkably managed to score a run without the benefit of a hit. There were no more no-hitters in 1963 but the Colt .45 team did manage to win an impressive 16 shutout games.

In 1964, an even more amazing event occurred when pitcher Ken Johnson pitched no-hit ball against the Cincinnati Reds for nine innings and lost the game. In the bottom half of the decisive ninth inning, Pete Rose managed to get on base without the benefit of a hit and scored from third base when all-star Colt .45 second baseman Nellie Fox bobbled Vada Pinson's one-out ground ball. Johnson was the first and only pitcher in major league history to ever lose a no-hit game.

The Harris County Domed Stadium, more commonly known as the Astrodome, was completed in 1965 and the Colt .45's became the Astros, a name which sportscaster Howard Cosell said would never catch on. The first indoor baseball game in history was played on April 9, 1965, with President Lyndon Johnson, Governor John Connally and 47,900 other fans in attendance. They witnessed the Astros 2-1 exhibition game victory over the New York Yankees, which featured Mickey Mantle hitting the Astrodome's inaugural home run.

Astrodome, world's first indoor stadium, is the home of the Astros, Oilers and Hurricane.

Initially, the dome's clear skylights caused baseballs to disappear momentarily from the sight of infielders and outfielders chasing pop or fly balls. This unique problem was solved when the Astrodome's roof panels were painted off-white at the end of the 1965 season. Another first in the history of baseball was recorded at the opening of the 1966 season when the park's natural grass, unable to grow under the new lighting conditions, was replaced by a synthetic surface known as Astroturf.

In 1967, the Astros, who continued to win over 40 percent of their games each year without registering a winning season, recorded their first no-hit, no-run game. Don Wilson, who struck out 15 batters in all, fanned home run king Hank Aaron for the final out, and beat the Atlanta Braves 2-0. Two more National League stars excelling for the Astros in 1967 were Rusty Staub, who batted .333, and Jimmy Wynn, who hit 37 home runs.

On April 15, 1968, the New York Mets played the Houston Astros at the Astrodome for 23 consecutive innings without either team scoring. This record-breaking scoreless tie was ended when the hapless Mets gave up an unearned run in the bottom of the 24th inning in a remarkable 1-0 Houston victory. Later that year the Astrodome was the site of another notable 1-0 game, a win by the National League over the American League as Houston hosted baseball's annual All-Star Game.

The Astrodome's attendance surpassed two million spectators annually during the first years of the stadium's existence but the major attraction was the baseball park and not the baseball team. The Astros improved, however, and won half of their games for the first time in 1969. That year, baseball history was made again by the Astros when Jim Maloney of Cincinnati no-hit Houston 10-0 on April 30th. The very next evening, against all odds of this ever happening, Don Wilson returned the compliment and no-hit Cincinnati 4-0.

Two losing seasons followed, but in 1972, with the legendary Leo Durocher as its manager, Houston registered its best finish ever, an 84-69 record. Cesar Cedeño, Doug Rader, Lee May, (acquired in a major trade for Joe Morgan) and Bob Watson provided the nucleus for a potent hitting attack.

Cesar Cedeño showed that he had superstar ability in 1973 when he batted .320, hit 25 home runs and stole 56 bases.

Don Wilson was deprived of completing his third no-hitter on September 4, 1974 when he was lifted for a pitch-hitter in a game that the Astros managed somehow to find themselves trailing, 2-0. His pitching replacement gave up one hit in the ninth inning, ending the team's no-hit bid.

In 1975, a year after Leo Durocher had retired, the Astros undertook a major rebuilding program under the direction of current manager Bill Virdon in an effort to lay the foundation for their first serious pennant contending team.

Larry Dierker no-hit the Montreal Expos in 1976, pitching the fourth hitless game in Houston's short history. That same year, J. R. Richard won 20 games, matching the feat first accomplished by Dierker in 1969.

The Astros finished third in 1977, but dropped to fifth the following year. In 1978, J. R. Richard became the first right-handed pitcher in National League history to strike out 300 batters in a season and Astro pitchers led the league in both team strikeouts and team shutouts.

The emergence of a strong Astro pitching staff in 1978 set the stage for the dramatic season of 1979. On April 7th, Ken Forsch pitched Houston's fifth no-hitter, this time against the Atlanta Braves. The Astros moved into first place early and were still there in the middle of September, the final month of the season, before they bowed to the Cincinnati Reds in the Western Division pennant race by 1 1/2 games. Bill Virdon was named Manager of the Year as the Astros finished with their best season, 89 wins and 73 losses. The Astros' performance as a pennant con-

tender was amazing considering the fact that the team had one of the lowest composite batting averages in all of baseball and hit only a few home runs.

In the free agent market, following the 1979 season, the star pitching staff of J. R. Richard, Joe Niekro (who won 21 games in 1979), Ken Forsch and relief specialist Joe Sambito was further enhanced by the acquisition of left-handed pitcher Nolan Ryan from the California Angels. Ryan pitched four no-hit games during his career, a major league record, and has led the American League in strikeouts. The offensive attack of Cesar Cedeño, Terry Puhl and Jose Cruz was bolstered, as well, by the re-acquisition of Joe Morgan from the Cincinnati Reds in the free-agent market.

As the 1980s began, Houston has completed its metamorphosis and is generally recognized as the National League Western Division's team to beat.

FOOTBALL

Failing to convince the National Football League to assign a franchise to Houston, Kenneth Stanley "Bud" Adams of Houston and Lamar Hunt of Dallas led a move to form the rival American Football League (AFL), which began in 1960. Adams headed the Houston franchise and named it the Houston Oilers.

Playing their home games at old Jeppesen Stadium, the Oilers were an immediate success. They won their first regular season football game on September 11, 1960, defeating the Oakland Raiders in San Francisco, 37-22. The first Oiler touchdown score came on a 43-yard pass from George Blanda to Charles Hennigan. On December 11th, the Oilers beat Buffalo in Houston to clinch the Eastern Division title. The first AFL Championship game ever played was won by the Houston Oilers, 24-16 over the Los Angeles Chargers as George Blanda completed 16 of 32 passes for 301 yards and three touchdowns before 32,880 fans in Houston.

The second season started out just as successfully when, with Hurricane Carla threatening the game, the Oilers defeated the Oakland Raiders by the score of 55-0. During the 1961 season, quarterback-place kicker George Blanda kicked field goals of 53 and 55 yards and, in one game against the New York Titans, threw seven touchdown passes, the all-time professional record. Billy Cannon scored five touchdowns for the Oilers in another game over the Titans in a 48-21 triumph at New York's Polo Grounds. Cumulatively, the Oilers became the first professional team to score over 500 points in a single season. On December 24, 1961, Houston won the second AFL championship with a 10-3 victory in San Diego over the Chargers. George Blanda was named AFL player of the year and Wally Lemm was named AFL coach of the year.

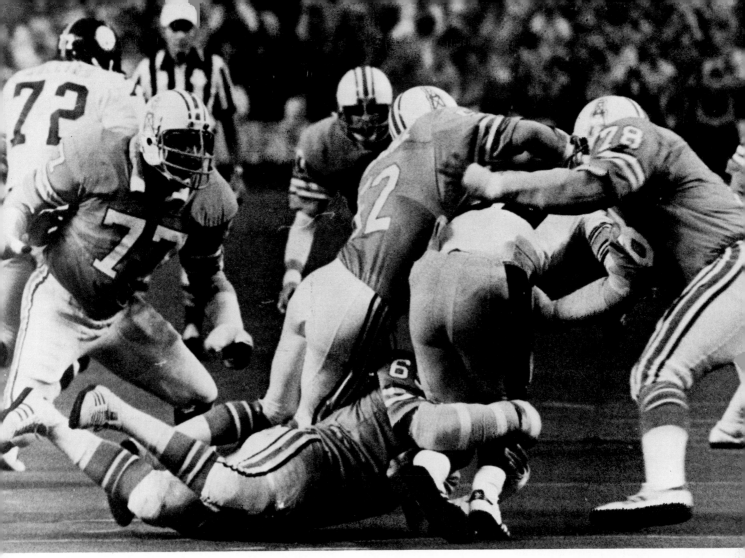

The Oilers, who continued to win in the offensive-minded American Football League, set an AFL scoring record on October 14, 1962 when George Blanda threw for six touchdown passes in a 56-17 win over the New York Titans. On December 15, they won their third consecutive Eastern Division Championship with a 44-10 win over New York as Charlie Tolar gained 107 yards in the game, making him the first Oiler to gain one thousand yards in one season. Houston's 1962 record was their best ever, eleven wins and three losses. Their third straight AFL Championship Game did not end as successfully as the first two but was memorable nonetheless. By the time the Dallas Texans kicked the decisive field goal to win 20-17 in double overtime, 77 minutes and 54 seconds had elapsed, making it the longest game in pro football history.

The Oilers' early success record was reversed in 1963 when they won six and lost eight. Between 1964 and 1966, they won no more than four games out of 14 per season. A change of location occurred in 1965 when the Oilers, failing to reach an agreement to play in the Astrodome, signed a $100,000 per year contract to play at Rice Stadium. In their new home a record crowd of 52,680 saw them defeat the New York Jets on September 12, 1965.

A significant change occurred on June 9, 1966

Houston Oiler action with Jim Young, No. 77, Robert Brazile, No. 52, Elvin Bethea, No. 65 and Curley Culp, No. 78.

when the American Football League merged with the National Football League. It was announced that in 1969, the Oilers would become part of the league's American Football Conference, largely made up of teams from the American Football League. A championship game, or "Super Bowl," would be played annually between winners of the two conferences.

An impressive record was set in an Oilers' game in the 1966 season when Houston held Denver to no first downs in a game—a league record—as they beat the Broncos, 45-7.

The Oilers completed a metamorphosis of their own in 1967 when they clinched the Eastern Division title and became the first team to go from last place to first in one season. Confronted with their first opportunity to reach the Super Bowl, the Oilers were decisively beaten by the Oakland Raiders, 40-7 in the AFL Championship Game on New Year's Day.

The team's owners came to terms with Astrodome officials prior to the 1968 season and the first indoor professional football game was played there on August 1, 1968. Houston's record was 7-7 in 1968, which represented their best season until 1975. In the meantime, the team suffered through two 1-13 seasons in 1972 and 1973.

At the beginning of the 1975 season, Houston's present coach, O. A. (Bum) Phillips took over from the retiring Sid Gillman and promptly led the team to a 10-4 record, which fell just short of clinching a playoff spot in the difficult Central Division of the American Football Conference. The Oilers slumped to 5-9 in 1976, improved in 1977 and again became a winning team in 1978.

The new Houston Oilers really took shape on April 24, 1978, when the team traded three draft choices and another player to the Tampa Bay Buccaneers for collegiate draft choice Earl Campbell, an All-American at the University of Texas.

Running Back Earl Campbell (34) of the Oilers.

Campbell had seven 100-yard games in his rookie season and he was the main ingredient in Houston's appearance in the AFC playoffs. The Oilers defeated favored Miami and heavily favored New England in playoff games on the road before losing the AFC championship game 34-5 to the Steelers in icy Pittsburgh. Proud of their team despite the loss, 50,000 fans turned out to welcome the Oilers back to Houston.

The 1979 season was another success story for the Oilers and they again qualified for the playoffs. In the first playoff round, with three major offensive players injured and unable to participate, the Oilers stunned the San Diego Chargers and won. They again proceeded to beat the Miami Dolphins in playoff competition, giving them their second straight opportunity to knock off the defending World Champion Pittsburgh Steelers in an AFC Championship Game. But, playing their third successive playoff game on the road, the Oilers this time narrowly lost to the Steelers. Houston Oiler fans again turned out for another massive post-game rally at the Astrodome, with more than 70,000 people in attendance, many sporting "Lov Ya Blue" T-shirts.

Besides Campbell, key players responsible for Houston's success were quarterback Dan Pastorini, tight end Mike Barber, linebacker Robert Brazile, defensive end Elvin Bethea, wide receiver Ken Burrough and special team star Billy "White Shoes" Johnson. In early 1980, the Oilers traded Pastorini to Oakland for the Raiders' veteran quarterback Ken Stabler.

BASKETBALL

The city's basketball franchise, the Rockets, was acquired when the San Diego team of the National Basketball Association (NBA) was moved to Houston in 1971. The Rockets played on six different home courts during their maiden season in Texas but most of their games were played in the Hofheinz Pavilion between 1972 and 1975. Later, the Rockets moved to the brand-new 15,676-seat Houston Summit.

After a poor initial season on the court, Houston traded Elvin Hayes to Baltimore and switched from the Western Division to the Central Division. Playing the 81-game NBA schedule, the team dropped from a record of 34 wins in 1971-1972 to 33 in 1972-1973 and 32 in 1973-1974.

Led by forward Rudy Tomjanovich, the Rockets won 41 games in the 1974-1975 season and made the NBA playoffs for the first time since moving to Houston. After eliminating the New York Knicks in the first playoff round, the Rockets were eliminated from further playoff contention when they lost a five-game series to the Boston Celtics.

In 1975-1976, Houston dropped to 40 wins and failed to make the playoffs, despite the continued excellent play of guard Calvin Murphy. Murphy ranked tenth in the league in scoring, with a 21 points per game average. He was also third in assists at 7.3 per game and second in free throw percentage at 90.7 percent.

Acquiring 6'11" center Moses Malone from Buffalo during the off-season, Houston achieved its first winning season in 1976-1977, a 49-33 record which earned the team a second trip to the NBA playoffs. Playing before sellout crowds at the Summit, the Rockets beat the Washington Bullets in the first round, propelling them into the Eastern Division championship series against the Philadelphia 76ers, to whom they lost in six games; Houston coach Tom Nissalke was voted NBA coach of the year.

Injuries to Rockets' players dropped the team to last place, 38-54, in 1977-1978.

With the addition of basketball superstar Rick Barry from the Golden State Warriors on June 17, 1978, the Rockets reversed their one-year slump and, in 1978-1979, finished with their second best record ever: 47 wins and 35 losses, one game behind the Central Division champion San Antonio Spurs. Although failing in the playoffs, center Moses Malone was voted the league's most valuable player in a vote by NBA players. Malone led the NBA in rebounding with 17.6 rebounds per game and was fifth in scoring with 24.8 points per game. Also that year, Rick Barry set a new free throw percentage scoring record by hitting on 160 of 169 free throws, a 94.7 percent average.

The Rockets named Del Harris as head coach prior to the 1979-1980 season and the team proceded to win an NBA playoff berth, with a 41-41 record. The Rockets beat the San Antonio Spurs in the first round to qualify for the Eastern Division semi-final series, which they lost to the Boston Celtics in four games.

SOCCER

The city's large international community and a growing interest in the sport has made soccer successful in Houston. The only home-grown American soccer superstar, Kyle Rote, Jr., plays for the Houston Hurricane club of the North American Soccer League (NASL).

In the fall of 1978, a second professional soccer team was formed in Houston as a Major Indoor Soccer League (MISL) team known as Summit Soccer, began playing at the Houston Summit. In the 1978-1979 and 1979-1980 seasons, Summit Soccer was loaned several players from the NASL Houston Hurricane. The Hurricane's marked improvement during the 1979 season, when it was undefeated during regular season play, was partly credited to the additional training time afforded its players in the indoor league prior to the start of the regular NASL season. Hurricane players were able to play together

A stuff shot by Houston Rockets forward Moses Malone (24).

on Summit Soccer in 1979, but new NASL rules restricted the number of players that could do so in the 1979-1980 season.

HOCKEY

Despite the great success of Houston's first professional ice hockey team, the Houston Aeros of the World Hockey Association (WHA), the National Hockey League (NHL) decided to exclude Houston from its list of new teams when the WHA was merged with the larger NHL in 1979. Nonetheless, a professional hockey tradition was begun in Houston by the Aeros' key players, led by superstar Gordie Howe and his sons Mark and Marty. During the time that the Howes played at the Summit, Houston won two WHA championships. Despite the failure of the move to acquire an NHL franchise, ice hockey remained in Houston when the Central Hockey League included the Houston Apollos in time for the 1979-1980 season. The Apollos, the minor league affiliate of the NHL's Edmonton Oilers, play their games at the Sam Houston Coliseum.

COLLEGE TEAMS

The University of Houston Cougars, the Rice University Owls, the Texas Southern University Tigers and the Houston Baptist University Huskies compete in football, basketball and baseball in major US collegiate sports conferences. The University of Houston teams play at the Astrodome, competing in football, basketball and baseball in the Southwest Conference. The Cougars have played in the Cotton Bowl in Dallas three times, including their most recent appearance in January 1980.

A scene from Houston Motorcross competition, held each year at the Astrodome.

Rice University is a member of the National Collegiate Athletic Association (NCAA), the Southwest Athletic Conference (SWC), and the National Association of Intercollegiate Athletics for Women (NAIAW). Rice's male athletes compete in SWC football, baseball, basketball, track and field, cross-country, tennis, golf and swimming, and the school's female athletes participate in volleyball, basketball, track, swimming, tennis and cross-country in the NAIAW.

Houston Baptist University is a member of the NCAA and its men and women participate in basketball, tennis, golf, track and field and gymnastics in the Trans America Conference.

Texas Southern University participates in the Southwest Athletic Conference in football, basketball, baseball, track and field, tennis, and golf and a women's basketball team participates in the NAIAW.

PRO TOURNAMENTS

Tournament sports thrive in Houston, ranging from tennis and golf to rodeo and wrestling. The River Oaks Tennis Tournament, which is the last stop on the World Championship of Tennis circuit, offers a $50,000 purse to the winner and attracts top tennis players from throughout the world. Rod Laver, Ken Rosewall, Roy Emerson, Manuel Orantes, Brian Gottfried and Cliff Richey have played at River Oaks.

The Coca Cola Ladies Invitational Tennis Tournament brings top-seeded stars like Martina Navratilova, Billie Jean King, Tracy Austin and Chris Everet to Houston.

The Houston Open Golf Tournament at the Woodlands Country Club features leading golfers such as Lee Trevino, Gary Player, Arnold Palmer and Jack Nicklaus.

The Yamaha Gold Cup Motorcycle Races, with a $38,000 purse, are held at the Astrodome annually. The event features professional motorcyle racers in short track races and a steeple chase.

Championship wrestling is showcased weekly at the Houston Coliseum. Colorful professional wrestlers performing include Gorgeous Gino Hernandez and Tiger Conway, Jr. (both native Houstonians), José Lothario, Bruiser Brody, El Gran Markus and world champion Harley Race.

Professional and amateur boxing tournaments are held at the Coliseum and at the Astroarena regularly by both the World Boxing Council (WBC), the World Boxing Association (WBA), Golden Gloves and the United States Olympic Committee (USOC). Title fights have been staged by both the WBC and the WBA.

The biggest seasonal sporting event with a local flavor is the annual Houston Rodeo, which is one of the highlights of the Livestock Show. It features professional cowboys of the Rodeo Cowboy Association who compete in chuckwagon races, bareback and bronc riding, calf roping, bulldogging, barrel racing (for lady bronc riders) and bull riding.

ACKNOWLEDGEMENTS

Special thanks are extended to the following people and organizations for their assistance in making the book "Houston, City of Destiny," a reality: Adrienne Arnot, Gloria Barboza, Harry Benson, the Cameron Ironworks, Joseph Chow, the City of Houston, David Courtney, Kay Ebling, Jim Foley, Ramona G. Garner, Goodyear Tire and Rubber Company, David M. Henington, Ann Holmes, Edward L. Horn, the Houston Board of Realtors, the Houston Chamber of Commerce, Emil Karam, Rayford G. Kay, Geri Konigsberg, Frances Lawrence, Mike McClure, Tom Morton, Tom Murrah, Northwest Bank and Trust, Diane Olson, James E. O'Rourke, Rick Rivers, Greg Stangle, Susan L. Stubbs, Tenneco, Underwood Neuhaus & Co., Elizabeth Von Helms, Ed Wade, Dr. Jack Williams, Don Zullo.

The Editors

PHOTO CREDITS

Astrodome, p. 172; Astroworld, p. 145, 155, 161; Bill Basham, p. 142, 143; Norman Baxter (Courtesy Houston Natural Gas), p. 156-157; Bayou Bend Collection, p. 18; Brown & Root, Inc., p. 2, 69; Fred Bunch, (Houston *Post*), p. 9; Jim Caldwell, p. 125, 141; Cameron Iron Works, p. 76; Jeanne White Forristal, p. 97; Galleria, p. 151; Murray Getz, p. 158; Gittings, p. 89 (top right), 90 (top left); Goodyear Tire and Rubber Company, p. 66, 72; Greater Houston Convention and Visitors Council, p. 11, 12, 13, 16 (bottom), 33, 52, 55 (bottom right), 56, 57, 68 (top), 73, 75, 95, 117, 122, 123, 127, 128, 163, 167; Greenway Plaza, p. 87; Frank Grizzaffi, p. 136; Gulf Photo, p. 160; Harris County Heritage Society, p. 17, 22-31, 32 (top), 34 (top left, top left center, top right center), 35, 129; Jack Heard, p. 91 (right); Hickey-Robertson, p. 20; Houston Astros, p. 166; Geoff Winningham, Houston Ballet, p. 159; Houston Board of Realtors, p. 101, 103, 107 (bottom), 111, 113, 115, 120; Houston *Chronicle*, p. 131; Houston Library, p. 34 (bottom left), 36-42, 43 (left), 44-46, 48-50; Houston Oilers, p. 169, 170; Houston *Post*, p. 34 (top far right), 51, 53, 112 (top), 114; Houston Rockets, p. 171; Houston Symphony, p. 124; Houston Zoo, (R. Michael Bowerman) p. 153, 154; Hyatt Regency, p. 150, 164, 165; Owen Johnson, p. 10, 19, 64 (bottom), 77, 81-83, 85, 86, 89 (except top right), 90 (except top left), 92, 152; *KHOU*, p. 134; *KPRC*, p. 133; *KUHT*, p. 132; Emil Karam, p. 88, 126, 144, 146; Jim La Combe, p. 55 (top left), 105, 106, 107 (top), 112 (bottom), 147, 148, 162; Jon Lindsay, p. 91 (left); M. D. Anderson Foundation, p. 43 (right); NASA, p. 61 (bottom), 63, 64 (top), 70, 80; James E. O'Rourke, p. 87, 88, 155; Pervin Photographic Co., p. 61 (top); Port of Houston Authority, p. 67, 68 (bottom), 71, 98; Rice University, p. 121; San Jacinto Museum of History Association, p. 58; Anthony Sheppard, p. 21 (right); Ezra Stroller, p. 126 (top); Tenneco, p. 60, 62; Texas Medical Center, p. 78, 79; Texas Southern University, p. 140; Tony's Restaurant, p. 149, 158; John Tvetum, p. 14, 15, 16 (top); Underwood Neuhaus, p. 110, 118, 119; University of Houston, p. 6, 32 (bottom), 137; Uversity of St. Thomas, p. 139.

INDEX